WITHDRAWN

ALEJO CARPENTIER
AND HIS
EARLY WORKS

FRANK JANNEY

ALEJO CARPENTIER AND HIS AND HIS EARLY WORKS

TAMESIS BOOKS LIMITED
LONDON

Colección Támesis

SERIE A - MONOGRAFIAS, LXX

Depósito Legal: M. 30138-1980

Printed in Spain by Talleres Gráficos de SELECCIONES GRÁFICAS
Carretera de Irún, km. 11,500 - Madrid-34

for
TAMESIS BOOKS LIMITED
LONDON

CONTENTS

PREFACE

Canonized for his major works of the fifties and early sixties Los pasos perdidos, Guerra del tiempo, *and* El siglo de las luces, *Alejo Carpentier is a patriarch in the world of hispanic letters. His latest novels,* Concierto barroco *(Mexico, 1974) and* El recurso del método *(Mexico, 1974) have added to his stature, although their critical reception reminds us that the stage has widened considerably with the passing years. If that is so, it is partly because of Carpentier's own literary struggle to refocus the Latin American experience from new dramatic and linguistic perspectives and to stretch the broad frame of his own complex cultural heritage. The grateful reception abroad of his efforts has demonstrated to younger writers that there was a stage, and indeed a hungry audience, beyond the provincial world of our modern capitals.*

Carpentier has unlocked doors to the colonial past, the South American jungle, the rural bodegas, *and his symbolic characters have come forth upon the universal stage to don the livery of the moment—a failed revolutionary, a black king, a founder of jungle towns. We sensed the fragility of the actors, swept along by the forceful chords of a baroque ensemble, and we learn to sense and recognize the* basso continuum *beneath their brief solos.*

The young artist in search of a voice, of the 20's and 30's and early 40's, laboring in prose fiction with the renovating concepts stated discursively years later in the prologue to El reino de este mundo *(Mexico, 1949) and in* Tientos y diferencias *(Mexico, 1964), is the subject of this book. I intend to show the artist in his early evolutionary paths, isolating recurring themes and stylistic devices.*

The theme of regression, cast in primitivistic (¡Écue-yamba-Ó!) and individual («Viaje a la semilla») terms is dominant in Carpentier's early works. On the one hand his fiction evokes a world penetrated and determined by natural forces, on the other, the journey through time to the wellsprings of innocence in childhood. Regardless of the scope, it is still the same compelling theme of the return.

In his desire to fuse welt *and* trope, *Carpentier developed consistent stylistic procedures in these years. In my efforts to define these techniques, I prefer not to employ such misleading terms as «realismo mágico»,[1] but to*

---

[1] «Realismo mágico» is a critical term of relatively high frequency in Latin America, and one which due to lack of definition has become relatively worthless. The authors to whom is applied, in seeming recognition of that fact, avoid its use consistently. The problem stems from the obscure origin of the term. It was coined

allow a fresh definition of style to emerge. On the other hand, in the discussion of such devices as animism and reification, I am conscious that Carpentier has no unique claim upon them; indeed Marcel Proust used them abundantly in the evocation of a milieux far removed from Carpentier's, and as eminent linguists have pointed out, we use them ourselves in everyday speech. If this study has value, that value lies in the examination of the degree, the purpose, and the contexts of certain devices the author has used—in short, in the demonstration of a way characteristic to the author of expressing matter and thought.

In Carpentier's earliest works, where he cultivated black themes nearly exclusively, his style was directed toward the creation of a state of pantheistic vitality, where man is immersed and leveled in an active cosmos of matter. The artist's style in this period was a highly refined vehicle for his primitivistic vision of man and nature. As the anthropological framework of this vision melted away, the fusion of welt *and trope became more subtle, less the product of the conscious elaboration of effect than a frame of mind, a way of seeing Caribbean reality. Yet the forces acting in ¡Écueyamba-Ó! and in his early short works persist in all of Carpentier's fiction and the style there is discernible in its forward trajectory.*

The reader will find two virtually unknown stories by Carpentier —«Histoire de lunes» (1933) and «Oficio de tinieblas»— included in the appendix.

by a German art critic —Franz Roh— to describe the «new objectivity» which characterized some German artists rebelling against the extremes of expressionism during the entre-guerre period:

> The charm of the object was rediscovered. In opposition to Expressionism, the autonomy of the objective world around us was once more to be enjoyed; the wonder of matter that could crystallize into objects was to be seen anew. In an article written in 1924 I coined the phrase Magischer Realismus (magic realism) —magic of course *not* in the religious-psychological sense of ethnology. In 1925 the expression was attached as subtitle to my book, Nach-expressionismus (Post-Expressionism). The same year Hartlaub organized the important exhibition at his gallery in Mannheim with the title Neue Sachlichkeit (New Objectivity or New Realism) —a formulation I had avoided— to imply that we were not dealing here with a repetition of the more neutral realism of Courbet or Leibl. This New Objectivity was aimed in quite a different direction, seeking an approach to the autonomous sharpness of objects, as in the late Middle Ages, the Quattrocento, or to the revolutionary form-hardening classicism of David or Ingres. Moreover, the emphasis in relation to the objective world implied abstraction, not empathy...
>
> Franz Roh, *German Art in the 20th Century,* trans. Catherine Hutter (Greenwich, Conn.: The New York Graphic Society, 1968), pp. 112-113.

Roh contrasts such qualities of expressionism as «ecstatic subjects,» «suppression of the object,» «summary,» «monumental,» «dynamic,» «expressive deformation» with, respectively, the following qualities of the «new objectivity»: «sober subjects,» «the object clarified,» «thorough,» «miniature,» «static,» «external purification of the object.»

Although many of these qualities intuited by Roh could be transposed metaphorically to describe Carpentier's prose, particularly in light of the author's rebellion against surrealism and his own search for «lo real maravilloso», Roh's emphatic rejection of «religious» magic would appear to exclude authors like Carpentier and Asturias, who were concerned with the collective transfigurings of reality.

INTRODUCTION

Five of Alejo Carpentier's earliest works will be the subject of this book. Within this arbitrary period, I intend to pinpoint elements of the Cuban writer's nascent style, establish interrelationships among those works, and reach conclusions that will enhance the appreciation and comprehension of later works. The chronological approach was chosen in order to facilitate treatment of the evolution of the writer.

The implied division into periods is justified by the continuity of themes and artistic intent observable in the five works. «El milagro de Anaquillé» (Habana, 1927), ¡Écue-yamba-Ó! (Madrid, 1933), «Histoire de lunes» (París, 1933), «Viaje a la semilla» (Habana, 1944) and «Los fugitivos» (Caracas, 1946) all focus on aspects of the black world in the Caribbean. They are stations on the way to the stylized *El reino de este mundo* (México, 1949) in which the essences of this world are successfully captured in language. These works, with the exception of *Écue* and «Viaje a la semilla» have escaped critical attention, mainly due to the obscurity of their publishing circumstances.

The fact that there is to some degree a subject common to the five works appears to this writer highly advantageous for pointing out stylistic and thematic traits within a comparative framework, and thereby suggesting evolution. It is hoped that the observations and conclusions made about Carpentier's early period will shed a much needed light on central aspects of mature style; for example, his increasingly sophisticated use of primitive motif. In terms of thematic content, the «black period» has a key position in the trajectory of Carpentier's life-long and most obsessive theme —the eternal return.

As the author gains mastery over his subject matter in the early years, his Negro figures increasingly reflect universal problems, and tend less and less to reveal a debt to anthropology and the Latin American school of «nativismo.» Thus, the crowning achievement of the first period —*El reino de este mundo* of 1949— is a clear counterpart of Carpentier's later and most comprehensive novel, *El siglo de las luces* (México, 1962), although the former is almost entirely within the human context of Haitian ex-slaves and the latter within that of middle-class Cubans and French. Christophe, the black king and central figure of the first novel, and Hughes, the French Jacobin made governor of Cayenne in the second novel, both illustrate the limits of the charismatic hero, and are embodiments of a similar cyclical view of history. In like fashion, those elements of the black world which seem to have obsessed Carpentier in his earliest works —ritual, atavism, animism, and communion with nature,— appear in sublimated form in all of his later works, as the black world per se disappears. Instead of seeing only his subject, the artist began to see *through* his subject, not seeing only manifestations of animism, but seeing animistically.

When this incorporation occurred, the author no longer needed his subject. After a long apprenticeship in the «presencia faústica» of the Cuban Black,[2] the author turned his powers on a wider spectrum of reality beyond the confines of his laboratory. The first product of that liberation was *Los pasos perdidos* (México, 1953).

In this book I am concerned with this apprenticeship, for the secrets mastered then have served the author well, and can also serve the critic in his endeavor to penetrate to the roots of the Cuban's fiction. First, we must widen our sights to comprehend both the author and his context in an effort to appreciate his particular relationship to the world of his early fiction, as well as something of his dual perspective as an islander and a continental man of letters. Let us return to the awakening of primitivism.

> La larga nostalgia de los poetas del siglo xix y el halago cada vez más insistente, más concreto de los pintores del siglo xx no podían dejar de obtener algún día una respuesta del alma fascinadora que ya Baudelaire llamaba «La Superbe Afrique». Hace ya unos cuarenta años que la Gran Diosa de la fertilidad de Guinea, que podía admirarse en París en el Museo del Hombre, fue situada en arte al lado de aquellas figuras que se habían considerado como las más expresivas del genio de otros tiempos. En la estela de la estatua, el ojo moderno penetrando poco a poco en la diversidad sin límites de objetos llamados de «origen bárbaro» y percatándose así de su rico desdoblamiento en el plano lírico, se hacía consciente de las fuentes incomparables de la visión primitiva. Llegó a amarla tanto, a desearla tanto, que aún a costa de un milagro quiso apoderarse de esta visión.[3]

> ... ...

> Nuestra inveterada inclinación a corear el último grito literario de Francia o de Alemania determinó en los escritores isleños una espectación alborozada por lo africano. Por primera vez el impulso extranjerizante nos jugó una buena partida. El camino hacia París o hacia Berlín, hacia Blaise Cendrars o hacia Leo Frobenius, nos condujo a nuestra propia casa. Buscando lo extraño dimos

---

[2] Alejo Carpentier, *El reino de este mundo* (México: Compañía General de Ediciones, 1969), p. 15.

[3] André Breton, «El surrealismo en la pintura» (New York: 1942), quoted in Fernando Ortiz Fernández, *Wilfredo Lam y su obra vista a través de significados críticos* (Habana: Ministerio de Educación, Dirección de Cultura, 1950), p. 1.

con lo propio... algún tesoro oculto debía esconderse bajo la piel oscura cuando el mundo todo se daba a su hallazgo...[4]

... ...

Nuestra poesía afrocriolla es un eco de la moda europea; consecuencia más que iniciativa propia.[5]

There are many factors involved in the artistic awakening of the Afro movement in the Antilles in which Carpentier participated from both sides of the Atlantic. Undoubtedly the first and most significant of these factors is the discovery abroad, at the dawn of this century, of the world of primitive art by the Expressionists, and later, the Cubists. According to De Salerno[6] the realm of primitive art was virtually blocked out of the Western artists' experience until the Expressionists' discoveries because of the hegemony of the mimetic tendencies of classical theory.

The German expressionist painters were the first to understand primitive art and successfully incorporate its principles (the *Brücke* painters, 1904; the Blue Rider group, 1912). Expressionism, according to De Salerno, was «stimulated by primitive art at least as much as, if not more than Cubism, and was particularly concerned with form as expression.»[7] In the same period, Picasso's direct plundering of the primitive expressive techniques of the African mask (Les Demoiselles d'Avignon, 1907) was accompanied by that of Modigliani (Head of a Woman, 1904) and in sculpture, by Brancusi (The Kiss).

These pioneers of primitivism sought in the aesthetic sense the simplification and deformation of forms free from the burden of individualized detail and the weight of cultural or temporal reference:

As they tried to discover how African Negroes were capable of conjuring up, through very simple, elementary forms, an atmosphere of intense spirituality, the artists of the Rue Revignan were struck by a process of geometric simplification which was exemplified in practically all of these imported carvings. They observed that details were either omitted entirely or indicated very roughly; only marked by bold planes, bulbous masses, sharp notches, or violent projecting angles. Thanks to an almost complete elimination of accidental aspects of texture and to the placing of a vigorous emphasis —quite intuitively— on structural relations and proportions, the Negroes succeeded in suggesting with almost overpowering force a mysterious order, not thrust upon passive objects by an organizing intelligence but existing, as it were, *at the very core of the things themselves.*[8]

[4] Juan Marinello, *Literatura hispanoamericana* (México: Ediciones de la Universidad Nacional de México, 1937), p. 84.

[5] Ramón Guirao, *Órbita de la poesía afrocubana* (La Habana: Ucar, García y Cía., 1938), introduction, p. XXII.

[6] Luigi de Salerno, «Primitivism,» *Encyclopedia of World Art* (New York: McGraw Hill, 1958), pp. 705-706.

[7] Ibid., p. 710.

[8] Georges Lemaitre, *From Cubism to Surrealism in French Literature* (Cambridge: Harvard University Press, 1947), p. 77.

In the philosophical and emotional sense the European primitivists sought a regeneration through contact with the vital forms of civilizations that had not been touched by the blight of war and industry. Genuine primitivism, whether in art or literature, usually involves the dual search for regeneration in spirit as well as form.

James Baird describes primitivism as partially a product of «cultural failure,» the «loss of a regnant and commanding authority in religious symbolism, since religion is (here understood as) the ultimately effective symbolic authority in the total culture of a race.»[9]

Such a loss of authority, documented broadly in Spengler's *Decline of the West,* and demonstrated in Jarry's *Ubu Roi,* existed in the chaotic years surrounding the First World War. The response to the social disintegration of these years was extremely varied. While the German lyrical expressionist writers' «tragic fate was to perish on the shoals of rigid bourgeois society»[10] others were trying, in Jung's words, to «break into Oriental palaces that our fathers never knew,» letting «the house that our fathers built fall to pieces.»[11] Many followed in one way or another, the tracks of Gauguin —his flight from «accursed Europe» and his stance against bourgeois existence. Often only achieved in the imagination, seldom physically realized, the escape to earlier cultures, whether aimed primarily toward aesthetic or spiritual rejuvenation, was paradoxically a prime factor in the shaping of what we consider modernism. The phenomenon of the dehumanization of the arts, as described by Ortega y Gasset,[12] is to an impressive degree a result of the contamination with the art of civilizations less preoccupied by the individual than by the inherited myths of their culture. The modern artist, freed (or exiled) already from nature by such challenges to mimesis as Kant's *Critique of Pure Reason,* discovered that the «primitive» peoples, although close to nature, had traditionally enjoyed a high degree of freedom in their interpretation of its forms.[13]

It was natural that the visual art of primitive cultures should exert a direct and wide-spread influence on the plastic arts, and later on music. These forms, if not more highly developed than the verbal arts in primitive societies, were at least more accessible to, and readily incorporated by, the European sensibility. The search for close parallels in European literature to the tremendous explorations into primitive arts by sculptors and painters is for the most part a vain one for this reason.

[9] James Baird, *Ishmael* (Baltimore: Johns Hopkins Press, 1966), p. 16.

[10] Walter H. Sokel, *The Writer in Extremis* (Stanford: The Stanford University Press, 1959), p. 55.

[11] Quoted in Sokel, ibid., p. 55.

[12] José Ortega y Gasset, *La deshumanización del arte* (Madrid: Revista de Occidente, 1958).

[13] According to Sokel, op. cit., p. 9, «The *Critique of Pure Reason* unmasks the world as the product of our mind and declares the supernatural unknowable. With these two blows Kant shatters the foundation for art as mimesis and art as revelation.»

For the most part those writers whose interest in primitive societies was awakened and who actually did travel and write were not able to, or did not attempt to create new styles for portraying newly discovered realities. André Gide, José Más, and Blaise Cendrars, described, exalted, and compiled, in the wake of the German Frobenius (who made his first voyage to Africa in 1912), but for the European writer there was no new way of seeing equivalent in force to Van Gogh's revelation at Arles or Gauguin's Tahiti.

Perhaps the only significant area of relationship is found in the early German lyrical Expressionists. It is safe to say that there is a valid parallel between the compulsion for violent undiluted colors and exaggerated, simplified forms of the painters (particularly Franz Marc) and the desperate need to identify with the primary forms of existence on the part of such writers as Paul Zech, Georg Trakl, Elske Lasker-Schuler, Alfred Brust and Franz Kafka. In a sense theirs is the negative expression of the forces behind primitivism; a form of suicide and regression taken to its last boundaries by Kafka. The forms of human existence are unbearable —the cities, even the human body being—, and the poet seeks to identify with the uncontaminated realms of plant and animal. In a play by Alfred Brust, *The Wolves* (1921), the need of the protagonist to regress to a state of nature is expressed in the fatal desire to become a wolf. Gregor Samsa's desire for regression to another state is similarly realized in Kafka's *Metamorphosis*.

The most apparent link between Primitivism and Expressionism was made in García Lorca's *Romancero Gitano* of 1928. Following the Expressionist playwrights' tendency towards abstraction of character into basic qualities, Lorca rose above the social polemics (as in Kaiser's plays of industrial villains), and the aberrant fixations (of Brust, for example) of the movement through his relationship with the Spanish poetic tradition.

In the externalized archetype «de bronce y sueño» of Lorca's poems and dramas, the Antillian writers during the early stages of the *Afrocriollo* movement saw a close parallel and often a source their aims often to the point of imitation:

> La poesía Afrocubana... fraguada en moldes impropios bajo un firmamento retórico de lunas y panderos de cobre repujados por los caldereteros del barrio gitano de Granada, herido de relucientes aceros de Albacete, entraña ya un acercamiento sincero...[14]

Yet even prior to the publication of *Romancero Gitano,* the Puerto Rican poet Luis Palés Matos wrote «Pueblo Negro» in 1925, the first poem of his Afro-Antillian period, culminating in 1937 with the publication of *Tuntún de pasa y grifería.* Later poems in this collection show the direct influence of Lorca. «Pueblo Negro» is the first real bridge between the visual arts writing of the European primitivists and the genuine experience

---

[14] Ramón Guirao, *op. cit.,* p. XIX.

15

of the Antillian writers. The search for the form of a primitivistic vision of vitality in the poem makes «Pueblo Negro» a literary parallel to the experiments of the Expressionist painters, and to the Cubists. No such literary parallel exists in European letters.

The first two lines of «Pueblo Negro» betray a Symbolist orientation; nevertheless it goes far beyond the initial invitation to flight. Palés' «Africa» is *realized* in form:

> Esta noche me obsede la remota
> visión de un pueblo negro...
> Mussumba, Tombuctú, Farafangana—
> es un pueblo de sueño,
> tumbado allá en mis brumas interiores
> a la sombra de claros cocoteros.
>
> La luz rabiosa cae
> en duros ocres sobre el campo extenso.
> Humean, rojas de calor, las piedras,
> evapora frescuras vegetales
> en el agrio crisol del clima seco.
>
> Pereza y laxitud. Los aguazales
> cuajan un vaho amoniacal y denso.
> El compacto hipopótamo se hunde
> en su caldo de lodo suculento,
> y el elefante de marfil y grasa
> rumia bajo el baobab su vago sueño.
>
> Allá entre las palmeras
> está tendido el pueblo...
> Mussumba, Tombuctú, Farafangana—
> Caserío irreal de paz y sueño.
>
> Alguien disuelve perezosamente
> un canto monorrítmico en el viento
> pululado de úes que se aquietan
> en balsas de diptongos soñolientos
> y de guturaciones alargadas
> que dan un don de lejanía al verso.
> Es la negra que canta su sobria vida de animal
> la negra de las zonas soleadas   [doméstico;
> que huelen a tierra, a salvajina, a sexo.
> Es la negra que canta,
> y su canto sensual se va extendiendo
> como una clara atmósfera de dicha
> bajo la sombra de los cocoteros.
>
> Al rumor de su canto
> todo se va extinguiendo,
> y sólo queda en mi alma
> la u profunda del diptongo fiero,
> en cuya curva maternal se esconde
> la armonía prolífica del sexo.[15]

[15] Luis Palés Matos, *Poesía* (San Juan: Editorial Universitaria, 1964), p. 239.

The experimental, plastic nature of the poem is evident. Palés, in his imaginary landscape, erases rigid contours, flattens out and remolds the stuff of reality. There are abstractions of objects —«el elefante de marfil y grasa»— and exaggerated stylized solidification —«el compacto hipopótamo se hunde en un caldo de lodo.»— There is a similar preocupation with volumes here —«baobab,» «elefante,» «hipopótamo,»— that characterize the African-inspired sculpture of Brancusi,

But the «canto monorrítmico» in the second part of the poem moves us back from the dreamed landscape to the interior of the poet, to the starting point of his poetic vision, and into the phenomenon of the medium itself. We are no longer in the dream-realms of Mussumba, but in Puerto Rico; the woman is «la negra que canta su sobria vida de animal doméstico,» in whose familiar song Palés perceives an ideal language. Palés' poetic epiphany is in anticipation of the new possibilities of his medium —a preview of the fusion of music and language in «jitanjáfora,»— of sculp-ture and poetry in his successful search for a plastic vocabulary. «Pueblo Negro» is the *ars poetica* of the poet in which he contemplates the essential elements of form and sound which comprise his aesthetic vision, and procedes toward their fusion. This fusion is at its deepest level a search for the adequate expression of an existing life-style which, neither Spanish nor African, eludes the traditional images of a European heritage:

> Podrías ir de mantilla,
> si tu ardiente sangre ñáñiga
> no trocara por madrás
> la leve espuma de España.
>
> Podrías lucir, esbelta,
> sobriedad de línea clásica
> si tu sol. a fuerza de oro,
> no madurase tus ánforas
> dilatando sus contornos
> en amplitud de tinaja...[16]

The Antilles, here personified, is given heavy, sun-blazoned forms har-monized in the plastic image of «tinaja.» The «tinaja,» symbolic of the craft of earlier cultures, serves as contrast to the «sobriedad de línea clá-sica.»

The Puerto Rican gave the first evidence in 1925, that the primitivist vision in the Antilles could be, in the words of Nicolás Guillén, «modo» rather than «moda,» [17] and that the conquest of form was synonymous with the conquest of identity. At the same time artists of the stature of Palés, Carpentier and Guillén brought the perspective of their essentially European culture to bear on their subject, investing the *comparsa* with the irony of

---

[16] Ibid., p. 241.
[17] Nicolás Guillén, «El negro cubano,» *Hora de España* (Valencia), Vol. XI, 1937, pp. 38-39.

2

Valle-Inclán (as Palés' «Preludio en Boricua»), the *ingenio azucarero* with Zola's naturalism (Carpentier's *¡Écue-yamba-Ó!*) or the «manigua cubana» with Lorca's mythification (Guillén's «La llegada»).

In Cuba, the «supervivencia» of African culture, the energetic efforts in the realm of anthropology by Fernando Ortiz, and the existence of cultivated writers, painters and musicians contributed to the dual task of creating, in Carpentier's words, «una fisonomía propia a lo criollo» and establishing «contactos con intelectuales de Europa.» These were some of the factors involved in the particular dynamism of the Cuban scene of the 20's and 30's and specifically in the birth of the Afro-Cuban movement.

Three giants stand behind the Afro-Cuban artists —Picasso, García Lorca, and Stravinsky— whose direct disciples were the painter Wilfredo Lam, the poet Nicolás Guillén, and the composer Amadeo Roldán. The influences of those Europeans were so strong and unmistakeable that these Caribbean artists, although profiting abundantily from their tutelage, often betray debt in their early works. The road to originality was at least in part provided by two factors; the first was the existence of a vast source of material in the Cuban culture itself, to which the young artists had legitimate and «exclusive» claim —the «cantos de cabildo,» comparsas, liturgies, centuries-old guarachas, «sones.» The other factor was the existence of a vitally related movement in the different arts, to an extent of a common endeavor. In the cross-fertilization between artists and mediums a «fisonomía propia» emerged that distinguished these artists and writers from those of similar interests abroad and elsewhere in Latin America.

> Con la aparición del negrismo se establece entre nosotros una corriente de simpatías, un ligamento que nos lleva a una introspección más cabal, amplia y certera del alma negra... no es un injerto ni un pegote, sino retorno también a la formidable tradición folklórica ininterrumpida que comienza en el llamado «poeta gallo» o «de puya» de los cabildos africanos...[18]

The spirit of collaboration was manifest in all the arts: Amadeo Roldán and García Caturla composed elaborate settings for poems by Guillén and Palés Matos; Carpentier wrote the libretti for Afro-Cuban ballets scored by Roldán («El milagro de Anaquillé» of 1927, «La Rebambaramba» of 1928), and collected paintings by Wilfredo Lam whose themes echo his own. Guillén credits the anthropologist Fernando Ortiz with being his prime influence, and Ortiz himself spanned all the diverse activities in his monographs on the poetry, painting, and music of the movement.

Carpentier, looking back as a participant in the movement, sums up the forces behind it and the significance of the Negro for the creative artists in the 20's and 30's:

> La presencia de ritmos, danzas, ritos, elementos plásticos, tradicionales, que habían sido postergados durante demasiado tiempo en virtud de prejuicios

---

[18] Alejo Carpentier, *La música en Cuba* (México: Fondo de Cultura Económica, 1946), p. 309.

absurdos, abría un campo de acción inmediato, que ofrecía posibilidades de luchar por cosas mucho más interesantes que una partitura atonal o un cuadro cubista... Los ojos y los oídos se abrieron sobre lo viviente y próximo. Por otra parte, el nacimiento de la pintura mexicana, la obra de Diego Rivera y de Orozco, habían impresionado a muchos intelectuales de Cuba. La posibilidad de expresar lo criollo con una nueva noción de sus valores se impuso a las mentes... Fernando Ortiz, a pesar de la diferencia de edades, se mezclaba fraternalmente con la muchachada. Se leyeron sus libros. Se exaltaron los valores folklóricos. Súbitamente, el negro se hizo el eje de todas las miradas. Por lo mismo que con ello se disgustaba a los intelectuales de viejo cuño, se iba con unción a los juramentos ñáñigos, haciéndose el elogio de la danza del diablito. Así nació la tendencia afrocubanista, que durante más de diez años alimentaría poemas, novelas, estudios folklóricos y sociológicos. Tendencia que, en muchos casos, sólo llegó a lo superficial..., pero que constituyó un paso necesario para comprender mejor ciertos factores poéticos, musicales, étnicos y sociales, que habían contribuido a dar una fisonomía propia a lo criollo.[19]

A reading of *La música en Cuba* (México, 1946) reveals that for Carpentier, as for others in the movement, the newly awakened interest in the Black was many-sided: he was a source of lore; a creator and performer in the historical sense and in the present; a human cypher to «Cubanidad» as a meaningful definition of being.

On the other hand the marginal and often maleficent rôle played by the white man in Carpentier's early fiction provides a backdrop of colonial decadence for the vital drama of the Black. In *¡Écue-yamba-Ó!*, «Histoire de lunes», «El fugitivo» and *El Reino de este mundo,* only a handful of whites appear, and in general they are the dregs of humanity, chained to vices and deteriorating institutions in a kind of forlorn exile. Often only their images or effigies are present, always seen as incongruous and absurd, almost as unwanted remainders of a lost civilization. The white middle-class Cuban, who might somehow reflect the author's own identity, is totally absent.

In *Écue* the American presence is felt but seen only in advertisements: «En un cartel de hojalata, un guapo mozo de tipo estandarizado blandía un paquete de cigarrillos: It's toasted!»

The black wagon-drivers are created at the weighing station by an old Italian (the only white character to appear in the novel) «antiguo hidalgo italiano, arruinado por la guerra y su esteticismo improductivo, movilizaba todas las prácticas encaminadas a engañar inicuamente al mísero machetero en beneficio del colono...»[43]

The other whites are represented in the Goyesque portraits hanging in the Prado jail which depict a decadent, syphilitic aristocracy of the colonial epoch: «El óleo había plasmado sus ojos bizcos, sus avariosis, sus pechos constelados de toisones, rosarios y medallas, así como sus escudos seccionados por campos y gules. Codicia, privilegios reales, escapularios. Tanto Monta y mal de Nápoles.»[44]

---

[19] Ibid., p. 236.

In «Histoire de lunes» (Paris, 1933) the lone white character is the churchman who shuts the door on the procession of African idols. In «El fugitivo» as in *El reino de este mundo* the white man is seen as a degenerate slaver whose life is characterized by cruelty and folly. In the latter work his European habits are put in a ridiculous light: recall also the protagonist-author's emphatic rejection of Mouche, the French pseudo-existentialist in *Los pasos perdidos.*

El reino de este mundo, perhaps most revealing in this sense, realizes the destruction of Western culture and the total exiling of the whites within the scenario of the Haitian revolution. In a sense the novel is the apocalyptic staging of Spengler's *The Decline of the West.* In place of the «ludiones» and machines of the modern sector, primitive idols are erected in hieratic supremacy.

The white man, then, though appearing infrequently in Carpentier's early period, is associated with four classic institutions of oppression in Latin America —prison, the Church, slavery, foreign imperialism.

Neither, however, is the Black free of the taint of the corrupting forces of civilization; he cannot be a figure of pure primitivism, reflecting as he must the dominant culture and being inevitably linked to its fate. This is seen by the early Carpentier as the ultimate irony and even tragedy of the Black; Menegildo loses his rural innocence within the walls of the Prado jail under the warped scrutiny of the «alcaldes coloniales.» Christophe is condemned in *El reino de este mundo* because in the last analysis he has done little more than ape the European court. Many of the Afro-Antillian writers vacillate between the ideal of undiluted primitivism and negritude (as in Nicolás Guillén's «Llegada» for example) and the often bitter knowledge of the corruption of that ideal by the forces of poverty and oppression or by the Black's own duplicity (as in Palés' «Preludio en Boricua»). In the case of Palés and Guillén, the conflict is resolved with humor and the creation of semi-comic figures, the best example of which is «El Duque de la Mermelada» of Palés. In Carpentier the conflict is manifested in a tense naturalism which approaches the grotesque. Like other Antillian artists, Carpentier sees the Black world through a telescope. When seen through the large magnifying end, it is the «triste lujuria» of an impoverished proletariat; when seen through the small distancing end the perspective of myth shapes and purifies vision.

* * *

In 1920 Carpentier returned to Havana from Paris where he had been since the beginning of his secondary education, studying at the Lycée Jeanson de Sailly and becoming in his words a «pianista aceptable.» When he matriculated in the University of Havana as a student of architecture in the same year, he was 16 years of age, already with a richly variegated cultural background. Only one year after his return to Cuba he was writing a column for *La Discusión* entitled «Obras Famosas.» Later in the year he left the University for another trip to France, abandoning abruptly his ambitions as architect (his father's profession) if not his interest in the field. On his return to Cuba «se dedicó completamente al periodismo» and contributed articles of art and literary criticism to *El Heraldo de Cuba* and *La Discusión*. During this period of activity as a newsman, Carpentier also became involved in politics, specifically in the «abortada revolución de Veteranos y Patriotas» of 1923,[20] which significantly, seems to have constituted an excursion into the absurd for him. However sterile the route of activism proved, more productive channels were opened by the formation of the «Grupo Minorista,» an outgrowth of the previously mentioned revolutionary group. «El Grupo Minorista» was the Cuban version of avant-garde groups throughout Latin America at this time, and its members were the human conductors for literary ideas from abroad, and the organizers of local manifestations of the modern spirit.

> Al calor de la abortada revolución de Veteranos y Patriotas (1923), que fue típico ejemplo de pronunciamiento latinoamericano, sin cohesión, ni dirección, ni ideología concreta, algunos escritores y artistas jóvenes que se habían visto envueltos en el movimiento, sacando provechosas enseñanzas de una aventura inútilmente peligrosa, adquirieron el hábito de reunirse con frecuencia, para conservar una camaradería nacida en días agitados. Así se formó el Grupo Minorista, sin manifiestos ni capillas, como una reunión de hombres que se interesaban por las mismas cosas. Sin que pretendiera crear un movimiento, el minorismo fue muy pronto un estado de espíritu. Gracias a él se publicaron revistas; se establecieron contactos personales con intelectuales de Europa y de América, que representaban una nueva manera de pensar y de ver. Inútil es decir que en esta época se hicieron los «descubrimientos» de Picasso, de Joyce, de Stravinsky, de los seis, del Esprit Nouveau y de todos los «ismos». Los libros impresos sin capitulares andaban de mano en mano. Fue el tiempo de la «vanguardia», de las metáforas traídas por los cabellos, de las revistas tituladas, obligatoriamente, «Espiral», «Proa», «Vértice», «Hélice», etc. Además, toda la juventud del continente padecía, en aquellos años, de la misma fiebre.[21]

Three years later, the sophisticated review, *Avance,* which for three years (1927-1930) would inform Cuban intellectuals of universal art currents, was founded by «Los Cinco» (Jorge Mañach, Juan Marinello, Francisco Ichaso, Martín Casanovas, and Carpentier).

Although neither the «Grupo Minorista» or «Los Cinco» was a primarily political group, the concept of art held by these young men was closely tied to political aims, and often bent towards the common struggle against the overt dictatorship of Machado who gained power in 1925, and the continuing denunciation of North American capitalism. Carpentier and an associate were jailed in August 1927 for signing a manifesto. There he wrote the first draft of *¡Écue-yamba-Ó!* between August and March 1928 when he was provisionally freed. Soon after he escaped to France with a group of French newsmen, using Robert Desnos' passport. Once in France, the doors were opened for him to the principal figures of French artistic movements.

---

[20] Ibid., p. 235.
[21] Ibid.

21

What of Carpentier's literary preferences in the early years? As the author has told us, the novels of Dumas, Salgari, and Verne lent fuel to his dream as an adolescent of being «hombre de acción.» From his father, an admirer of the works of Blasco Ibáñez, Baroja, and Galdós, he inherited a strong feeling for the Spanish novel, which in a recent interview he still extols over the «recintos casi familiares» of the French novel.[22] These early preferences leave their mark in a most noteworthy way on Carpentier's historical novel, *El siglo de las luces*.

Carpentier, years later, was to describe himself and those of his generation as «envueltos en las olas del nativismo» in the 20's, and his frequent praise of authors such as Rómulo Gallegos, José Eustacio Rivera, and Ricardo Guiraldes, make it reasonable to conjecture that he had read the principal works of that tradition (for example, José Eustacio Rivera's *La vorágine* of 1924, Güiraldes' *Don Segundo Sombra* of 1926, the early works of Gallegos) before leaving Cuba in 1928.

Although Carpentier, after his first novel, departs radically from the nativist perspective, and consistently condemns the trend as a necessary evil, «un paso necesario» towards significant fiction, in a passage from *La música en Cuba* he delivers a paradoxical justification for the emphasis on regional themes during the times:

> Los adversarios de las tendencias nacionalistas que prevalecen hoy... en casi todas las naciones del Nuevo Mundo, se valen a menudo de un argumento polémico que es, poco más o menos, el siguiente: inspirarse en música de negros, de indios, de hombres primitivos, no es un progreso; desligarse de la gran tradición artística europea, sustituyendo las grandes disciplinas de la cultura occidental por el culto del vodú, del juego ñáñigo, del batuque, del candombe, equivale a renegar de las raíces más nobles de nuestra idiosincrasia, colocando un tambor en lugar del clavicordio.
>
> Sin embargo, los que así razonan olvidan demasiado que el compositor latinoamericano, vuelto hacia Europa en busca de la solución de sus problemas estéticos, no oye hablar más que de folklore, de canto popular, de ritmos primitivos, de escuelas nacionalistas...[23]

It was, then, a consciously cultivated artistic regionalism well irrigated by the flow of the current and the classic French works through Cuban bookstalls. This was possible, according to Carpentier, through the diligence of a bookseller named Morlhoon in keeping his shop well-stocked with the works of most of the significant and avant-garde French writers. Carpentier describes the «culto a Anatole France,» the fact that «se leía Zola» and that «en Cuba se leía Proust tal vez antes que en cualquier otro país del continente.»[24] Most significant is Carpentier's summary dismissal of

[22] Reyes Nevares, Beatriz, interview with Alejo Carpentier in *Cuadernos de Bellas Artes* (México), June 1964, p. 83.

[23] *La música en Cuba, op. cit.,* p. 251.

[24] César Leante, «Confesiones de un escritor barroco,» *Cuba,* Año III, no. 24, April 1964, p. 32.

the Cuban letters of the time: «Miguel Carrión era el único escritor importante en ese tiempo en Cuba.»

This brief commentary shows the preponderance that French authors must have had in Carpentier's personal library during this time. And Carpentier's singling out of Carrión only reinforces this observation, pointing back to Zola as a key force in his literary formation. A Cuban critic describes Carrión and the literary ambience surrounding him:

> Por este tiempo se había impuesto ya en el país un nuevo patriciado de «generales y doctores», una alta burguesía al servicio del capital monopolista norteamericano, que dominaba sobre una pequeña burguesía alimentada con sus migajas. El proletariado, informe todavía, no era aún favorable al socialismo de Diego Vicente Tejera y de Carlos Loveira, el mejor novelista del período, cuyas obras... constituyen agudas denuncias de la realidad política y social del país. Loveira... es el tipo de los escritores de esta Primera Generación Republicana en quienes la amargura ante el desorden social y administrativo se impone con tal fuerza que anula la esperanza y el propósito de un gesto superador. *Como en Zola, a cuyo naturalismo adscriben sus obras, los novelistas más importantes de este período —Loveira, el médico Miguel de Carrión (1875-1929)— describen la decadencia social de su patria como un proceso de incurable degeneración, y esta amargura contagia las primeras producciones de los autores más jóvenes...*[25]

The mines of Zola's *Germinal* and the *ingenio azucarero* of Cuba, brought closer by a generation of patriotic but embittered literary realists, such as Carrión, and its literary offspring (the Luis Felipe Rodríguez of *La pascua de la tierra natal,* 1923, for example) were still inseparable in Carpentier's conception of social struggle of his time. The Zolaesque tradition survived in the propitious climate created by the proletarian currents of the twenties in art, which for many Latin Americans were most powerfully channeled by the Mexican muralist Diego Rivera.

It is also necessary to mention the effect of the avant-garde poetry of Latin American on Carpentier —the «nueva industria; la de la metáfora a toda ultranza... la del ultraísmo.»[26] That Carpentier was familiar with the iconoclastic imagery of authors such as Huidobro, Girondo, Greiff, and his compatriot Mariano Brull, is evidenced in the abundance of verbal pyrotechnics of his first novel. Carpentier describes his full participation in the «chacota,» referring to the period as «una época que padecíamos todos en América Latina... las tendencias mecanistas, ultraístas, futuristas, nos hizo mucho daño... la metáfora había que usarla en una forma totalmente desaforada...»[27]

Carpentier's relationship to his enviroment as reflected in his early literary works, was determined above all by the Cuban's unique perspective,

---

[25] José Antonio Portuondo, *Bosquejo histórico de las letras cubanas* (La Habana: Editora del Ministerio de Educación, 1962), p. 51.
[26] Enrique Anderson-Imbert, *Historia de la literatura hispanoamericana* (México: Fondo de Cultura Económica, 1964), p. 14.
[27] Mario Vargas Llosa, «Cuatro preguntas a Alejo Carpentier,» *Marcha* (Montevideo), 1246, 12-III- (1963), p. 31.

as American and, in Claude Fell's words «presque Américaniste,» the latter being a condition inherited from two generations of Carpentiers. In his earliest works this perspective was manifested in a compensatory, myopic slavery to detail and documentation which only with time was he able to surpass, using his intrinsic distance to see beyond the elements of his raw material.

Juan Marinello in a chapter on the early years of Carpentier characterizes his compatriot «con el crítico amor que merece»:

> Alejo Carpentier es, como se sabe, una de las sensibilidades más finas y cultivadas de las nuevas generaciones. Su curiosidad generosa iguala a su capacidad técnica. Es tan artista como hombre de letras, tan ansioso de primitivismos como esclavo de refinamientos. En relación con lo cubano se agrava ésta su posición contradictoria. Vivió entre nosotros largos años; partió hacia París en la primera juventud, pero acusada ya, en armoniosa precocidad, su personalidad artística. Tenido en La Habana como extranjero... vivió entre nosotros una peregrina indefinición: lo criollo le atrajo poderosamente; sintió de cerca lo africano trasplantado a la isla, el son mulato, el tono colonial, pero no pudo redimirse la extranjería. Impelido por su sed artística y su hambre inquisitiva trabó contacto esotérico con nuestros negros y frecuentó cabildos y bembés. Los vio por dentro, pero no se metió en ellos; les sorprendió el perfil, les robó el acento, no les llegó a las vísceras recónditas. Si para muchos cubanos blancos y aun para algún cubano negro, la intimidad afrocriolla en sus valores más definidos, es teatro y pintoricidad, ¿no habría de serlo para un adolescente nacido en la vieja cultura y que había ido hacia lo negro como a una fiesta de los sentidos y una prueba de sus capacidades cultas? [28]

Although Carpentier participated fully in local movements and activities, both literary and political, in some senses he was a marginal man, with the detached perspective of the inquisitive phenomenologist, «ansioso de primitivismos.»

Carpentier's literary conception of the Negro bears little relationship to that of the general vein of the *Afrocriollo* poets such as Guillén and Ballagas. While the latter poets were primarily interested in the Black of «carne y hueso» and his immediate Cuban ambience, Carpentier's Black, in spite of the trappings of localism, betrays the aspirations of the primitivist; he is an archetypal being, a symbolic force that the author seeks to evoke and achieve. Aiming beyond the local existence of the Cuban Negro, Carpentier tries to arrive at the essence of atavism, of the «Africanía» of the Black. Thus the author's works focus on the liturgical, the ritual, the supernatural elements that he has discerned in the Caribbean.

This is not to say that Carpentier's primitivism did not find sympathetic vibrations among Cuban artists; many Cuban painters of the time (Antonio Gattorno and Víctor Manuel for example) were painting in the tradition of Gauguin. In music, composers such as García Caturla and Amadeo Roldán, influenced by Stravinsky, made extensive use of the most primitive instruments for their percussive ensembles. The Cuban art of the time,

---

[28] Marinello, *op. cit.*, p. 171.

nourished by close contact with European movements, contains an air of synthesis, to which Carpentier contributes. Even in the poetry of Nicolás Guillén there is a dimension of primitivism (as in «Llegada» and «Sense-mayá»), inspired, as he has maintained, by the anthropologist Fernando Ortiz.

Thus many forces are identifiable in the early writings of Carpentier, not all of which are compatible. «El milagro de Anaquillé» of 1927 and *¡Écue-yamba-Ó!* of 1933 reveal the author at cross-purposes between polit- ical and aesthetic goals, caught between the dual tendencies of populism and *Barroquismo* of the 20's, between the resuscitated verse of Góngora and the massive social forces mobilized in Diego Rivera's proletarian art. And as I have suggested, Carpentier the primitivist is at odds, in the author's first works, with Carpentier the naturalist.

I. «EL MILAGRO DE ANAQUILLÉ»

In the years prior to his incarceration and subsequent exodus from Cuba, Carpentier's scant literary production was closely related to the musical life on the island. Inspired by the example of Stravinsky's musical primitivism, [29] Carpentier, with the composer Amadeo Roldán, sought to capture the folkloric essence of Cuban life by welding gesture to music in four choreographic works. «El milagro de Anaquillé» (1927). «La rebambaramba» (1928) —two Afro-Cuban «ballets»— and «Mata-Cangrejo» and «Azúcar» were the first experiments with forms which Carpentier would cultivate abundantly in Paris beteen 1928 and 1933. There he collaborated with well-known composers such as Darius Milhaud, Villa-Lobos, and Marius Gaillard in the composition of farces, musical poems and works in the «teatro bufo» tradition.

As a primitivist Carpentier was primarily interested in the ritualistic aspects of the African cults. As musicologist he was aware of the central and sacred rôle of music in the realization of the functions of ritual. Thus, by combining gesture and music of «lo Afrocubano», he undoubtedly considered the new «ballet» —«género que casi no se ha explotado»— to be capable of a deeper, more complete and accurate representation of the rustic elements of Cubanidad to which he was attracted. He exhorts other Cubans to write «ballets o argumentos de acciones coreográficos explotando el inacabable acervo de nuestros elementos genuinos.» [30]

As a white man of European background, Carpentier saw in this genre the possibility of distilling the essence of his primitivist vision through the concentrated and multidimensional performance of stage. However this very condition condemned him to a peripheral stance focusing on his subject «desde fuera,» as a mine of lore to exploit artistically:

> Lo cierto es que el «ballet» y el drama o comedia musicales de asunto criollo afrocubano nos abren una cantera riquísima de temas por explotar.[31]

[29] *La música en Cuba* gives ample testimony of the direct influence of Stravinsky in those years, and of the excitement generated by the composer's use of primitive instruments which were of course highly familiar to most sophisticated Cuban musicians.

[30] Alejo Carpentier, prologue to «El milagro de Anaquille,» *Revista Cubana*, VIII, April-June 1937, p. 145.

[31] Ibid., p. 145.

With this posture in relation to his material, Carpentier recalls the traditional, colonial literary exploitations of black themes, embodied in the «teatro bufo» of Creto Gangá (which Carpentier discusses in a chapter of *La música en Cuba*) in which the Negro is used as the basis for the picturesque and the linguistic frivolity inherited from Góngora and Lope's treatment of the theme. Carpentier is in a sense the sole reviver of the ambience of this forgotten genre; «La rebambaramba» was a projection into the past «sugerido por la contemplación de un grabado de Mialhe representando comparsas del Día de Reyes frente a la vieja iglesia de San Francisco.» [32] Carpentier, like the «bufo» writers wished to exploit «lo folklórico» for the entertainment of a sophisticated audience. Yet Carpentier's Afro ballets are more ambitious and unmistakeably modern by virtue of their serious musical, socio-political, and primitivist dimensions.

«El milagro de Anaquillé,» which Carpentier says dates from 1927, provides a rather interesting vantage point from which to consider the author's black period, and contains in embryo some important tendencies. Ten years after writing «El milagro,» Carpentier decided to publish the text in *Revista Cubana,* accompanied by a prologue. In the latter, undaunted by the fact that all of his «ballets» had been «momentáneamente inmovilizados... sin salida inmediata,» he prides himself that «gracias a 'La rebambarada,' al 'Milagro de Anaquillé,' a 'Liturgia,' a 'Manita en el suelo,' Amadeo Roldán y García Caturla han podido escribir partituras —que marcan fechas capitales en la historia de nuestra música.»

«El milagro,» subtitled «misterio coreográfico en un acto» is indeed, as Carpentier's introduction prepares us, «una muestra curiosa» of a little-known genre. It contains in the brief space of seven pages, elements of the colonial farce —the «bufo»— in its somewhat burlesque display of local types, the allegory and social realism of proletarian drama in the early 20's, the *esperpento* of Valle-Inclán, and avant-garde Pirandellian devices of overt artifice in stage props. The dramatis personae consist of: «El Business Man (personaje enmascarado),» «El Marinero,» «La Flapper,» «El Diablito,» «El Guajiro,» «Los Jimaguas (personajes enmascarados y atados por el cuello con una cuerda),» «ocho cargadores de caña,» «tres guajiros,» «tres guajiras.» The «Business Man» and the «jimaguas» «deben parecer irreales y monstruosos, moviéndose como autómatas... los guajiros... lucirán semblantes pálidos... los cargadores de caña (negros) actuarán con un sincronismo perfecto, ejecutando simultáneamente los mismos gestos.»

The stage directions reflect a stylized poverty with two «bohíos» with «techos de guano,» that belong to the «Guajiro» and the «Iyamba.» The hut of the «Iyamba,» «de forma más primitiva,» is peaked with a horn, and there is a «San Lázaro chillón» hanging from the door. The flat horizon of a canefield, broken by the «mole geométrico» of a sugarmill with «tres chimeneas exageradas» is the backdrop for the action.

There are eight short scenes, each comprising an elaborate gesture. In Scene I, the «guajiros» arrive at the «bohío» and to the accompaniment of a guitarist, begin the zapateo (the text contains musical cues).

[32] Ibid., p. 145.

The «Business Man, masked grotesquely and wearing golf pants, intrudes on the «guajiros» in Scene II; he carries a camera and a bicycle pump, and begins inspecting the «guajiros» «como si fuesen caballos de raza.» Then he claps his hands, and as he shouts «O.K.,» Scene III begins with the sailor and the flapper dancing ragtime. While the couple dances, the «Business Man» busily covers the «bohíos» with the «clásicos ludiones» of North American commercialism «Ice Cream Soda,» «Wrigley's Chewing Gum.» Finally, with the bicycle pump he inflates a huge skyscraper.

In Scene IV, the «Business Man» sets up his camera and is engaged in taking shots of the couple in different poses.

The entrance of the black cane-cutters starts Scene V. They move «en fila, lentamente, *hieráticamente.*» Their arrival interrupts the «Business Man's» photography, and infuriated, he watches them destroy the advertisements. He protests, but the «Iyamba» «lo hace retroceder con una mirada.» The cane-cutters sit forming a circle around the «Iyamba» and the ritual fetishes.

Scene VI is the choreography for an elaborate «Náñigo» initiation rite including the dance of the «Diablito.» The «Business Man» looks on with interest, sitting in a film director's chair. He instructs the sailor and the flapper to dress in outlandish costumes, indicating that they mix with the «fieles,» all with the idea of making a new film.

In Scene VII the cane-bearers reject the couple; there is a confrontation between the «Business Man» and the «Iyamba.» The «Business Man,» armed with his tripod «como una lanza... destruye el altar a golpes.» «Los fieles» move to take him, but are paralyzed by *una fuerza inexplicable* (italics mine). It is the «Jimaguas» —«dos enormes muñecos negros, casi cilíndricos... con aspecto sobrenatural, implacable.»— The «Business Man» «retrocede aterrorizado» as the «Jimaguas» «avanzan bailando pesadamente.» The grotesque figures tie a noose around the «Business Man's» neck and the sky-scraper collapses «como un muñeco de goma.» The cane-carriers «alzan los brazos al cielo»; slow curtain.

The piece is an obvious social allegory in which the «genuine» powers of the believers («los fieles» is the recurring name given the cane-cutters) are triumphant over the illusory power of the economic imperialist as suggested by the deflated skyscraper. In the clash of styles and values, the Black, the exploited member of Cuban society, attains victory through his close relationship to supernatural forces, his total indifference to the vulgarity of commercialism —in short, through his purity.— The vehicle for the denouement is the miracle —the notion of *collective epiphany* so important in Carpentier's later work— of the «Ñáñigo» deus ex-machina who exorcises the cultural evils embodied in the «Business Man.»

With regard to the artistic conception of the work, the first thing that strikes the reader is the nature of the characters. They are achetypal representations of ethno-cultural groups whose intrinsic qualities are frozen hyperbolically in gesture and mask. Carpentier is not interested in the typical in its quotidian sense; his Black here is not the one who might most accurately depict «Cubanidad,» but rather the one most capable of evoking «Africanness» —«El Iyamba,» or «shaman.» The white man is similarly abstracted and stylized in his antagonistic rôle as foreign imperialist.

In his prologue, Carpentier describes another work, written three years posterior to «El milagro» —«Manita en el suelo» (1930). In this «farsa para títeres y actores» the dramatis personas reflect a similar tendency: «En 'Manita en el suelo'... escrito para el compositor Alejandro García Caturla, movilicé personajes tales como la Virgen de la Caridad del Cobre, el Capitán General de España, Juan Odio, Juan Indio y Juan Esclavo, el Chino de la charada, Candita la Loca, El Gallo Motoriongo, y Papá Montero...»

This mixture of archetypes embodying either ethnic (Juan Indio, Juan Esclavo), moral (Juan Odio) or folklórico (El Gallo Motoriongo, Papá Montero) values would seem to illustrate Carpentier's simplistic and programmed conception of Caribbean themes at this time.

Yet even here in the earliest stages of Carpentier's career as a writer one of the salient characteristics of his mature works is already in evidence a way of looking at man and history that determines the structure of, among other works, his two historical novels, *El reino de este mundo* and *Siglo de las luces,* in which the action results from the clash between human groups while individuals play minor rôles. Carpentier would remark to Claude Fells in 1965:

> Le roman sud-américain doit montrer la transformation de groupes en mouvement, en action. C'est pourquoi mes romans ont peu de personnages. Mon prochain roman «El año '59»... sera d'ailleurs un roman sans personnages. Les cas individuels ne sont plus posibles. Le roman est devenu un moyen d'explotation de certaines collectivités, et un lien entre le particulier et l'universel...[33]

Carpentier projects for a forthcoming novel the next logical step from the creation of archetypes, the abandonment of character altogether, while the archetype is the embodiment of collective, not individual, truths.

The archetypes in «El milagro de Anaquillé» are conveyed entirely through gesture, as there is no dialogue in the «ballet.» It is interesting to find this mode of presentation at such an early stage in Carpentier's work, since in varying degrees it is to be a constant in his works. Antipodal to the psychological novelist's analysis of man's interior working and equally alien to the technique of dialogue, Carpentier at his most characteristic is exceedingly visual, even cinematographic in his conception of subjects. Like his often-praised Goya, he desires to bring man from the depths of himself to the flat surface, fixing him in his most intense attitudes and gestures: «Todo en nuestro ambiente puede transcribirse en gestos, cantos, coros, o ritmos.»[34]

---

[33] Claude Fell, «Rencontre avec Alejo Carpentier,» *Les Langues Modernes,* 59 année, 3 (May-June 1965), p. 109.
[34] «El milagro de Anaquillé,» *op. cit.,* p. 146.

The gestures of the «Iyamba» are imperious, invested with authority. The cane-cutters' movements are made with «sincronismo perfecto.» When they arrive on the stage, it is «hieráticamente.»[35] The «Guajiro,» contrastingly, is represented as «pálido» and «medroso»; dramatically he has no genuine function, unless it is to complete the impression of poverty and exploitation.

In «El milagro de Anaquillé» can be found the beginnings of Carpentier's discoveries of the «real maravilloso,» an aesthetic and philosophical criterion not consciously elaborated until more than twenty years later in the prologue of El reino de este mundo (México, 1949). In the latter, Carpentier, in reaction to the artificialities of the surrealist's world, states that he composed El reino de este mundo, «dejando que lo maravilloso fluya libremente de una realidad estrictamente seguida 'en todos sus detalles'.»[36]

Similarly, in the prologue of «El milagro» Carpentier wrote proudly that he incorporated «sin modificación alguna el ritual coreográfico de las ceremonias de iniciación Afrocubanas.» However the use of the «real maravilloso» is quite different in the two works. Ritual barely surpasses mere choreography (although it may not be fair to judge the work without the musical context) in the earlier work, and again in ¡Écue-yamba-Ó!, but in the later El reino de este mundo Carpentier was able to include ritual in the thematic fabric of the novel.

Another element in the artistic conception of the piece is that of the grotesque, the esperpento, the absurd and farcical, which would seem to be incompatible wth the serious prime moving forces of the play —social allegory and primitivism.

There is an air of the grotesque in the staging. On the door of the «Guajiro» shack is painted «un chico que mira con expresión medrosa, con toda la mano metido en la boca.» The «Iyamba's» shack is «rematado por un cuerno» on the thatched roof. The chimneys of the sugarmill loom «muy exageradas» on the horizon. The «Business Man» and the «Jimaguas,» as representatives of antagonistic forces, «deben parecer irreales, monstruosos.» The «Business Man's» mask «duplica el volumen de su cabeza,» while the «Jimaguas» are enormous dolls with «gruesos ojos blancos y saltones.» The skyscraper collapses at the end like «un muñeco de goma.»

The musical side of the ballet presents a partial explanation for this conscious use of grotesque motifs. If indeed, as Carpentier has stated, «El milagro» was inspired by Stravinsky, it is not unlikely that the Cuban writer had the mixture of primitive rhythms and orchestral grotesques, of the playful and the sinister, characteristic of the «Rite of Spring,» present in his imagination when he choreographed this piece for Roldán.

It is also through the grotesque, as in the case of Palés Matos, that Carpentier achieves his distance from the material of the social drama. For

[35] Frances Weber, a penetrating critic of Carpentier's fiction, employs the word «hieratic» to describe the author's tone in «El acoso,» It is interesting that a stage direction early in the writer's career, could foresee a style, and a characteristic way of looking at reality. See Frances Weber, «'El acoso': Alejo Carpentier's War on time,» PMLA LXXVIII, 4, Sept. 1963, pp. 440-448.
[36] El reino de este mundo, op. cit., p. 15.

simultaneous with the delivery of a «message» is the presentation of the absurd incongruities of the stylized microcosm of Caribbean society conceived in the piece, the forms of which act as relief, in a way parallel but, not equivalent to, comic relief.

The grotesque, as Kayser has demonstrated, can be an aesthetic category, as well as an exploration into unknown recesses of the mind and human existence. The grotesque of forms used in a light burlesque, almost decorative sense, is found in Carpentier's ballets, in manifestations quite similar to Palés' Valle-Inclanesque «grandes Cocorocos» and «Tembandumbas,» as the exaggerated, formalized and semi-comic figures evocative of, if not directly inspired by, ritual costume. The grotesque as exploration into unknown realms of existence, inextricable from the grotesque of forms, is a constant in Carpentier and naively manifested in the «Jimaguas.»

There are several elements of «El milagro» that represent characteristics of Carpentier's vision, and show what place the tiny ballet holds in relation to the author's later works.

First, the notion of collective drama is a constant and dominant mode of artistic conception in Carpentier's career as novelist, to which he seems to have returned in his latest and unpublished novel *El año '59*. In «El milagro» the antipodal archetypes are limned out in the ultratheatrical elements of costume (costumes attain symbolic importance in later novels, notably in *Siglo de las luces*), mask, and the gesture that freezes, stylizes humanity. As Carpentier matures, the archetypes themselves will move into the background, wearing their inherited livery of the day, while the confrontation of human groups, ideas, and above all, styles, comes to the foreground as the focal point.

While Carpentier in «El milagro» simplistically breaks down Caribbean society into three component groups or styles —Black, Guajiro, foreigner— he will later search for a truer, more difficult reality —the «tercer estilo» resulting from the symbiosis of races and cultures in the Caribbean.

The ballet demonstrates the incipient gestation of «lo real maravilloso» and the fundamental rôle played by the black culture in the genesis of this literary philosophy. The «real maravilloso,» although theoretically the aesthetic of the real that transcends itself through inherently marvelous conjunctions and luminosities not imposed by the author («dejándose que lo maravilloso fluya libremente de una realidad estrictamente seguida en todos sus detalles»), is of course inevitably an intellectual condition —a predisposition to accept «lo maravilloso» in the real and also an aesthetic criterion, and a latent mysticism operating through faith. Relatively primitive peoples are in a sense Carpentier's collaborators, since through faith they are able to achieve this condition, to attain access to the «real maravilloso,» the ultimate manifestation of which is the miracle. Thus, Carpentier often projects his vision *through* the «collective unconscious» of primitive peoples, investing thereby the elements of reality with a new intensity and harmony as in the projected animism of later works. Through this perspective the division between reality and imagination is abolished, and the miracle becomes reality. Thus one can explain Carpentier's fascination with the primitive and medieval aspects of the chroniclers of the conquest of America, with Ponce de León, and other visionaries.

In «El milagro de Anaquillé,» Carpentier projects his dramatic conception through the «Ñáñigo» consciousness and the «Jimaguas,» the projections of collective faith, are indeed incarnated on the stage. As the surrealists aim at erasing the false boundaries between the individual subconscious as manifested in dream and the exterior world of objects, Carpentier has a similar ambition on a collective scale —to erase the margin between faith and deed, resulting in miracle, or the collective epiphany at the most intense level.

The Black in addition to his rôle as martyr in the immediate economic and historical sense, is also a cultural hero, through his imagined indifference to bourgeois (specifically North American bourgeois) values, through his belief in the supernatural. Following Breton's description of the primitivist, Carpentier, for whom black culture took on the dimensions of a revelation, «quiso apoderarse de esta visión a costa de un milagro.» In his early stages, the naive method used to possess this vision was to lift chunks of reality out of their context in an attempt to transplant them into fiction. But the connecting arteries, branching from a clearly understood set of «contextos» (the term he will later use —in *Tientos y diferencias*— to describe this vital need) were not there, and the «Ñáñigo» episodes in his early works, although brilliant, die in isolation from the whole of his vision of the Caribbean. It was, in seeming paradox perhaps, Carpentier's apprenticeship with the surrealists while in Paris that would help him find the connections between the «merveilleux» and the «quotidian.»

II. ¡ÉCUE-YAMBA-Ó!

Shortly after the founding of the review *Avance,* which from 1927 through September 1930 was the principal organ of the avant-garde in Cuba, Carpentier and Martí Casanovas were arrested for signing a manifesto against «el asno con garras».

During his seven month in the Prado jail in Havana, Carpentier turned out the rough draft of *¡Écue-yamba-Ó!* («God be Praised» in «Ñáñigo» dialect), «novela Afrocubana» which six years later he published in Madrid (Editorial España, 1933). Since Carpentier had managed to flee Cuba in March 1928, he had ample time before publication to polish and make additions to his novel during the important formative period of his years in Paris. Just how much of it he changed cannot be ascertained; however it is probable that certain surrealistic touches were added in Paris, while the basic conception remained true to the first draft.

All of the preoccupations evident in «El milagro de Anaquillé» carry over into *¡Écue-yamba-Ó!.* The theme of the exploitation of the Cuban Black by American capitalism is again central, although the white North American does not appear as a character, but rather as a kind of Orwellian presence, manifested in effigy or commercial signs, and in obscure transactions.

The same incongruous combination of social and aesthetic aims that in «El milagro de Anaquillé» resulted in the bizarre novelty of «protest ballet,» in *¡Écue-yamba-Ó!* might be described as a novel-social document. However, in terms of proportion the social commentary is low in *Écue* compared to the welling up of artistic ambitions observable in it.

As in «el milagro de Anaquillé» these social and aesthetic preoccupations are related to the dominating force in the novel —the philosophy of primitivism. The values of the Black —not the ordinary Black, but rather the Black endowed with the African heritage of «occult» knowledge— are offset against bourgeois commercialism in the abstract. Through these values the Black gains the status of martyr and, to some extent, cultural hero. His identity is confirmed and upheld in ritual and knowledge of the occult. Yet for all his hieratic disdain for materialism, Carpentier's Black falls prey in the naturalistic mode to the forces of sex and violence, doomed to repeat a futile cycle of «navajazos» and rebirth.

The dramatic conception is similarly programmed in the two works, as the archetypal (if not stereotyped) view of human groups set off and counteracting persists in the novel.

Through very diverse means, ranging from poetic prose to elaborate documentary, *¡Écue-yamba-Ó!* intends to capture the essence of the black world of Cuba. The human vehicle for this act of penetration is the archetype Menegildo whose unfolding life of successive «iniciaciones» into the occult, into sexual fulfillment, and finally, into the «hampa Afrocubana» of Havana, is meant to give the reader an inside perspective compensatory to Carpentier's own erudite view.

Through Menegildo Carpentier seeks to accomplish his primitivist goal —to arrive at the marrow of life, to reduce it to its most elemental acts and rituals, to comtemplate man denuded of all the artificial contexts of modern society and Western culture.

In this plan, infancy, sex, violence, and death represent moments of truth wherein man is reduced to animal stature, yet placed in contact with the fundamental mysteries of the cosmos. The rural Black, seen to be in close contact with these forces, is for Carpentier a most useful instrument.

Menegildo, after an infancy of co-habitation with a veritable bestiary of tropical animals, is described by Carpentier in adolescence:

> ... No sabía leer... pero en cambio era ya doctor en gestos y cadencias. El sentido de ritmo latía en su sangre... cuando golpeaba una caja... reinventaba la música de los hombres...[37]
>
> ... ...
>
> Sus músculos respondían a la labor impuesta como piezas de una excelente calidad humana... sus ojos, más córnea que iris, sólo sabían expresar alegría, sorpresa, indiferencia, dolor o lubricidad...[38]

Complementay to the elemental nature painted by Carpentier here, is the profund ontology of Menegildo and the Cuban Black, maintained in atavism:

> Pensaba muchas veces en la mitología que le había sido revelada, y se sorprendía entonces de su pequeñez y debilidad ante la vasta harmonía de las fuerzas ocultas... En este mundo lo visible era bien poca cosa.[39]
>
> ... ...
>
> Estaba claro que ni Menegildo, ni Salomé, ni Beruá habían emprendido nunca la ardua tarea de analizar las causas primeras. Pero tenían, por atavismo, una concepción del universo que aceptaba la posible índole mágica de cualquier hecho... volvían a hallar la tradición milenaria —vieja como el perro que ladra a la luna— que permitió al hombre, desnudo sobre una tierra aún mal repuesta de sus últimas convulsiones, encontrar en sí mismo unas defensas instintivas contra la ferocidad de todo lo creado. Conservaban la altísima sabiduría de admitir la existencia de las cosas en cuya existencia se cree.[40]

---

[37] Alejo Carpentier, *¡Écue-yamba-Ó!* (Buenos Aires: Xanadú, 1968), p. 31.
[38] Ibid., p. 31.
[39] Ibid., p. 54.
[40] Ibid., p. 54.

As in «El milagro de Anaquillé,» the primitive is counterpoised against the other world of bourgeois capitalism:

> ... Ante *ellos* llegaba a tener un verdadero orgullo de su vida primitiva, llena de pequeñas complicaciones y de argucias mágicas que los hombres del Norte no conocerían nunca.[41]

In *¡Écue-yamba-Ó!* Carpentier explores many dimensions of «lo primitivo.» With the impulse of cultural primitivism he enters into the atavistic, the «más allá» of Africa, and the folkloric —the national myths of «la gran época de 'Manita en el suelo', los curros del Manglar y la Bodega del Cangrejo»; in his cosmic primitivism he seeks to capture the essence of ontology in documentary fashion, and the world of infancy.

While primitivism gives the positive generating force to *¡Écue-yamba-Ó!* the novelistic conception is naturalistic. In schematic fashion, man is reduced to a pawn of biological and economic forces, subject to their cyclical, seasonal movements, victimized by the machine that mixes his sweat and blood with the cane-sap and by the hurricanes and fires that plague the islands. It is not a long way from the mines of *Germinal* to the sugarmills of *Écue,* and Carpentier has not hesitated to draw the geneological line:

> Au début du XXième siècle, l'influence du naturalisme français de Zola a été capitale. Zola jouissait d'une véritable audience en Amérique Latine. Il se rendait par exemple jusqu'à une mine ou à un lieu de travail déterminé, puis il écrivait un roman à propos de ce qu'il venait de voir. Mais il faut se détacher de cette observation. Ainsi dans mon premier roman: *¡Écue-yamba-Ó!,* j'ai suivi un chemin absolument parallèle: J'ai voulu écrire un roman sur les Noirs de Cuba, présenter une vision nouvelle d'un secteur de la population cubaine. Mais je me suis depuis lors opposé à la réédition de ce livre, car je considère que ma vision est fausse, parce que partielle et trop rapide. L'animisme, le «merveilleux» qui tient une si grande place dans la vie des paysans cubains, m'avait complètement échappé. Je n'avais pas saisi cet état d'esprit «laïco-mystique» qui fait qu'un paysan cubain qui entre dans une forêt peut saluer les arbres et leur parler. Une vision locale et ruraliste d'un pays ne signifie rien.[46]

And later in the Vargas Llosa interview, referring in this critic's opinion to the naturalistic influence, Carpentier denies the novelistic conception itself of *Écue*: «No corresponde a mi manera actual de concebir la novela.»[47]

In terms of Carpentier's «novelística» we can accept this extreme act of disinheriting a first novel. As the author becomes capable of feeling and capturing ever-deeper relationships between man and nature, through the dimensions mentioned by the author himself of «animism» and the «merveilleux,» he abandons the more simplistic schemata of naturalism.

[41] Ibid., p. 61.
[46] Fell, *op. cit.,* p. 110.
[47] Vargas Llosa, *op. cit.,* p. 31.

Yet traces of the naturalistic vision persist even in his urban novel *El acoso,* some 20 years later. Furthermore, as I intend to demonstrate, in many senses Carpentier's disavowal is not totally justifiable, since many of the key elements of his vision of man and nature are found within the first novel.

The most and accurate comments on *Écue* have been made by Juan Marinello in a chapter that is as much wise counsel to a countryman as good criticism. Reacting primarily as a Cuban, Marinello is rigorous in his critique of his friend's efforts to capture an ethnic and national reality. His aim is the schism between «el impulso humano» (the attempt to render living character, through dialogue and psychological penetration) and «ambición literaria» (the purely aesthetic pretensions of the novel).

> Si Alejo Carpentier hubiera querido darnos una visión exclusivamente estética de lo Negro Cubano, o hubiera preferido que lo exótico fuese contraste de la pupila blanca, su libro, cualquiera que fuese su nivel, poseería unidad íntima... Menegildo ve por primera vez el mar y su grito de animal en pasmo queda roto, invalidado ante un mar literario... mar realista, mar sobrerrealista. Mares irreconciliables, océanos de dos continentes que se dan la espalda...[48]

Summing up, Marinello injects a note of hope for the young writer:

> Y Alejo Carpentier posee capacidad paternal, es decir, lealtad amorosa —antena vibrátil, tentáculo sediente— para transformar esta bella historia Afrocubana en un canto épico de sangres espesas y profundas, en un canto que, por ser de todos los hombres, sea también nuestro.[49]

I concur with Marinello's judgement in that the central flaw of *Écue* is one of perspective. Carpentier not having found *the way* into his subject remains peripheral to it: *Écue* therefore is a book *about* magic and the primitive, while his later works are able in varying degrees to suggest a *state* of magic, or as Carpentier put it, «cet état d'esprit laïco-mystique».
Écue is a vital, ambitious book, in which many often incongruous «miras» are brought to bear on the subject: there are unmistakeable elements of «ultraísmo,» Lugonesque imagery, surrealism, expressionism, as well as the naturalism, primitivism and futurism which are the central forces of the book. The aim, here, is to remove the extraneous and reveal the permanent, truly organic elements of the author's vision which remain and evolve.

[48] Marinello, *op. cit.,* p. 173.
[49] Marinello, p. 175.

Construction

Story

The plot is very simple, as naturalistic plots tend to be. Menegildo is born in the atmosphere of rural poverty of the Cué shanty. The father, Eusebio, swindled by the sugar companies into selling his canefields at a low price, buys a team of oxen with the proceeds. Thus, he acquires the position of wagoneer at the sugarmill which he will pass on to his son, Menegildo, when he comes of age, The young Menegildo undergoes the successive initiation involved in rural adolescence, survives the routine dangers of cohabitation with scorpions and «cangrejos cicuatos,» and as emblem of his coming of age, is given the job of wagoneer in charge of the oxen. The placidity of this life is transformed by an «encuentro» with Longina, the concubine of a Haitian cane-cutter, on a dark path. Afflicted by desire, Menegildo seeks the counsel of Beruá, the local «brujo,» who furthers the adolescent's knowledge of the occult and aids him through witchcraft in the seduction of Longina. The two become lovers but are discovered by the enormous Haitian, Napoleon, who administers a nearly fatal blow to Menegildo. The latter staggers back in the night to the Cué hut where he slowly convalesces.

The final stage of initiation —that of «machismo»— is begun with the arrival of Antonio at the Cué home. Antonio —the epitome of Habana's «guapería hampona»— determines the shape of Menegildo's subsequent world. After a drinking bout with his new mentor, Menegildo determines to get revenge on the Haitian Napoleon. He seeks out and knifes his rival, and after the subsequent arrest, is taken by the authorities to Habana where he is incarcerated in the Prado jail. The months in jail are the final confirmation of his manhood within the value system of his «Ñáñigo» peers, and once he is freed through the workings of Antonio, he is accepted into one of the city brotherhood cults.

After tasting the perils and pleasures of Habana for some time, Menegildo's sect is attacked by a rival group and he, along with others, dies in the fracas. In the last chapter the pregnant Longina returns to the Cué shack, bearing the bad news to the family. She is at first rebuked, finally accepted, and then redeemed when she gives birth to Menegildo's child.

Outwardly then, the form is that of one human life, from beginning to end. It would be close to the picaresque in form, a genre to which Carpentier is strongly attracted,[50] were it essentially episodic and socially oriented. However, *Écué* is an arrangement of fixed scenes around the life of Menegildo —scenes which often bear little more than a contextual, as opposed to an active and vital relationship to the individual character. Carpentier's focus was on phenomena and description rather than on character and episode. Thus here are three chapters entitled «Paisaje» as well as «Temporal,» «Fiesta,» «Incendio,» «Mitología,» and «Política,» which all

---

[50] Reyes Nevares, *op. cit.*, p. 84.

correspond to phenomena quite peripheral to the inner life of the character. The latter is at best, representative of themes and as a person, undeveloped and flat. The mode of *static sequence,* associated with the creation of a one dimensional character is not necessarily an inferior or outdated one; Carpentier uses it to great advantage and in a truly modern fashion in «El camino a Santiago.»

Then if neither character study nor social criticism is the purpose in unfolding Menegildo's life, one must look for other patterns and conjunctions in the structure of fixed arranged scenes to draw closer to the meaning.

¡Écue-yamba-Ó! is divided into three sections: «Infancia» (1), «Adolescencia» (11) and «La Ciudad» (111), comprising eleven chapters (forty-six pages), sixteen chapters (seventy-six pages) and fourteen chapters (eighty-eight pages) respectively. The book is 217 pages (forty-three chapters) in total length.

In Section 1 —«Infancia»— there are eleven chapters but in terms of clear significant divisions only six are discernible. These are:

Section 1

a) Scenes of the «ingenio» (Chapter one): Carpentier narrates, in descriptive fashion, the dynamic start of the «zafra» in the canefields. The author here seeks to weld the natural, the human, and the mechanical processess of the harvest through imagery.

b) The birth of Menegildo and the ambience of the black cane-cutter's shack (Chapters two and three): The birth is described as a routine element of country life, treated matter-of-factly by the midwife and mother, yet given relief by semi-grotesque touches of the author. Menegildo is «horrendo trozo de carne amoratada.» Pigs and lizards are part of the event.

c) Menegildo explores the wonders of the Cué hut —the world of insects and the hidden altar of «Ñáñigo»— from the magical perspective of infancy. Bitten by a poisonous crab, he is cured by «oraciones» (Chapters four and five).

d) History of economic exploitation.

e) Study and eulogy of «lo primitivo» as manifested in the emerging character of Menegildo and elemental music he inherits (Chapter seven). Animals collaborate subtly in this music.

f) Cyclone —man versus the elements (Chapters eight, nine, ten and eleven): This section is an extended study, with a poetic interlude (Chapter nine) of man's inferior relationship to the elements under the extreme condition of cataclysmic disaster. Man is reduced to a primeval state of naked terror.

Central elements and relationships in Section 1

The three natural phenomena of harvest, birth, and cyclone (*a*, *b*, *f*) are the framework for Section 1. The first two, normally symbols of fertility and hope of men, are treated ambiguously, depicted as the incipience of a perennial cycle of exploitation in which man and plant are sacrificed to the «gigante diabético» of the mill. The last section (*f*) of Part 1 closes this diminutive view of man, converting him into a plaything of the force of the cyclone. However, in schematic fashion, Carpentier shows that the truly native elements —man and plant alike— resist the cyclone, while the foreign are destroyed.

Here the authentic relationship with the land is shown to be a virtue which enables the Black to pass the test of survival, or perhaps vice-versa, the survival allows the Black to pass the test of authenticity in Carpentier's terms. It is only when man and nature, seen as one by Carpentier, are enslaved by economic forces that both are denigrated, and victimized.

The middle sections (*c* and *e*) are ventures into the primitive cosmos and of childhood, and into the exposition of cultural primitivism. Both of these sections, as opposed to the three discussed above, evoke the inventiveness of man in perceiving «lo real maravilloso.» They depict the positive relation of the Black to his environment —significantly, as child and as artist.

The child through the freshness of his vision understands intuitively fantastic dimensions in the mundane objects of the hut:

> La tabla más tosca sabe ser mar tormentoso con un maelstrom en cada nudo... Eclipses y nubes en la piel de un taburete iluminado por el sol... desde allí el mundo se muestra como una selva de pilares que sostienen plataformas, mesetas y cornisas pobladas de discos, filos, y trazos de bestias muertas...[51]

Carpentier chooses to reveal the ocult world of «santos» and «orishas» to the reader in the childhood section. Through the infant's eyes, the family altar is a «mágico teatro» of intriguing statuettes; it becomes real through the child's capacity for faith. Through the evocation of childhood, Carpentier achieves an intensified expression of primitivism —and the first example of a consciously elaborated magical universe.

The section of cultural primitivism (*e*) is written on the level of discursive consciousness, and attempts to describe the timelessness of the art of the primitive drummers, relating it to «edades remotas... Bajo el signo de una selva invisible.» For Carpentier, this music is a product of a distillation of nature itself, and the medium of communication with everything basic: «Música de cuero... huesos y metal» and animals respond to the «extraño maleficio sonoro.»

Each section of the first part is an exploration in differing dimensions of the relationship of the Black to his environment: on the whole it shows an early and self-conscious effort of the artist to create what he would later

---

[51]   *¡Écue-yamba-Ó!, op. cit.*, p. 21.

term the authentic «contextos» of the novel. Here the artist has mapped out his subject, aiming for, characteristically, a totality in an almost architectural sense.

In this special relationship to environment, the Black becomes the instrument of Carpentier's perpetual war on time, and the medium of communication with the primitive «illo tempore.» Petrified in the most fundamental attitudes, archetypal gestures and ritual acts of harvest, birth, childhood, music and violence, the Black becomes timeless in the cyclic, eternal recreations of mythic times:

> Their meaning [that of human acts] their values, are not connected with their crude physical datum but with their property of reproducing a primordial act, of repeating a mythical example... His [the archaic man] is the ceaseless repetition of gestures initiated by others.[52]

The artistic aim of Carpentier then coincides with that of primitive ontology in the elimination of unwanted time dimensions, and in the creation of the single, permanent time of ritual: «Siempre he tratado de establecer una relación de tiempo sin tiempo entre el pasado, el futuro y el presente.» [53]

Thus, as seen from the invaluable perspective of Carpentier's early work, the author's complex manipulations of time in *Pasos perdidos* and *Guerra del tiempo* take on a new light. In *Écue,* the suspension of time is a product of the primitivist vision of the author who sees time as the primitive himself sees and enacts his —as never-ending repetition of the fundamental acts, the denial of materialism and the empirical time of human progress. Increasingly as seen in «Viaje a la semilla» this suspension becomes an overt goal rather than product, but the important relationship between Carpentier's use of time and his primitivism, seen clearly in his Black cycle, is consistent. Even in *El siglo de las luces,* the basic conception of time is that of ritual; in that novel, revolution is conceived as the great ritual of mankind, successively repeated under the different blasons of Christ (in the conquest of America), Robespierre, and, the reader is tempted to project, Fidel. As ritual, revolutions perform the needed function of regeneration, yet as ritual they must sacrifice, in Carpentier's eyes, any claim to originality or even to longevity of effect.

Thus, *Écue* is a series of rituals which repeat an elemental archetype. Seen in this light, Parts II («Adolescencia») and III («La Ciudad») are both expansions, and repetitions of Part I («Infancia») leading to the final repetition which completes the circle —that of Menegildo's death and rebirth through his son.

In Part II —«Adolescencia»— there are eight discernible sections. In section (*a*) (Chapters 12-13) Menegildo, having reached the required level of maturity, is initiated in the intricacies of the family altar: this scene

[52] Mircea Eliade, *The Myth of the Eternal Return* (New York: Bollingen Foundation, 1965), p. 83.
[53] Vargas Llosa, p. 32.

is a continuation of the childhood scene in Part I wherein he discovers the altar figurines. Section (b) (Chapters 14-15) is a costumbrista description of different Black groups in the mill.

Section (c) (Chapters 16-21) is the central and focal section and describes Menegildo's «encuentro» with Longina, his initiation into sex, and the use of the occult for sexual purposes. Love is described «desde afuera,» as a ritual act with a prescribed sequence. The act itself is simultaneously animalized and stylized in a sensual pastoral ambience. Carpentier here aims for the pagan simplicity set off with elegant language.

Section (d) is a digressive discussion of the past and slavery.

Section (e) is the parallel study of a cataclysmic fire with the violence it engenders on the canefields, and the violence of sexual desire. The saving, fertility-bringing rain and the «cópula de la tierra» is accompanied by the sex act of Menegildo and Longina.

Section (f) is the convalescence of Menegildo after the jealous Napoleon's revenge. A curing rite is instrumental.

Section (g) (Chapters 26-28) is the arrival of Antonio which begins Menegildo's final stage of initiation —into «ñáñiguismo»— and his descent into the city.

The three focal elements in Part II are sex, nature, and the occult, all brought together in the center section (e) in the symbolic ritual love act. Part II, then, demonstrates a logical progression from Part I; in the latter the natural process of the harvest was welded to human life through imagery, followed by the birth of Menegildo. Part II seeks the same goal —to weld the human to the natural forces of fertility and violence, represented by rain and fire, in the crucible of the sex act. In this section (e) naturalism gives way to a lyrical pathetic fallacy, a full, even epic celebration of the primitive and elemental couched in poetic language.

After this epic celebration of life, Menegildo embarks on the road which leads inexorably toward the final ritual act of violence —his death, the last of the three interrelated rituals of birth, sex and death which form the focal points, or stations, of the life cycle and of the book.

Part III is a departure from the themes of the first two parts, and is characterized by various apocryphal digressions in tone and emphasis, yet it returns ultimately to the central themes.

In section (a) of Part III (Chapters 29 and 30) Menegildo is escorted by train from his rural ambience to the new world of the city, and his incarceration. In section (b) (Chapters 31-33) Carpentier makes an elaborate realistic description of jail life based obviously on his own concurrent experience. In section (c) (Chapter 34) Menegildo is freed and explores the foreign ambience of the city.

All the central sections, (d), (e), (f) and (g), are essentially rituals: section (d) (Chapters 36-37) is the documentary elaboration of the «Ñáñigo» initiation rite in which Menegildo takes part. Section (e) (Chapter 38) is the portrayal of rites of childhood, and the natural creativity of children in the invention of myth. This section is closely related in style and theme to the childhood section of Part I and both are significant examples of «lo real maravilloso.» Sections (f) and (g) (Chapters 39-41) are excursions, or digressions, into the phenomenon of popular «espiritismo»: section (g) terminates in a ritual gang war and the death of Menegildo. In the final section (h) (Chapters 42-43), Longina leads us to the symbolic return to the Cué hut and the beginning of a new cycle in the birth of the young Menegildo.

Part III for the main part, can be considered as an extended, choreographed ritual; it is filled with moments of brilliant description, yet with the exception of the childhood scene and the return of Longina, and possibly the initiation rites, which significantly, take place outside the city, it is mostly apocryphal in relation to the first two parts. In this section Carpentier attempts to complete the picture of the Black *welt* by drawing the urban dimension. But as he has cut the roots of his character in translating him into the foreign urban environment, he has cut his own roots, those of naturalism and primitivism, which were the simplistic aesthetic principles in the genesis of the novel. Only years later is Carpentier able powerfully to suggest the teluric forces in the urban environment.

However, in this third part, Carpentier achieves a measure of unity with the first two when in the last two chapters, through the stylized almost Lorcean violence of the gang fight, Menegildo participates in the third and final ritual of his cycle —his death— and returns to his ambience in the rebirth of his namesake. Throughout Carpentier, using the trajectory of a human life as the principal of unity, emphasizes the natural-impersonal and cyclical phenomena of harvest, cataclysm (fire and hurricane), reproduction and violent death. The construction of the elements and their rhythm is an attempt to weld these natural and human cycles: the fate of man with sugarcane, and the parallel movements of fertility and violence in man with those in nature.

Style

It is within this formal frame, in the realm of style, that the author's intentions and the most accurate picture of the book can be seen. Through the author's choice of vocabulary and image, i.e. the varying degrees of comparison (metaphor or simile), pathetic fallacy, and finally metamorphosis (suggested or realized), we can trace the novel's true course towards its goal of the fusion of man and nature. The artistic realization of this goal was one of the constant and primary endeavors in all of Carpentier's works in his first period and was seen by him to correspond to the essence of his subject.

Before proceeding to a discussion of the concrete techniques Carpentier used for this end, it may be wise to reiterate the essential duality of the author's conception of man and nature in *Écue*. In the naturalistic vision man, plant, and animal are linked in the bio-economic cycle and both man and nature are martyred to abstracted forces as in Thrall's description:

> The fundamental view of man which the naturalist takes is of an animal in the natural world, responding to environmental forces and internal stresses and drives, over none of which he has control or full knowledge.[54]

Yet in Carpentier's primitivist view, the rural black man, partly through his knowledge of the occult, and because of his special rapport with the forces of nature, can gain ascendancy and achieve a superior harmony with nature. Therefore man is seen in a shifting relationship with nature, at times exalted, because of it at times seemingly denigrated, even to the extent of the grotesque.[54 a]

Among the myriad methods one might use in a discussion of style, perhaps the most obvious would be the spotting and classification of all the images of the book. One could, as Ricardo Fernando has done with *Écue* in an unpublished thesis,[55] distinguish among other classifications: futuristic, Lugonesque, ultraistic, and surreal in this immature novel. However, this method does not accomplish much in the critical effort to reach the center of the book and particularly in this stage of the author's development. For the author, by virtue of his extremely variegated cultural formation and youth, was pulled in many directions in the writing of the novel, towards the political, towards the rarified irony of the post-modernist, towards the descriptive orgy of the naturalists. Therefore, one must look beyond these digressions of the spirit, towards the structure of imagery of the work. If the effort to grasp this structure is successful, we not only confirm our interpretation of the book through the examination of recurring sensuous embodiments and images, but also limit the discussion to what is central, since of the many breeds of imagery evidenced in *Écue*, only those organic to theme are in any sense functional, and merit discussion.

The first page of a Carpentier novel is usually an overture in which the principal themes are stated in compressed, often semi-poetic form. Thus in *Écue*, the author establishes the affinities between the rural Black and the land through a consciously elaborated parallelism. The growth of the cane is described from the point of view of the old Usebio Cué:

> Para él la caña no encerraba el menor misterio. Apenas asomaba entre los cuajarones de tierra negra, se seguía su desarrollo sin sorpresas. El saludo

[54] Willian Thrall and Addison Hubbard, *A Handbook to Literature* (New York: The Odyssey Press, 1960), pp. 301-302.

[54 a] Pedro Lastra has described the conflict of *¡Écue-yamba-Ó!* as one between the «mundonovista» tendencies which still were important in the thirties, and the conviction of young artists that the effort to depict local reality was questionable in a «mundo que ahora era sentido en su radical fragmentación.» See Pedro Lastra, «*¡Écue-yamba-Ó!*,» *Eco* (Bogotá), Vol. XXIII/1-2, nos. 133, 134, May-June 1971, p. 53.

[55] Ricardo Fernando, unpublished thesis on Alejo Carpentier, Princeton University, 1969.

de la primera hoja. Los canutos que se hinchan y alargan, dejando un pequeño surco para el «ojo.» El visible agradecimiento ante la lluvia anunciada por el vuelo bajo de las auras. El cogollo que se alejará algún día en el pomo de una albarda. Del limo a la savia hay encadenamiento perfecto. Pero hecho el corte, el hilo se rompe bajo el arco de la romana... La locomotora arrastra millares de sacos llenos de cristalitos rojos que todavía saben a tierra, pezuñas y malas palabras. La refinería les devolverá pálidos, sin vida. De la yunta terca, que entiende de voz de hombres, a la máquina espoleada por picos de alcuzas.

Como tantos otros, Usebio Cué era siervo del Central. Su pequeña heredad no conocía ya otro cultivo que el de la «cristalina.» Y a pesar del trabajo intensivo de las colonias vecinas, la producción de la comarca entera bastaba apenas para saciar los apetitos de San Lucio, cuyas chimeneas y sirenas ejercían, en tiempo de zafra, una tiránica dictadura. Los latidos de sus émbolos... podían alterar a capricho el ritmo de vida de los hombres, bestias y plantas.[56]

The rural Black, through his total knowledge of the natural processes, sees the land and its products as an extension of himself, «que no encerraba el menor misterio.» To evoke this special rapport Carpentier makes sophisticated use of personification and animism in his effort to suggest the forces of the «zafra» and Cué's point of view. These images reach their culmination in the expressionistic image of the cane «que se alejará algún día en el pomo de una albarda,» which in describing the actual scene of the felled cane tied to the saddle and being taken away on a horse, suggests animistically an autonomous action of the cane itself, or a life parallel that of man.

To Cué the appearance of the first leaf is «saludo,» and the rain is received on the canefields with «visible agradecimiento» by the growing plant-life. The sugar suffers as if imbued with the life of the workers who produced it, returning from the foreign refineries «pálido... sin vida.» Then Carpentier tightens the parallelism of man and nature describing the yoke of mechanistic exploitation as affecting both in the same terms: «Sus émbolos... podían alterar a capricho el ritmo de vida de los hombres, bestias y plantas.»

Important in the artistic elaboration of the unity of man and nature is the more or less traditional mode of pathetic fallacy. Throughout the novel, nature provides a sympathetic background for the rural characters, echoing their rituals and dramatic moments. Related to this plastic, affective use of natural elements is Carpentier's use of «animal contexts,» or at times motifs, for dramatic effects during particular key incidents of the book. Then of course, the reverse appears, man as a context of nature, dwarfed and leveled by the cataclysms of the hurricanes and fires.

Thus in the scene of Menegildo's birth, Carpentier surrounds the event carefully with the accompaniment of animals. When Salomé feels the pangs of delivery, «Era como si le ladraran en las entrañas... Se dejó caer sobre su cama de sacos, rodeada por el cloqueo de las gallinas que acudían en bandadas.»[57] The pigs take advantage of the situation to invade the patio

[56] *¡Écue-yamba-Ó!* p. 7.
[57] Ibid., p. 17.

soiling the clothes «con e'jocico.» A lizard, «fallando el salto a una mosca fue a caer sobre el vientre de la criatura arrugada y húmeda.» When Menegildo is old enough to crawl around the hut he discovers a bestiary within the four walls:

> Interrumpió el amoroso coloquio de alacranes, cuyas colas, voluptuosamente adheridas, dibujaban un corazón de naipes al revés... los insectos han trazado senderos, fuera de cuyos itinerarios se inicia el terror de las tierras sombrías, habitadas por arañas carnívoras... Menegildo cortó el viviente cordón de una procesión de bibijaguas que portaban banderitas verdes. Más allá un lechón lo empujó con el hocico. Los perros lo lamieron, acorralándolo debajo de un fogón ruinoso. Una gallina enfurecida le arañó el vientre. Las hormigas bravas le encendieron las nalgas.[58]

It is clear that Carpentier exaggerates the presence of animals and insects in these instances to suggest the instinctive level of the child's world, and «lo real maravilloso» of his perspective which transforms the commonplace into the enchanted. This willed artistic regression to the animal world of infantile sensory impressions is carried out more programmatically in «Viaje a la semilla.» Carpentier's explorations into the child's perspective are a lyrical variation of his primitivism.

In *Écue,* music, particularly the elemental music of the cult drummers, is as childhood, a medium for contact with the primordial world of animals. Thus, Carpentier surrounds the session of musicians with animal contexts. Through their sacred music, man influences the elements, attracting animals through some arcane power of communication and regression, as if the music were a time-machine capable of transporting man back into a ritual «illo tempore,» or even beyond into the dawn of man's evolution.

> Los sones y rumbas se anunciaban gravemente, haciendo asomar hocicos negros en las rendijas del corral... otro de los virtuosos rascaba la dentadura de una quijada de buey rellena de perdigones... Los instrumentos casi animales y las letanías se acoplaban bajo el signo de una selva invisible... En las frondas las gallinas alargaban un ojo amarillo hacia el corro de sombras entregadas al extraño maleficio sonoro.[59]

Later in a similar scene, describing the chaotic zeal of some Jamaican gospel singers in the streets, Carpentier uses the animal context for semi-grotesque effects:

> El Señor misericordioso sabía encolerizarse. Quien no montara en su ferrocarril bendito, corría el peligro de no conocer el paraíso... Los perros del vecindario ladraron desesperadamente, y los graciosos soltaron trompetillas muy criollas. Una vaca ·en trance de parto, lanzó mugidos terroríficos detrás del santuario. Los cantares, impasibles, se prosternaron, viendo tal vez al Todopoderoso y su gospel-train bienaventurado... y el cántico estalló nuevamente en los gaznates

---

[58] Ibid., p. 2.
[59] Ibid., p. 31.

de papel de lija. Una mandíbula de lechón a medio roer produjo una ruidosa estrella de grasa en el tambor del trío espiritual.[60]

In describing the «brujo» Beruá's hut, Carpentier attempts to create a natural setting evocative of a primordial state of nature:

> El bohío del viejo Beruá se alzaba al pie de un mogote rocoso, agrietado por siglos de lluvias y roídos por una miríada de plagas vegetales. Algunas cañas bravas, ligeras como plumas de avestruz, jalonaban su base, orlando el manto casi impenetrable del enorme cipo —urdimbre de espinas, tubos de savia dulzona, verdosas ciempíes y orquídeas obscenas.[61]

Menegildo's sexual initiation is achieved against an elaborately developped natural setting which mirrors the germination of the boy's desire culminating in the love act itself.

> Una peculiar vibración de la atmósfera denunciaba la llegada de la primavera, con su destilación de savias, su elaboración de simientes. El limo se resquebrajaba, ante un hervor de retoños. Los caballos soltaban las lanas del invierno. El rumor constante de la fábrica se sincronizaba con un vasto concertante de relinchos, de persecuciones en las frondas, de carnes aradas por la carne. Los grillos se multiplicaban. El mugir de los toros repercutía hasta las montañas azules que la bruma esfumaba suavemente. Un primer nido había sido descubierto por los macheteros del cañaveral cercano... Encima de ellos [los amantes], bajo cúpulas de hojarasca, los cocuyos se perseguían a la luz de sus linternas verdes, mientras el rumor sordo del ingenio danzaba en una brisa que ya olía a rocío.[62]

The passage is an intensification of the book's constant parallelism between the forces of man and nature. In the act of love, those parallel lines are confluent and Carpentier's tone rises to the level of epiphany in celebration of the climactic fulfillment of both.

In the central scene of the book, the parallelism is wrought more clearly both in action and style: the violence of fire on the canebrake is as an echo of the sexual desire of Menegildo, who deserts the fire-fighting crew to steal into Longina's hut and possess her. The release and satisfaction of the lovers is echoed by the rain which fertilizes the land and extinguishes the fire in the coupling of heaven and earth. The parallelism is dramatized by a rather traditional use of personification characteristic of the novel.

> Gruesas gotas comenzaron a rodar sonoramente por las pencas del techo. Las nubes se desgarraron en franjas transparentes y la tierra roja estertoró de placer bajo una lluvia leve y compacta. Un perfume de madera mojada, de verdura fresca, de cenizas y de hojas de guayabo invadió la choza. Todas las fiebres del Trópico se aplacaban en un vasto alborozo de savias y de pistilos. Los árboles alzaron brazos múltiples hacia los manantiales viajeros. Un vasto

---

[60] Ibid., p. 64.
[61] Ibid., p. 79.
[62] Ibid., p. 89.

crepitar de frondas llenó el valle. Ya se escuchaba el rumor de la cañada, acelerada por la impaciencia de mil arroyuelos diminutos.

El incendio agonizaba. Una que otra columna de humo jalonaban la retirada de las llamas. En el sendero, las herraduras besaban el barro...[63]

When Antonio and Menegildo meet with other members of the cult to enter the «bodega» where the members are assembled «se aventuraron entre dos albardas y ocho patas, echando una mirada al interior de la bodega.»[64] In this scene even the politics of the «ñáñigos» is given an animal context, and the popular mythology is permeated by animal figures:

> ...Había quien votara por el Gallo y el Arado. Otros confiaban en Liborio y la Estrella, o en el Partido de la Cotorra. La lucha se había entablado entre el Chino-de-los-cuatro-gatos, el Mayoral-que-sonaba-el-cuero, y el Tiburón-con-sombrero-de-jipi... La mitología electoral alimentaba un mundo de fábula de Esopo, con bestias que hablaban, peces que obtenían sufragios y aves que robaban urnas de votos...[65]

In addition to the use of pathetic fallacy and animal contexts Carpentier on several occasions makes direct comparisons by simile or metaphor between man and animal. When Salomé is great with child, the pains seem to her «como si le ladraran en las entrañas.»[66] The cult drummers in the middle of an improvisation, «jadeantes, sudorosos, enronquecidos... se miraban como gallos prestos a reñir.»[67] In the worst of the hurricane, the Cué family, «agazapados, revueltos, boca en tierra como los camellos ante la tempestad de arena, grandes y chicos se preparaban a resistir hasta el agotamiento.»[68] The old «brujo,» Beruá, has hands «llenas de escamas como lomo de caimán.» Salomé's sisters are «prolíficas como peces.»[69] Menegildo, caught by the police after his assault on Napoleón, «se dejaba llevar mansamente, como buey que tiran del narigón.» Paula Macho, before the hurricane, «...pasó por la carrilera saltando sobre los palines como una cabra.»

These metaphors indicate a direction towards the culminating point metamorphosis, a phenomenon that has exerted a strong fascination on of Carpentier throughout his literary life, and which he has tried to suggest in one form or another in nearly all of his works. Although *¡Écue-yamba-Ó!* does not consciously, as do his later works, construct actual metamorphoses, the suggestions of changing of states are many in the novel. These are valuable to point out, in the light of the increasing importance of metamorphosis in Carpentier's work.

Metamorphosis may be defined as spiritual or physical change of form, substance or structure, as transformation by external or internal forms.

---

[63] Ibid., p. 102.
[64] Ibid., p. 122.
[65] Ibid., p. 122.
[66] Ibid., p. 17.
[67] Ibid., p. 205.
[68] Ibid., p. 46.
[69] Ibid., p. 108.

As a cultural belief, metamorphosis is characteristic of most «early» cultures and known to Western civilization primarily through Greek myth. By the time of Ovid, however, metamorphosis had become in the Western world a literary device, divorced from current religious practices. Since then, metamorphosis has entered into many distinct forms of literary expression in both the popular and sophisticated domains, sometimes linked to specific folkloric beliefs, sometimes used for purely aesthetic effect, and often in a combination.

Metamorphosis in modern times is a staple of fantastic literature of all types, as in Stevenson's *Dr. Jekyll and Mr. Hyde,* Oscar Wilde's *Picture of Dorian Gray*, Clemente Palma's *El Príncipe Alacrán*, Mérimée's *Lokis,* Balzac's *Sucubis,* and so on. Perhaps under the spell of the Gothic in literature, most modern writers of the fantastic have lost sight of the lyrical and ontological connotations of metamorphosis, using it as a tool in the creation of the grotesque and «espeluznante».

The expressionists, although related in their use of metamorphosis to the modern creators of the fantastic and grotesque, made an original and profound use of the motive, employing the transmutation of realms as a concrete embodiment of personality disorder. But perhaps even more than to the modern spirit, the expressionists, and Kafka in particular, were related to the dark visionaries of late Medieval and early Renaissance Europe —Bosch and Breughel for example— in their fearless exploration of the absurd, and in their need to embody the «innomable.» Carpentier in his writings has on several occasions expressed his particular interest in precisely these artists, to say nothing of his affinity with Goya, after whose «Caprichos» he named the chapters of *El siglo de las luces.*

Carpentier's conception of metamorphosis is not alien to any of these traditions and perhaps the most striking feature of it is his bringing together the literary tradition of the fantastic and the ontological tradition of an early culture. What Carpentier does then may seem in a sense redundant, as a curious doubling of perspective, that is writing of that which is per se fantastic (the occult) while using the techniques of fantastic literature. His goal has clearly been to make them work together in a new synthesis of the sophisticated and the primitive so that the European sensibility does not interfere with capturing of subject, «dejándose que lo maravilloso fluya libremente de una realidad estrictamente seguida...». In short, it is an anti-metaphorical style. Thus the importance of metamorphosis increases in Carpentier as the *realized* metaphor, in which the tenor fuses with the vehicle. Instead of the constant comparison implying that man is *like* nature, Carpentier aims toward the more effective idea that man *is* nature, and that, the forces of regression exert a constant pull on him. The images discussed below, because more direct than simile, more insistent than metaphor, suggest the metamorphosis of man, and his fusion with nature.

In nearly every epiphany of *Écue,* Carpentier has added a peculiar, perhaps unconscious choreographic detail. Recalling that his first works were choreographic, and that he has written that «todo en nuestro ambiente se puede transcribir en gestos,» this detail merits consideration.

The main characters, when approaching transcendent experiences are often depicted in the posture «a gatas,» the characteristic posture of child and animal. This physical posture represents an «achicarse» before the great forces of life, a regression to a humble almost prehuman state of instinctive receptivity in which man, stripped of his humanity in the outward sense, can participate again in the wonder and terror of nature. Man in Carpentier receives the transcendent moments of his life in a paradoxical, but perhaps innately Christian attitude of prayer or grovel: thus prostrate he can ascend. Menegildo's first sally into the world, and Carpentier's into the «real maravilloso,» is undertaken «a gatas»:

> Como nadie escuchaba sus gemidos, *emprendió a gatas un largo viaje* a través del bohío... Menegildo aprendería, como todos los niños, que las bellezas de una vivienda se ocultan en la parte inferior de los muebles.[70]

In the moment of maximum primordial terror in the hurricane, «*Usebio gateó entre los restos* del bohío,» finding refuge in «la fosa abierta.» The Cué's are «vaciados de ideas... El temblor del perro había contagiado al hombre.»

In the same scene, Carpentier suggests the metamorphosis of man into plant, as both are reduced in the storm: «Empapados, tiritantes, los hombres parecían listos a colaborar con la incipiente podredumbre de los escombros vegetales.»

In the first love scene, Menegildo «andaba a paso de potro,» and Longina, on seeing him approach tried to flee «con nervioso sobresalto de corza.» In the second scene of love, the metamorphosis is further suggested:

> Pero Menegildo estaba seguro de que Longina estaba ahí. El instinto se lo decía.
> *Entró a gatas en la choza* triangular. Se oía una leve respiración en la sombra. *Un olor que le era bien conocido lo guió* hacia Longina.[71]

In addition to the posture, Carpentier attributes Menegildo with the heightened olfactory sense of the animal. Guided by a scent, on all fours, Menegildo ceases conscious control control over himself, surrendering instinctively to the stimulus of the female. Further when Beruá gives Menegildo his first exposure to the occult, he is reduced to a kneeling position:

> «¡Arrodillao!»
> Cuando el mozo hubo obedecido, Beruá encendió una vela. Un estremecimiento de terror recorrió el espinazo de Menegildo... se hallaba por vez primera, ante las cosas grandes...[72]

---

[70] Ibid., p. 21.
[71] Ibid., p. 102.
[72] Ibid., p. 83.

Similarly in the second childhood epiphany, which within the context of the city is a lyrical digression, Carpentier describes the entrance into the secret world of children and into the birth of ritual: «...Por el hueco de una tapia penetraban *a gatas* en un jardín lleno de frutales sin poder y hierbas malas, donde puñados de mariposas blancas se alzaban en vuelo medroso...»

The willed regression-metamorphosis is elaborated in the paragraph. The boys cross the garden and enter their hiding place:

> Era aquella la Cueva de las Jaibas. Pescando en la costa los chicos habían envidiado muchas veces a los cangrejos, que solían ocultarse en antros de roca llenos de sombras glaucas y misteriosas dependencias. *¡Cuánto hubieran dado por tener el alto de un erizo y poder penetrar también en esos laberintos de piedra!* Ahora, en esa casa inhabitada hallaban el escondrijo apetecido. Cada cual era «jaiba» y aceptaba que aquella habitación se encontraba en el fondo del mar. Si alguno abría las ventanas, todos morirían ahogados.[73]

The scene of collective spiritism which precedes the death of Menegildo depicts the experience of «bajando el santo» as a progressive, crescendo changing of states which culminates in a total surrender of individual humanity and the immersion into a marginal lycanthropic euphoria: «Los animadores habían dejado de pertenecer al mundo... las voces de la maquinaria humana se extravían en licantropía de bramido, gemido, grito agudo.»[74]

In the death scene, after Menegildo has received a mortal wound, Carpentier describes the dramatic moment when Longina enters into the presence of death in the following terms:

> Un bulto se movía entre las hierbas. Longina se acercó *a gatas*. Menegildo yacía de bruces, cubierto de sangre tibia... estaba gris, vaciado de sangre, con la yugular cortada por una cuchillada. Su herida se había llenado de hormigas...[75]

Death has no metaphysical significance. Man is erased from the human scenario; his body is rapidly reincorporated into nature and turned fodder in the cycles of decay and regeneration. In this scene, Carpentier intentionally has Menegildo's death occur outside, «entre las hierbas,» although the wound was received indoors. Within minutes, the ants begin their work of reincorporation. His mate, «a gatas,» discovers the reality of death and knows the elemental pain of solitude. Death is the final metamorphosis, the ultimate return in which man finds total union with nature.

The notion of ultimate experience as a regression is a constant in the works of Carpentier, and in these varied examples we can see its first manifestation —not solidified enough to be called theme perhaps, but recurring obsessively. In the early works, Carpentier was primarily inter-

[73] Ibid., p. 184.
[74] Ibid., p. 209.
[75] Ibid., p. 211.

ested in regression as a state, induced by the occult or achieved in moments of intense communion with nature, or a circumstance, suggestive of metamorphosis. Progressively the Cuban became more ambitious with the theme, employing the dimension of time in the endeavor to recapture «le temps perdu» in personal and historical terms. In «Viaje a la Semilla» the reversal of time induces the regressive metamorphosis of man and setting. Finally, in *Los pasos perdidos,* the theme of regression becomes a total evasion; leaving the constrictions of the contemporary frame of the protagonist, the author, through the symbolic use of the spatial dimension, arrives at «los umbrales de la civilización.»

Carpentier's attraction to metamorphosis and the occult in evidence here leads him inevitably towards the fantastic in literature, still related to the occult in the early works. In *Écue,* he was too closely bound by the naturalistic mode of social realism to participate in the freedom of the fantastic. Carpentier himself implicitly denies any connection with fantastic literature, preferring to hide his craft under such easily misleading terms as «lo real maravilloso.» Yet «lo maravilloso» does not simply flow «libremente,» particularly from the pen of an author as painstaking as Carpentier.

The Crossing of the Realms

Metamorphosis is the most obvious, the most final, and important (in a thematic sense) manifestation of a broader characteristic of Carpentier's writing which can be called the crossing of the realms. This refers to a quality, which although noticed by many critics (Ricardo Alegría's study on «realismo mágico,» for example), has been analyzed only very partially. This quality is the insistent, deliberate confusion of the distinct realms of matter in his fiction, the animate with the inanimate, the human with the animal, in every possible combination. The principal effect of this quality on the reader is a subtle bewilderment, or even a feeling of displacement, in the presence of a world in which the basic divisions of matter are deftly shuffled. The reader must reorient himself to the unexpected relationship between things, people and animals, and in so doing discovers a new potential in the organic quality in man.

The most widely used figure in literature —the metaphor— is germane to this quality, since metaphor seeks to relate, in most cases, elements of distinct realms. «Her teeth were wondrous pearls» relates an element «pearls» from the inanimate world with one from the human and animate world «teeth». Actually, more than «relating,» the poet accomplishes linguistically a substitution of the latter by the former, and sensorially, a fusion of the two. Carpentier's style, however, is increasingly antithetical to the metaphorical style. The metaphor is the unfettered flight of the imagination moving freely between the diverse realms of existence. People in the metaphorical poet's hands can become for instants of their existence, gazelles, trees, statues, stars; a thought can be an avalanche,

51

a bird's flight. Yet the reader, although illumined for a brief instant by the swift journey between realms, can return to the original.

Carpentier's style is more insidious than metaphor, and more ambitious. He avoids overt comparison, seeking through other means to achieve not a comparison, but an actual confusion of realms. It is with these other means that we are concerned here. Carpentier's tropes preserve the identity of the tenor the thing or person undergoing change yet conceive such things with new, and often alien properties sometimes in unusual relationship with their surroundings. Carpentier stays often within strict limits to achieve what are often fantastic effects; indeed he is highly cinematographic, relying as does on the camera, on angle distortion, juxtaposition, montage and accumulation for his most powerful effects. The total effect of a passage of this kind, can be more powerful than most metaphorical prose, because the changes operative on the elements of reality become organic and osmotic, with the newly wrought, growing identity. The realms, once crossed in a subtle literary shuffling, are no longer alien and do not recross as in the inevitable spring-like action of metaphor.

The principal techniques and figures observable in this process are five:

the anthropormorphic techniques of animism, personification, and the related impossible attribution;

the surrealistic technique of juxtaposition, which is a kind of free association, along the outer margins of realism;

expressionistic characterization as the reduction of character to several basic mobiles;

reification and zoomorphic animalization of people;

decorporalization in the independence of members of the body, which is often achieved with synecdoche.

The aim of this study is to describe Carpentier's intentions in using these tropes and techniques, and their dramatic effect, in his early work. There, these techniques are illuminated by their original literary function —the suggestion of the primitive and occult. In his early works, Carpentier was primarily concerned with the wedding of style to primitive ontology; thus, there are fertile relationships between trope and myth. Carpentier's increasing use of animism, personification, lycanthropic and anthropormorphic images was in good measure the attempt to recreate the essence of the intuited primitive's world vision through the ultra-conscious manipulation of these techniques. Trying to attune his soul and senses to the world of the Cuban Black, his literary arms were those of his European heritage. For in technique Carpentier did not radically depart from the European exploration of the occult. Only in the synthesis of trope and reality, made possible partly by direct participation in the ambience of the occult, did Carpentier offer a truly original contribution.

Animism in the Crossing of the Realms

Animism has been defined as the «belief that natural objects, natural phenomena, and the universe itself possess souls,» [76] and the «tendency to explain all the phenomena in nature not due to natural causes by attributing them to spiritual agency.» [77]

The word «animism» is primarily known to us in this mythological sense, yet it has become a category of linguistics of relatively wide currency. Since in Carpentier's case both categories have relevance and often become one, they will be considered here.

According to J. C. Froelich animism is the basic element of all Black religions in Africa: «Tous les éléments d'un monde dynamique en équilibre instable sont mus par la force vitales.» [78] This vital force, which is in all objects and people, is the «agent d'un véritable animisme qui constitue la base même de la 'weltanschauung' des Négro-Africains.» [79] Of the three evolutionary degrees which theoreticians have distinguished in religious forms, animism is the first, followed by polytheism and monotheism.

The African has developed «l'idée de la personalisation de tout, de l'unité de toute chose et de la possibilité de remplacer une chose par une autre ou de transformer un objet en un autre... Cela suppose la négation du principe d'identité et de spécifité, et la croyance aux métamorphoses les plus étranges: le magicien peut se faire bête, vent ou pierre, il peut transformer une pirogue en auto, un potiron en carosse.» [80]

The relationship between animism and metamorphosis is here made clear; both are expressions of the latent «force vitale» in all matter, the latter being the extreme expression of this power.

That Carpentier was conscious of the importance of animism in the mythological sense has been shown on several occasions in interviews and essays. For Carpentier, as for Froelich, animism is central to any attempt to portray the realities of primitive cultures. In his description of the «contextos» for the American novel in *Tientos y diferencias* (México, 1964) the first mentioned element is animism:

> Supervivencias de animismo, creencias, prácticas muy antiguas, a veces de un origen cultural sumamente respetable, que nos ayudan a enlazar ciertas reali-

[76] *The Random House Dictionary*, ed. Jess Stein (New York: Random House, 1969), p. 59.

[77] *The Encyclopedia Americana* (New York: The Americana Corporation, 1964), Vol. I, p. 714.

[78] J. C. Froelich, *Animismes* (Paris: Editions de L'Oronte, 1964), p. 53.

[79] J. C. Froelich, p. 51.

[80] J. C. Froelich, p. 55.

dades presentes con esencias culturales remotas, cuya existencia nos vincula con lo universal-sin-tiempo.[81]

In the interview with Fells the author criticizes *Écue* for having missed the essential factor of animism. «L'animism, 'le merveilleux,' qui tient une si grande place dans la vie des paysans cubains m'avait complètement échappé.»[83] Actually, this criticism is only partially true.

Of particular interest, in addition to the importance Carpentier places on animism, is the conjunction of animism and the «merveilleux»; indeed they become inseparable in his creative process.

Linguistically, animism as a mode of expression can be found in the most commonplace everyday speech, and in the most elaborate poetic illusion.

In everyday speech we tend to use animistic modes of description to give dramatic relief to the essential features of a scene, and in doing so eliminate what may be factually essential but unnecessary dramatically. For example, «the door opened abruptly,» «the ball leapt from the pitcher's hand,» «the trees leaned away from the wind's assault,» «his pen skated across the paper» all eliminate the true agent of the action and concentrate on the action itself as if it were autonomously performed by the object.

This separation of agent from action or cause from effect leads Richter to consider animism as a fundamentally impressionistic technique which consist in presenting «en el punto central la impresión sensorial desligada de sus causas y de tal manera que aparece como representación principal lo que antes era parcial y accesorio.»[83]

However when animism becomes integral to the artist's total vision, to his aesthetic program, to his interpretation of the world, it is a response to an inner compulsion, not to a merely sensorial stimulus. It is not difficult to distinguish a fundamentally impressionist use of animism from an expressionist one. Furthermore, the surrealists, in their interest in magic and the subconscious —one might say the magic *of* the subconscious,— often explored and released the latent forces of objects in their visions in a manner which could be termed animistic:

Les meubles font alors place à des animaux de même taille qui me regardent
fraternellement.
Lions dans les crinières desquels achèvent de se consumer les chaises.
Squales dont le ventre blanc s'incorpore le dernier frisson des draps.[84]

[81] Alejo Carpentier, *Tientos y diferencias* (México: Universidad Nacional Autónoma, 1964), p. 24.
[82] Fell, *op. cit.*, p. 109.
[83] Charles Bally, Elise Richter, Amado Alonso, Raimundo Lida, *El impresionismo en el lenguaje* (Buenos Aires: Imprenta de la Universidad de Buenos Aires, 19), p. 57.
[84] André Breton, «Vigilance,» *An Anthology of French Surrealist Poetry*, ed. J. H. Matthews (Minneapolis: University of Minneapolis Press, 1966), p. 69.

As we have mentioned, Carpentier's *entente* with the Surrealists began after he had finished the rough draft of *Écue* and taken up residence in Paris. His contacts with the movement before that time were peripheral: his friendship with Desnos and articles in Havana journals on modern painting. Yet tendencies can be found in *Écue* —one of which is animism— that if not properly speaking *within* Surrealism, demonstrate a leaning or affinity which found resonance and amplification during the Paris years.

Carpentier's pronouncement that «l'animisme m'a complètement échappé» is not based on his actual writing. It is true that his power of suggestion of «las fuerzas ocultas» was not at this time as highly developed as in succeeding works. Yet already his obsession with the «potencias movilizables» was given expression in *Écue,* and to some degree realized stylistically, as the following examples of «animism» and other devices demonstrate.

Animism in Écue is wedded to the Black's conception of the universe, as expounded discursively early in the novel:

> Se sorprendía de su pequeñez ante la vasta harmonía de las fuerzas ocultas... lo visible era bien poca cosa... entre los hombres existían potencias movilizables... *El espacio... se mostraba lleno de fuerzas latentes, invisibles,* fecundísimas, que era preciso poner en acción... un muñeco de madera, bautizado con el nombre de Menegildo, se vuelve dictador de su doble viviente... *el aire es un tejido de hebras inconsútiles que transmite las fuerzas invocadas... Si se acepta como verdad indiscutible que un objeto pueda estar dotada de vida, ese objeto vivirá.* La cadena de oro que se contrae anunciará el peligro. La pata de ave hallada en la mitad del camino se liga precisamente al que se detiene ante ella, ya que, entre cien, uno solo ha sido sensible a su aviso... bajo su influjo los tambores hablaban.[85]

Of interest in the effort to capture Carpentier's earliest stylistic expression of these ideas, is the opening page of Chapter 13, a description of a landscape. Significantly in the novel this description follows directly the above discursive statements, and may be seen as Carpentier's attempt to use them while the ontological concept of animism was still warm in his mind.

> Era raro que Menegildo saliera de noche. Conocía poca gente en el caserío y, además, para llegar allá, tenía que atravesar senderos muy obscuros, de los que se ven frecuentados por las «cosas malas»... Sin embargo, aquel 31 de diciembre, Menegildo se encaminó hacia el Central, a la caída de la tarde, para «ver el rebumbio.»
>
> Algunos merengues mofletudos, anaranjados por un agonizante rayo de sol, flotaban todavía en un cielo cuyos azules se iban entintando progresivamente. Las palmas parecían crecer en la calma infinita del paisaje. Sus troncos, escamados de estaño, retrocedían en la profundidad del valle. Dos ceibas solitarias brindaban manojos verdes en los extremos de sus largos brazos horizontales. Las frondas se iban confundiendo unas con otras, como vastas marañas de gasa. Un pavo real hacía sonar su claxón lúgubre desde el cauce

---

[85] *Écue,* p. 54.

de una cañada. El día tropical se desmayaba en lecho de brumas decadentes, agotado por catorce horas de orgasmo luminoso. Las estrellas, ingenuas, como recortadas en papel plateado, iban apareciendo poco a poco, en tanto que la monótona respiración de la fábrica imponía su sordina de acero a la campiña.[86]

First of all, although the prose is written in an elevated descriptive style, the first pragraph conveys Carpentier's intention to relate this description to Menegildo's presence, if not precisely to his point of view. The small piece of indirect dialogue further emphasizes this: «tenía que atravesar senderos muy obscuros, de los que se ven frecuentados por *'las cosas malas.'* » Thus immediately we feel the discrepancy, or break between the somewhat stylized descriptive prose that follows and the presence of Menegildo, who has been upstaged.

Nonetheless the passage is important because it is one of Carpentier's first attempts to suggest «lo primitivo» through the sheer power of style, without the aid of action or dialogue. As is immediately observable, the dominating factor in the imagery is the animistic spirit; no human or animal agents appear, no action as such takes place, yet the author is able to create a landscape filled with movement. Note the number of actions Carpentier describes, using verbs of motion:

merengues... flotaban;
azules... se iban entintando;
palmas... parecían crecer;
sus troncos... retrocedían en la profundidad;
Dos ceibas... brindaban;
Las frondas... se iban confundiendo;
El día... se desmayaba;
Las estrellas... iban apareciendo;
La respiración de la fábrica... imponía su sordina;

The animism here observable is mixed: a very traditional use of personification, some distinctly modernist imagery, one ultraistic image, and even alliteration. As far as images of pure animism, there perhaps are only two or three, where the object acquires autonomy, divorced from agent:

— «Las Palmas parecían crecer en la calma infinita del paisaje» (would be animistic were it not for the indicator «parecían»). (*Sus troncos... retrocedían en la profundidad* del valle.)

— «Las *frondas se iban confundiendo* unas con otras» (divorces the process of blurring contours from the agent, the effect of encroaching darkness on vision. The use of periphrastic plus present participle adds momentum to the «action»).

— «Las estrellas iban apareciendo.»

Personification is of course closely related to animism but can be distinguished because it does not really give autonomy to the thing; it, like

[86] Ibid., p. 59.

animism, ignores the true agent, but substitutes another false, a human, one. Usually it is a kind of applied metaphor in which things and phenomena are humanized, and thus more closely related to pathetic fallacy than animism which bares the working of the brute «fuerza vital,» unhumanized, uncompared, and autonomous, for example:

— «Dos ceibas... brindaban manojos verdes en los extremos de sus largos brazos horizontales.»

— «El día tropical se desmayaba en lecho de brumas.»

— La monótona respiración de la fábrica imponía su sordina.»

Still side-by-side with a traditional view of nature, a fresh and more original one can be seen emerging with the use of animism. The animistic spirit will continue to dominate Carpentier's prose, causing his descriptions to vibrate with the strange life of awakened matter.

Further on in the book, the first page of the third and last section, «La Ciudad,» is a piece of extended descriptive prose related closely, yet more elaborately developed than the preceding one:

La bruma demoraba todavía en las hondonadas, cuando Menegildo fue conducido a la pequeña estación del Ingenio por una pareja de guardias rurales. El mozo se dejó caer en un banco de listones haciendo descansar sus muñecas esposadas sobre las rodillas. El andén estaba desierto. El día se alzaba lentamente. De cuando en cuando, una locomotora, con los focos encendidos aún, se escurría sobre los rieles azules arrastrando rejas de caña. Tanques rodantes de miel de purga, con grandes iniciales blancas sobre fondo opaco, descansaban en vía muerta, como formidables salchichas de hierro. Un vagón frigorífico, con costillares en acordeón, aguardaba el momento de ser llevado hasta Chicago. Crecían mangas de agua y discos de señales en la luz naciente. Cadenas y ganchos aguardaban presa, dejando gotear el rocío sobre las hierbas mojadas. Una valla anunciadora mostraba un dirigible tirando de un pantalón irrompible. Un retrato de anciana con cuello de encajes, al que los chicos habían pintado bigotes y quevedos, pregonaba las virtudes de un compuesto vegetal destinado a aminorar los padecimientos de la menopausia.[87]

As in the previous example, Carpentier uses a mixture of personification and animism to give life to the inert scene of the railroad station, and to establish unexpected liaisons between incongruous objects. The difference between the two passages most immediately observable is that, in the latter passage, Carpentier for the first time in the novel applies his technique to an urban environment. He flexes his style to animate and incorporate the disparate, the anachronistic, and suggest the absurd resulting from the gratuitous connections. This is the first example in Carpentier of what he is later to call «el tercer estilo; el estilo de las cosas que no tienen estilo.» [88]

[87]   Ibid., p. 129.
[88]   *Tientos y diferencias, op. cit.,* p. 17.

By isolating the instances of animism and personification the nature of Carpentier's endeavor becomes more apparent: La bruma... demoraba; El día... se alzaba lentamente; Tanques... descansaban; Un vagón, con costillares en acordeón... aguardaba; Mangas de agua y discos... crecían; Cadenas y ganchos... aguardaban presa; Una valla anunciadora... mostraba; Un retrato de anciana... pregonaba.

Of particular interest here is the fact that «El andén estaba desierto.» Menegildo, escorted onto the platform, «se dejó caer en un banco.» Thus the human element is virtually absent, or in Menegildo's case, totally inert, while the inanimate objects are much more suggestive of life. The railroad car, «con costillares en acordeón» which suggests a tense compression, waits in silence, as the aggressive looking chains, hooks «aguardaban presa», the signal-disks, and waterspouts grow animistically in the early light. An advertisement presides over the scene, and the anachronistic «anciana con cuello de encajes» hawks a modern absurdity with the use of «pregonar» which suggests a loud and aggressive attitude.

Thus we have a clear case of the animistic spirit and its rôle within the concept of the crossing of the realms. Carpentier releases and distorts the potential of objects which come to the foreground in menacing or absurd attitudes, while the human elements fade into the background surrounded by a self-generated chaos as they surrender their normal rôle as agent. It is indubitable that this aesthetic characteristic is related to Carpentier's diminutive view of man in relation to the cosmic forces of nature and history.

Another example, closely related to the two previous ones, gives further evidence of the animistic spirit in Carpentier:

> El día echó a andar por el valle. Mil totis asomaron sus picos negros entre las hojas. Despertó el pescador noruego de un anuncio de la Emulsión, con su heráldico bacalao a cuentas; se hizo visible el rosado fumador de cigarrillos de Virginia, plantado en campiña cubana por el imperialismo comercial de hombres del norte. Las sirenas de la ciudad, las chimeneas del puerto, elevaron sus quejas en la lejanía, sin que la fiesta detuviera su ímpetu.[89]

Another instance of animism, which reccurs throughout Carpentier's works in one form or another, is the way in which the author is able to suggest the effect of idolatry on the popular imagination. Gradually, Carpentier's prose assimilates the mystical relationship of the believer with the idols, crosses, and fetishes that serve as intermediaries to the absolute. The Cuban becomes ever more capable of evoking the reverence, anguish, or dread of «los fieles» before the looming symbols of «el más allá»:

> Un estremecimiento de terror recorrió el espinazo de Menegildo... A la altura de sus ojos una mesa cubierta de encajes toscos sostenía un verdadero conclave

---

[89] *Écue*, p. 170.

de divinidades y atributos. Las imágenes cristianas, para comenzar, gozaban libremente de los esplendores de una vida secreta, ignorada por los no iniciados. En el centro, sobre la piel de un chato tambor ritual, se alzaba Obatalá, el crucificado, preso en una red de collares entretejidos... Changó... blandía un sable dorado... Vestidos de encarnado, con los ojos fijos, los Jimaguas erguían sus cuerpecitos negros en un ángulo de la mesa.[90]

The continuous, inexorable yet impossible action of the idols («blandir,» «alzarse,» «erguirse») prolonged by the imperfect tense, become animistically, logical extensions of the character of the objects. As in other examples, Carpentier's descriptions departing from the natural order of things do not seen like departures, because they stay within the boundaries of an aesthetic logic. In his later works, the author supplants the normal laws of causality and sequence so subtly that the reader tends to accept the new code without being entirely aware of the displacement.

To illustrate the increasing importance of this device, one can look ahead to the novella «El acoso» where the metaphysical dread of the central character is one of the major concerns of the novelist. In several dramatically key moments, instruments of the performers of Beethoven's symphony and the cross of Christ become hieratic and disconcerting autonomous symbols of divine persecution, objects seemingly moved by some latent «force vitale»: «iban a sus altos sitiales los trombones, erguíanse los fagotes en el centro de las afirmaciones.» [91]

And later in the novella as the hunted man seeks refuge in a church:

Una iglesia se iluminó en la noche... El acosado se acercó lentamente a la Casa ofrecida; pasó bajo la ojiva de uno de sus pórticos laterales, y se detuvo deslumbrado, al pie de un pilar cuya piedra rezumaba el incienso... Sonó un órgano... Allá, plantada en un ara de encajes, se alzaba la Cruz, dibujada en claro por el cuerpo de Cristo. Tal era el pasmo del hombre ante la realidad venida a su ruego, que no podían musitar sus labios las plegarias aprendidas del pequeño libro...[92]

In this brilliant scene from «El Acoso» the central character is reduced to a pathetic, incoherent puppet before the menacing autonomous presences in the church. Animism is used throughout the novella to suggest the omnipresence of Fate, which is the Christianized «force vitale» in the novella along side of the pagan and the occult. The aspect which interests me here is the expanded use Carpentier gives to a device conceived in his early period and linked to a specific cultural ambience.

[90] Ibid., p. 83.
[91] Alejo Carpentier, «El acoso,» Guerra del tiempo (México: Compañía de Ediciones S. A., 1958), p. 142.
[92] Ibid., p. 251.

The following two examples, which fall short of being animistic by virtue of the indicator «parecía,» show nevertheless the author's early concern with animism and his still peripheral grasp of it:

> Bailó [el Diablito] cara al levante, invitando al sol a salir; amenazó, bendijo... *Parecía capaz de hacer rodar las piedras o llamar las larvas que se retorcían* entre los linos de la laguna cercana.[93]
>
> ... ...
>
> *Erguida* sobre una suerte de plataforma portátil, precedida por la murga de los Bomberos del Comercio y llevada entre dos policías, *la sagrada imagen parecía bailar,* a su vez, sobre las cabezas de la multitud. *Cobres ensalivados y clarinetes afónicos entonaban* en tiempo lento... el aire de «Mira, mamá, cómo está José.» [94]

In another scene, Carpentier links animism again to Black faith. When Menegildo disuades Antonio the latter with a «talismán»:

> Antonio se levantó súbitamente, echándose una mano al bolsillo:
> — ¡Mira cómo está el diablo!
> En sus dedos crispados, entre cinco uñas rosadas, un pequeño collar de cuentas negras se retorcía como una culebra herida. Lentamente, Antonio alzó la mano hasta las narices del adversario, cuyos ojos espantados fijaban el extraño objeto viviente. Dio un salto atrás:
> — ¡Oye! ¡El diablo está duro!
> ... Menegildo reconstruía mentalmente la ceremonia de preparación de aquellos talismanes... aquellas cadenas, que *se doblaban en espiral, formaban el 8, dibujaban un círculo, se arrastraban y palpitaban sobre el corazón del hombre con una vida tan real como la que hacía palpitar el corazón del hombre.*[95]

Again with the occult, Carpentier uses animistic imagery in an episode of popular «brujería» near the end of the book, to suggest the presence of spirits in the house of Cristalina Valdés:

> Lenín, Allan Kardek y el Crucificado estaban alineados en una mesa, en busto y efigie para presidir la fiesta... Los mismos transmisores parecían divertirse. El rosal, movido por la brisa, acariciaba la testa de Allan Kardek con sus espinas pardas. Lenín parecía meditar bajo el brazo izquierdo de la cruz... *la puerta arcana se entreabría...* Callaron los tambores.[96]

In addition to the instances observed in connection with pathetic fallacy and animism, personification *per se* abounds in *Écue*. As mentioned in the discussion of form, personification supports and enhances the parallelism of man and nature elaborated in the book, as in the extended images of the

[93] Ibid., p. 201.
[94] Ibid., p. 181.
[95] Ibid., pp. 201-202.
[96] Ibid., p. 204.

sugar process at the beginning of the novel. Furthermore, in the Goyesque portrait of the cataclysmic hurricane, the hurricane is personified: «Las ranas de una charca ascienden por la columna de agua que aspira una boca monstruosa.» [97]

The same type of «cosmic personification» is observable in Carpentier's image of the city. From the Prado jail, the sky is seen as the victim of the appetite of the personified city:

> El firmamento circular del marino, ya mordido por los dientes de la ciudad, se va desmenuzando en parcelas de luz dentro del edificio penitenciario, proyectándose en rectángulo cada vez más estrechos.[98]

The association, even collaboration, of the jail with the city in the act of devouring the very substance (firmamento) of the natural world, is of course consistent with Carpentier's philosophy of primitivism as further developed in the antagonistic rôles played by jungle and city in *Los pasos perdidos.*

After *¡Écue-yamba-Ó!,* Carpentier ceases to use personification in the traditional sense associated with pathetic fallacy, and chooses instead to use it, along with animism, in connection with the suggestion of the occult forces in the Black world. In his most sophisticated use of personification —found in *El reino de este mundo*— Carpentier narrows the gap between personification and animism, more to suggest the raw «force vitale» of things, than to humanize them.

Crossings in the Opposite Direction

Whereas the techniques of pathetic fallacy, animism and personification suggest the life of objects, tending towards the creation of an anthropomorphic universe of interacting things, brought to life in unsuspected harmonies, another body of techniques frequently used by Carpentier suggest precisely the opposite —the «thingness» or the «animalness» of man. The techniques involved here are principally those of reification, juxtaposition, and to a lesser degree, the reduction or animalization of character, i.e. that mode of conceiving character not as a complex pattern of interior workings, but almost as the abstract embodiment of a quality. All of these techniques are of course, related by their dehumanization of man.

On the one hand Carpentier's tendency to reify his characters is but one microscomic manifestation of his diminutive view of man in relation to the forces of history and nature. As Claude Fell remarks:

---

[97]   Ibid., p. 43.
[98]   Ibid., p. 137.

> Ce qui intéresse le romancier, c'est en réalité l'analyse des rapports qu'entre-
> tiennent la nature, l'histoire et l'homme. A cet égard, l'attitude de Carpentier
> est claire; pour lui, l'évènement dépasse l'homme, le déconcerte, le balaie
> parfois, mais à travers les idéés l'homme retrouve une prise sur le réel.[99]

Thus even in *El siglo de las luces,* where the rôles of men are inflated, as is the scenario, by the magnitude of the «crise de valeurs» and the mere geography of the French Revolution, man is depicted as a mere actor-agent who chooses his rôle only to the extent that a player may choose his costume from the limited wardrobe of history. At the end of the novel, the two protagonists, Esteban and Sofía, are swallowed up anonymously in the rebellion of the populace following Napoleon's invasion of Spain. They literally disappear while the last lines of the book focus on the painting that symbolizes the dormant potential for revolutionary catharsis: man will serve this potential which is cyclically reawakened, yet he will perish anonymously in his merely supporting rôle.

An examination of the fate of Carpentier's protagonists reveals the consistency with which the author deliberately chooses to minimize their relative stature at the end of his novels. *El acoso,* which has many examples of reification, becomes itself a systematic instrument of reduction and elimination enforced by the hieratic tones of classical pathos, until the final abstract erasure of the «acosado». In *El reino de este mundo* Henri Christophe, similarly reduced in the overwhelming presence of fate, is sunk upon his death into the wet concrete of his own one lasting creation —his mountain fortress. In «Los fugitivos» the protagonist is torn apart by the dog he had once befriended and his bones haunt the area.

Carpentier's characters rarely transcend their function, and never overflow the borders of their dimensions or attain anything near autonomy. They can embody forces and principles, yet not generate them; they can participate in movements yet not affect their course lastingly. Carpentier has published one installment of his novel *El año '59.* It is a novel without characters, written from a belief that there is no more room in modern fiction for «casos individuales.»[100] Seen from the perspective of *El milagro de Anaquillé, ¡Écue-yamba-Ó!,* and other works of his early period, this plan is not surprising.

Yet the notion of reification should not be confused simply with a negative rendering of character. As we are trying to suggest, it is not only the product of a definite philosophical outlook, but also an element of aesthetic vision, particularly of the crossing of the realms. In his reification of human characters Carpentier illustrates the precepts of Ortega's *Deshumanización del arte,* and exhibits his essential modernity. Although his penchant for the Spanish baroque writers may indicate an earlier source, Carpentier predates many of Robbe-Grillet's experiments in the new objective style.

---

[99] Fell, *op. cit.,* p. 110.
[100] Ibid., p. 105.

Often Carpentier reifies humans in a way closely related to modern painting. A highly visual writer, his works abound in scenes in which humans, singly or in crowds, are used as purely plastic elements juxtaposed against or merged with their surroundings. Matisse's functionally mimetic figures in interior scenes offer a parallel. In Carpentier's desire to «plasmar» total scenes, to suggest unexpected relationship and new syntheses, man is often seen descriptively merely as an ingredient or a blotch of color on a teeming canvas.

Reification in Carpentier can be merely a plastic device, or, as best evidenced in *El acoso*[101], can be instrumental in the creation of a depersonalized static universe. This universe is a powerful vacuum in which the suspension of «lo humano» suggests a state of primordial chaos, which is the animistic interaction of things, or the unseen hand of Fate. Reification is the «other side» of animism: it is ultimately, in the early Carpentier, welded to primitivism. It is the vision the doubtful and fluctuating sovereignty of man in a universe of occult forces and autonomous matter in *Écue-yamba-Ó*.

To introduce the examination of Carpentier's use of reification the following «cuadro costumbrista» is useful:

> Atontado por la baraúnda, cegado por las luces, Menegildo entró en la bodega de Canuto. Aquí también se bebía, junto a una «vidriera» que encerraba cajetillas de Competidora Gaditana, ruedas de Romeo y Julieta, boniatillos, alegrías de coco, jabones de olor, carretes de hilo y moscas somnolientas... Varios cantadores guajiros improvisaban décimas, sentados en los troncos de quiebrahacha colocados en el portal a guisa de bancos. Los caballos asomaban sus cabezotas en las puertas, atraídos por el resplandor de quinqués de carburo en forma de macetas... Las flores poéticas nacían sobre el monótono balanceo de salmodias quejosas. Las coplas hablaban de trigueñas doradas a la orilla del mar, del zapateado cubano y de gallos malayos, de cafetales y camisas de listado; *todo iluminado con tintes ingenuos, como las litografías de cajas de puros.*[102]

Camera-like, Carpentier begins this «cuadro» by focusing his attention on the rustic merchandise of the «bodega» in a detailed fashion, savoring the brand names and the products which represent a certain style of life. The accumulation of local character is a very important aspect of the style. In the midst of this stampede of objects. Carpentier inserts man; however the «guajiro» singing «décimas» which completes the picture is in fact organic to it. What separates this «cuadro costumbrista» from a thousand others by young localist writers, is a certain artistic consciousness of distance that confuses the realms of art and life to achieve a unity of both. The «guajiro's» song of «trigueñas doradas a la orilla del mar,» «gallos malayos, cafetales,» and so on, readily insinuates itself into the atmosphere of the «bodega,» harmonizing with the accumulated atmosphere of «alegrías de

---

[101] Frances Weber, «'El acoso': Alejo Carpentier's War on Time,» *PMLA* LXXVIII, 4, (Sept. 1963).
[102] *Écue*, p. 69.

coco,» «jabones de olor,» «ruedas de Romeo y Julieta» and «guajiros sentados en los troncos de quiebrahacha.»

Carpentier's stylized portrait of «guajiro» life is doubled and enhanced by the popular stylization and the romanticized self-image of the «guajiro,» as projected in the song. Thus when Carpentier says at end of the portrait, «todo iluminado con tintes ingenuos, como las litografías de cajas de puros,» the «todo» includes both the described scene and the song; that is, the «cuadro» Carpentier wishes us to see is not the crude reality of a rural «bodega,» but rather a reality once removed, of a popular lithograph «iluminado con tintes ingenuos,» and enhanced by imagination. It is a subtle «transposition d'art,» as practiced by Valle-Inclán.

The role of man or the «guajira,» in this picture is that of an aesthetic element. It is part and parcel in the accumulation of popular images; a figure drawn from a cigar box, not «un ser de carne y hueso.»

In another instance, the aesthetic reification becomes more strikingly discernible. Menegildo, having been apprehended for his crime, steps off the train in Havana under guard, and Carpentier seeks to communicate the swirl of impressions caused by the strange environment:

> Menegildo surcó el gentío, escoltado por sus guardianes. Dejó a sus espaldas una hilera de Fords destartalados y se vio en una calle guarnecida de comercios múltiples. El Café de Versailles, con sus pirámides de cocos y su vidriera llena de moscas. El Louvre, cuyo portal era feudo de limpiabotas. La ferretería de los Tres Hermanos que habían embadurnado sus columnas con los colores de la bandera cubana. Y luego el desfile de ornamentaciones rupestres: los Reyes Magos del almacén de ropas; el gallo de la tienda mixta; la tijera de latón de la barbería Brazo y Cerebro. La funeraria La Simpatía, con un rótulo que ostentaba un ángel casi obsceno envuelto en gasas transparentes. *En un puesto de esquina tres chinos se abanicaban entre mameyes rojos y racimos de plátanos...*[103]

Although Menegildo is actually walking past the shops, Carpentier animistically reverses the relationship of viewer-object with the word «desfile,» giving the impression that the shop figureheads and signs are flowing past the observer «on parade.» It is an «atropello» of inanimate objects that come to the foreground in fortuitous seeming combination: the Three Kings, a chicken, an obscene angel, a pair of scissors. With this example of juxtaposition, we come close to Carpentier's relationship to surrealism, and his essential differences. Carpentier uses association and juxtaposition, yet he takes his materials and their dispositions from those made available by the environment he is depicting.

In the midst of this «atropello,» three living human figures are interrelated in such a way that we see them on the same level of existence as the signs and other paraphenalia: «tres chinos se abanicaban entre mameyes rojos y racimos de plátanos.» The Chinamen are purely aesthetic elements, reified by juxtaposition.

[103] Ibid., p. 136.

Earlier in the book, we find another example: «En el umbral de su tienda, *el polaco Kamín se erguía entre frascos y calcetines...*» [014] Similarly, in a description of an American bar near the ingenio, Carpentier deliberately confuses the animate with the inanimate through their juxtaposition:

> En el bar se alteraban todos los postulados del buen sentido alcohólico. La caoba, húmeda de Bacardí, olía a selva virgen. *Las cocktaileras automáticas giraban sin tregua, bajo las miradas propiciadoras de un caballito de marmolina* blanca regalado por una casa importadora de whisky...[105]

In a love scene, the author reduces Menegildo and Longina to two objects among the furniture of the room: «Cuando la luna asomó sobre los tejados del solar, *dos cuerpos se apretaban aún, tras de una puerta celeste, entre un jarro de café frío y una estampa de San Lázaro.*» [106] Furthermore, in the scene of Menegildo's initiation into sex, already discussed, the renewed reproductive activity of the springtime is «carne arada por la carne.» Longina as perceived by Menegildo's senses is «fruta chamuscada,» «resina fresca,» «ébano tibio,» «pasta de hogaza.» The participants of the seance of «brujería» towards the end of the book, are «dos ruedas de carne... como dos cilindros concentrados... Las manos multiplicadas se encendían sobre pieles de buey.» [107]

In these examples reification is a way of suggesting the incorporation of humans into nature and the cosmos, as well as their disappearance from the world of speech, thought, and personality: «los animadores habían dejado de pertenecer al mundo.» [108] The following example is perhaps one of the most illustrative of reification in Carpentier because it demonstrates both the aesthetic and thematic ranges of the device:

> Por el hueco de una tapia penetraba a gatas en un jardín lleno de frutales sin podar y hierbas malas, donde puñados de mariposas blancas se alzaban en vuelo medroso. Los cráneos rapados surgían como pelotas de cuero pardo entre anchas calabazas color de cobre viejo. Cada flor era herida por un prendedor de libélula...[109]

In this epiphanic scene of regression, Carpentier captures the correspondences of «cráneos rapados» and «anchas calabazas» poetically. These suggest a total immersion, an almost ideal state of thingness and belonging in the universe of form, shape and color creating an effect akin to mimesis. The heads, disembodied by the image of «pelotas de cuero pardo», are also a purely aesthetic element in the scene.

---

[104] Ibid., p. 63.
[105] Ibid., p. 68.
[106] Ibid., p. 162.
[107] Ibid., p. 208.
[108] Ibid., p. 208.
[109] Ibid., p. 184.

5

Although we have already mentioned aspects of Carpentier's conception of character in *¡Écue-yamba-Ó!,* it is germane, at this point, due to the connection with reification, to bring out his tendency towards expressionism. The essence of the Expressionistic mode of character portrayal is the reduction of character to a central quality. In the early Expressionist plays, for example, a tense man would become tension incarnate, the quality becoming more real than the person. Although Carpentier's most expressionistic piece in this sense is *El acoso,* the movement in this direction is manifest in *Écue* and intrinsic to his next work, «Histoire des lunes.»

Menegildo is, as we have noted, an archetype of Carpentier's primitivism. As a character he overflows the boundaries of humanity hyperbolically. He is something less and more than a man in Carpentier's hands; he is alternately thing, animal, superhuman machine, but always devoid of individual characteristics. At the beginning of his life, he is constantly referred to as «el rorro,» and at the end of it, he is «un bulto entre la hierba.» In his adolescence, «su deseo sólo había conocido mansas cabras con largas perillas de yescas y ojos tiernamente confiados,» a description of rural bestiality. After his first contact with Longina, «una palpitante alegría hacía oscilar un gran péndulo detrás de sus pectorales cuadrados, que ya conocían contacto de mujer.» The Futuristic imagery of machines in the case of *Écue,* is a manifestation of Expressionism resulting from reification, as in the earlier image of the cane-workers who «sincronizan sus caricias con los émbolos.»

In order to conclude our discussion of Carpentier's mixture of the universe of things and people which cross the realms in *Écue,* I shall discuss the section toward the end of the novel which contains many of the devices in a strikingly orchestrated fashion. The passage has been chosen to demonstrate how Carpentier's techniques of animism and reification work together in an extreme situation of «esperpento.» This section relates the explosion of cult rivalries at the end of the book, resulting in Menegildo's death. The stylized violence of the gang war makes it seem a graceful ritual, indeed the last ritual of Menegildo's cycle:

> Entonces sonó un ruido extraño: el ruido de las cosas anormales, que altera los ritmos del corazón. Longina, aterrorizada sin saber por qué, se agazapó detrás del barril de agua. Cristalina y Cándida echaron a correr, desapareciendo en la obscuridad. Hacia el son se veían *saltar sombras* en una *confusión de torsos y de brazos* alumbrados por *los faroles cuyos bombillos estallaban.* Una bandada de negros había surgido de la noche, arrojándose sobre los invitados. *Los tambores y calabazas volaron en el aire. Las mochas cortaron guitarras* en dos. *Se blandieron cuchillos* y palos. Las luces fueron pisoteadas. Cien *gritos hendieron* las tinieblas. Algunos *dedos tocaron sangre.*
>
> —¡Efó! ¡Efó!— gritó Antonio.
>
> Menegildo reconoció gente del Juego enemigo a la luz del último quinqué, que fue apagado de una patada. El mozo se arrojó en el montón, cuchillo en mano.
>
> Hubo carreras y choques. El *hierro topó con el acero.* Y cedió el empuje. Longina *vio pasar siluetas espigadas* por el pánico. Un negrazo pasó junto al barril... Gritó varias veces...

Pero viéndose sola, *esta sombra acabó también por desaparecer* en la obscuridad.
El silencio se llenó de grillos.[110]

Carpentier prepares us for the violent scene with the perception of the «ruido de las cosas anormales.» The ensuing eruption is indeed a chaos in which «las cosas» autonomously wage war and human agents are for the most part in indirect or partial evidence.

Before Carpentier introduces the true agent of the violence («la bandada de negros») the actions are performed animistically by the shadows, which is also reification in a sense; «hacia el son se veían saltar sombras.» Then the shadows are «una confusión de torsos y brazos», or an incorporeal mass. When the agents are mentioned, they are lumped together in a zoomorphic mass by the noun, «bandada.» The actions described from there on are purposefully used without mention of an agent, in the creation of an animistic chaos: «los tambores y calabazas volaron ... Las mochas cortaron guitarras (linguistic animism) ... Se blandían cuchillos (use of the impersonal reflexive to avoid agent) ... las luces fueron pisoteadas (passive construction to avoid agent) ... cien gritos hendieron las tinieblas (animism emphasized by synesthesis).»

The introduction of the human element «algunos dedos tocaron sangre», instead of suggesting the presence of imaginable people, suggests a non-particularized (through «algunos») autonomous action of the body members which contributes to the fantastic effect.

The animistic imagery continues with «El hierro topó con el acero» suggesting the autonomy of the weapons. Here the animism might be considered synecdoche, or substitution of the part for the whole; in any case the two devices are strongly related due to their essence-focusing characteristic. In an image of reification, «Longina vio pasar siluetas espigadas por el pánico.» Then Carpentier reifies the human figure that is reincorporated into the darkness: «esta sombra acabó también por desaparecer en la oscuridad.» By confusing the realms of matter and eliminating the human agent, Carpentier has created a powerful scene of violence, and an impression of disturbing chaos.

I hope those aspects of *¡Écue-yamba-Ó!* which anticipate the mature Carpentier now stand out in relief, capable of providing an organic base for the comprehension of later works. In *Écué* one finds Carpentier's earliest exploration of the theme of regression conceived in relation to the primitivistic interest in cult cosmogony. In form, Carpentier has tried to suggest the oneness of man and nature through the cyclical representation of the life pattern, and the concentration of these focal points of human life which best reflect the processes of nature —birth, sex, violence, death and regeneration. In terms of character realization, how Carpentier subordinates character to an archetypal primitivistic concept, serving the theme of regression. And more significantly there are instances in this

---

[110]   Ibid., p. 210.

flawed novel of the sustained effort to forge an adequate style for capturing the essence the Black world. This is the most significant product of *¡Écue-yamba-Ó!*, since by and large the self-conscious attempt to enter wholly into a distant social setting was unsuccessful and not to be repeated. Elements of style, however, the most significant of which have been examined in this study, were successfully employed in the endeavor to fuse trope and reality, and were to continue on in the author's repertoire of technique. The birth of a distinctive style can be sensed in *¡Écue-yamba-Ó!*, particularly in the crossing of the realms.

III. «HISTOIRE DE LUNES»

In 1928 Carpentier arrived in Paris, where his personality and talents assured him a prominent place in the fast moving milieu of European letters of the time, Paris was his home for 11 years, until 1939, when he returned to Havana. It was an active period in which the young Cuban made contributions in various media and art forms, and counted among his friends and acquaintances many celebrated figures in the arts, including André Breton, Tristan Tzara, Louis Aragon, Robert Desnos, Paul Eluard, Benjamin Peret, Yves Tanguy, and Pablo Picasso.

Yet in spite of his undeniable acceptance into the inner circles of the European art world, and in spite of the immeasurable wealth of experience he gained, Carpentier resisted strongly incorporation into the dazzling surge of movements and personalities. In Cuba he had devoured the latest imports on the shelves of Morlhoon's Bookstore with the natural impulse to establish a balance against the insularity of his homeland. But in Paris, the inner pendulum swung the other way; during those years he frantically embraced everything American, diving into the most remote chronicles of his own hemisphere:

> Me dediqué durante largos años a leer todo lo que podía sobre América, desde las *Cartas* de Cristóbal Colón, pasando por el Inca Garcilaso hasta los autores del siglo dieciocho. Por espacio de casi ocho años creo que no hice otra cosa que leer textos americanos.[111]

Like a tight-rope walker, Carpentier needed to feel himself in a reassuringly central position between two counter-balanced worlds. In his public statements he, quite naturally perhaps, exaggerated his «Americanness». Most revealing, in this light, is Carpentier's ambivalent public attitude towards the surrealist movement, in which he participated actively:

> Nunca me sentí el ritmo interior del francés... me parecía una tarea vana mi esfuerzo surrealista. No iba a añadir nada a ese movimiento. Tuve una reac-

---

[111] Much of this attitude is revealed later. See César Leante, «Confesiones sencillas de un escrito barroco,» *Cuba,* Año III, no. 24 (April 1964), p. 32.

ción contraria. Sentí ardientemente el deseo de expresar el mundo americano. Aún no sabía cómo... Pero el surrealismo sí significó mucho para mí. Me enseñó a ver contexturas, aspectos de la vida americana que no había visto, envueltos como estábamos en las olas de nativismo...[112]

Carpentier's obsession with «el mundo americano» was manifested equally as much in his writing as in his reading habits. The great majority of his creative work during these years concentrated on Antillian, specifically Afro-Antillian, themes. From Klaus Müller-Bergh's comprehensive look at Carpentier's activities at the time, the areas of his production can be summarized:

— *Poetry:* «Liturgia» and «Canción», two Afro-Cuban poems sent from Paris to Habana and published there in 1930 and 1931 respectively.

— *Musical collaborations:* with the French composer Marius François Gaillard: *Yamba-O* (Tragedia burlesca), realized at the Théâtre Beriza in Paris, 1928; *Poèmes des Antilles, neuf chants sur le texte de Alejo Carpentier,* Paris, 1929; *Blue,* poem set to music; *La passion noire,* cantata for ten soloists, mixed choir and «altoparlantes». With A. Garcia Caturla: *Manita en el suelo* (Afro-Cuban farce); *Dos poemas Afrocubanos, Mari-Sabel* y *Juego santo* for voice and piano. In addition, according to Müller-Bergh, Carpentier collaborated with Villa-Lobos and Darius Milhaud, and wrote the libretto for an opera by the father of electronic music, Edgar Varèse.

— *Short stories:* only two stories are known to exist from this period, «Histoire de lunes» (1933) and «L'Etudiant».[113]

— *Novels: El castillo de campana Salomón (Mitología de La Habana),* and *Semblante de cuatro moradas,* neither of which «vieron ni verán jamás la luz de la imprenta, porque el escritor tiene que tener coraje de echar polvo sobre muchas páginas aunque mucho esfuerzo le haya costado llenarlas ...».[114]

— *Film:* Carpentier wrote the text and synchronized the music for the French documentary «Le Vaudou.»

— *Radio:* Carpentier began working with radio in 1932, and in the period up to 1939 carried out projects for Études Foniric for which he became director. In collaboration with Desnos, Antonin Artaud and Jean-Louis Barrault he programmed readings of Poe, Whitman, Paul Claudel, Langston Hughes, Paul Eluard, and Rafael Alberti, among others.

— *Other activities:* In 1931 Carpentier became editor-in-chief of the short-lived journal *Imán,* which although defunct after only one edition, had the merit of attracting Pablo Neruda's manuscript of *Residencia en*

---

[112] Ibid., p. 32.
[113] Seymour Menton, «Asturias, Carpentier, and Yáñez: Parallels and Contrasts.» *Revista Iberoamericana,* XXV, 67 (Jan. 1969), p. 31. Menton cites «L'Etudiant» as having appeared in *Révolution Surréaliste* (Paris) in 1928. However we have not been able to locate the story with this information.
[114] Leante, *op. cit.,* p. 32.

la tierra. Neruda was paid rights of authorship, but the manuscript was forwarded to Madrid, and finally published by *Cruz y Raya* in 1934.

Concerning all the production of these years, Carpentier has only made public mention, to the best of my knowledge, of the two unpublished novels, in a manner clearly indicating his desire to bury them and the derogatory remarks already quoted with respect to *¡Écue-yamba-Ó!* Only the two poems—«Canción» and «Liturgia»—and one short story—«Histoire de lunes»—have been unearthed from this early period for this study. Although these are scant findings, they nevertheless shed valuable light on Carpentier in a formative period.

The poems, written in the then fashionable idiom of «jitanjáfora» in combination with authentic «Ñáñigo» dialect, are in celebration of the ritual aspect of Afro-Cuban life. Perhaps they are only valuable to the extent that they demonstrate Carpentier's continuing preoccupation with African themes, and something of the nature of that preoccupation. The poems are formalistic orchestrations of sound, striking for their hieratic seriousness and virtual absence of the familiar spirit of «chacota» which characterizes much of the Afro-Cuban poetry of, for example, Ballagas, Tallet or Guillén.

The first poem, «Liturgia», attempts to evoke the atmosphere of mystical climax of the «Ñáñigo» initiation rites, the same ritual documented in *Écue.* The elements are «el rojo altar de Obatalá,» «el diablito» («en su gorro miran ojos de cartón,») «los muertos que llaman,» «Papá Montero.» The second poem, «Canción,» is akin to some poems of Mariano Brull («Verdehalago» for example) and attempts to create a lyricism of pure sound by the momentum of euphony: «Al laba balahola / de bata y ola; / batacola de percal / blanca de cal / con encaje de nata.» Both poems attempt to achieve some status of ritual through incantation.

Of much greater importance is a short story which has escaped criticism to date, published in the December 1933 issue of *Cahiers du Sud* four months after Carpentier finished the final draft of *¡Écue-yamba-Ó!* Unfortunately we have been unable to ascertain whether the story, which appeared in French, was written originally in Spanish or French. The fact that it appeared in French in a Parisian journal, however, is significant in that it enables us to conjecture that Carpentier was aiming at European readers in a literary context of experimentation. Here he was perhaps expected, or felt the need, to make a distinctly American contribution which would nonetheless be modern in relation to the broad movements in which he had participated in Paris. Nothing was more modern and sought after at that time than primitivism with some claim to authenticity, through which Carpentier could find instantly a place in most of the vital movements from Expressionism to Cubism and Surrealism. Having arrived in Paris on the very crest of the wave of interest in Negro primitive art and culture, Carpentier's natural inclination towards primitivism must have been pushed even farther by the unavoidable fact that he was the «genuine article» in relation to the «primitivistes de boutique» that surrounded him. The consciousness of this superiority, is manifest in most of his esays and in the obvious relish with which he demeans the effete interest in «lo natural-primitivo» of some European writers and artists.

«Histoire de lunes» is the story of the Cuban boot-black who under the spell of a sorcerer undergoes metamorphosis into a tree, and disrupts the fabric of a rural village. It is both very American and very experimental; a fantasy rooted in a folk tradition, and the description of a magical reality. It is at once a concession to Surrealism and a stubborn adherence to nativism. Yet more than these contradictions might imply, it is a fruitful synthesis of Carpentier's American experience and his discoveries of a new freedom with the European surrealists.

«Histoire de lunes» is an incursion into the same world of *Écue*. The characters, the barber, and the disruptive central character, and the elements of cult warfare and ritual of the stem from the novel. The tendency towards expressionistic character portrayal seen in *Écue* is fully developed in «Histoire de lunes.» As in the latter the central character actually regresses to «las primeras formas», embodying rather than suggesting the qualities of the author's primitivism. «Histoire de lunes» is a polished microcosm of *Écue* and the animistic world of «postes que hablan, cráneos trepadores, vísceras que andan, hechiceros con cuernos, llamadores de lluvia y pieles agoreros» suggested in the latter. The central elements of sex, violence and the occult are stylized and compressed in the story. The theme of regression, tied again inextricably to primitivism, is distilled in the artistic form of a well-organized short story, in the structure of a myth.

To have written «Histoire de lunes» Carpentier must have become painfully aware of the shortcomings of *Écue*. The timing of the appearance of the story in relation to the publishing of *Écue* increases the plausibility of this conjecture. Absent from «Histoire» is the incongruous mixture of naturalism and primitivism found in *Écue*; the perspective is primitivistic and the action within the frame of occult practices. Absent also is the interpolation of social commentary, since in the story there is but one reference to social injustice, and it is made with ironic detachment. Furthermore, the overstatement of *Écue* gives way to the objective appearing, even understated, account of a story of violence and the occult. As opposed to *Écue*, here Carpentier is sufficiently detached to be less interested in the anthropological facts of his story than in the disposition of its elements. In a word, the distinguishing factor between the two works is distance —greater distance from character and immediate reality in the story than the novel. With the new distance, a note of irony creeps into Carpentier's prose, enriching it with ambiguity and humor.

«Histoire de lunes» foreshadows the tensely expressionistic *El acoso* with its the nameless characters and its marginal anti-social world of violence surrounding a manhunt. The theme of the clash of faiths and customs sharply perceived as the essence of a syncretic society, the almost perverse delight in anachronism and the incongruous which bloom as the grotesque, are all found in «Histoire de lunes» and carry on to *El reino de este mundo*.

«Histoire» is a keystone in the evolution of the style of «realismo mágico» because of the carefully cultivated tenuous balance between the real and the fantastic. Carpentier, of course, like the Surrealists, aimed at this erasing the distinction. The author, in this short story, enters into the spirit of a collective faith and describes events often from the angle of a chronicler, tempered by a baroque eye for complexity and antithesis.

The story takes place in a rural Cuban village. The whole village centers its life around the railroad station, where the arrival of «L'express» with its «nègre du pullman déposant des omelettes sur les tables», «Visages des femmes différents de ceux que l'on connaissait trop», and «le bossu du fourgon des postes», both breaks the monotony of rural life and provides a daily ritual for the indolent villagers.

But for Atilano, «le seul cireur du village», the arrival of the train means the commencement of his daily «crise»—his transformation into «Le Glissant», the half-man, half-tree, who violates the village women at night: «Mais c'était à l'heure exacte où les wagons entraient en gare que l'arbre commençait à pousser. Du moins ce que l'envoûtement faisait pousser comme un arbre ... Alors Atilano se levait péniblement ...»[115]

After the «Glissant» has begun his nightly attacks on the women, the rhythm of the village changes. Now only the children go to the station to meet the train. The men are planning the capture of Atilano and cursing

> ... ces putains de femmes qui s'étaient chuchoté la nouvelle en se gardant bien de tirer le verrou de leur fenêtre, la nuit. Ah! Ça porte chance d'être violée par un glissant, une bête de l'ombre, âme solitaire d'Elegba, bouc à face humaine, qui croit violer alors que l'on jappe de plaisir, en faisant patiner les phalanges sur son dos graisseux. Prétendre que sa semence de malheur guérit la stérilité, les enflures aux jambes et les rhumatismes, mieux que les emplâtres au sang de poule noires. Saloperies...[116]

The «Glissant» continues his nightly assaults and the townsmen take up arms. One morning in church, as the priest, is delivering a sermon on the «ténèbres honteuses de la sorcellerie», the call to meeting of a battery of «Ñáñigo» drummers in the distance empties the church. «Les fidèles marchaient vers la montagne», following the sound of the drums to the hut of a «brujo» whom they consult as to the true identity of the «Glissant».

In an invocation ceremony, the «orisha» reveals the identity of the «Glissant», but the revelation that Atilano has violated only women of one cult, «les Boucs», divides the men and transforms the manhunt into cult warfare. «Les Crapauds» defend Atilano against «les Boucs».

[115] Alejo Carpentier, «Histoire de lunes,» *Cahiers du Sud* (Paris), 20° année, no. 157 (Dec. 1933), p. 748.
[116] Ibid., p. 749.

The passengers on the daily express are bewildered by the air of chaos that reigns in the village, the sound of Chinese trumpets and cult drums.

> C'était simple pourtant. La guerre était déclarée. Les crapauds [Atilano's cult] avaient pris Atilano sous leur protection. A la tombée de la nuit, ils se faufilaient au long des murailles et des haies du quartier des boucs, couteau en main, pour défendre le glissant de toute agression. Maintenant il pouvait violer les femelles ennemies, avec l'approbation de tous les membres de sa confrérie. On l'aidait même à s'enduire le corps de saindoux, de cambois ou de graisse d'essieux. Pendant qu'il empoignait quelque femme nue, dont le nourrisson prenait la fuite entre les barreaux du lit, d'âpres combats se livraient dans l'ombre; le sang giclait, et souvent les crapauds accourus au bruit de la bagarre, ne trouvaient plus qu'un agonisant...[117]

With the arrival of the carnaval in honor of the patron saint of the village, the mayor hopes that differences will dissolve and peace will come to the village. For the parade, the «Crapauds» build a float with the effigy of the saint, «Notre-Dame-des-petites-oreilles», while the «Boucs» carry a «Saint-Lazare vivant» played by the fanatic barber.

However a rainstorm disrupts the parade, and when the «Crapauds» rush the effigy of the patron-saint into the church the priest «s'empressa de fermer les battants pour pouvoir dévêtir l'image, dont le manteau trempé commençait à déteindre».[118] His action shuts the «Boucs» and their «Saint-Lazare vivant» out in the rain, and they begin to pound in vain on the church door. «C'est alors qu'on vit Atilano sauter sur la plate-forme et renverser le Saint-Lazare vivant d'un grand coup d'épaule».[119] A fight breaks out, the police come, and the «Boucs» scatter. «A la porte de l'église, seuls, le Glissant et Saint-Lazare se roulaient toujours dans la boue, en brandissant des tronçons de béquilles».[120] Both are taken to jail.

> Saint-Lazare fut mis en liberté quelques heures plus tard, car il ne fallait pas prendre de mesures trop sévères envers un inspiré. Quant à Atilano, on le tira de sa cellule à l'aube pour le fusiller dans la cour de la caserne. Lorsque les Mausers se dressèrent vers lui, il cria:
> «Vous allez tuer un arbre!»
> Un arbre communiste, car le maire, par délicatesse envers les membres des confréries qui l'avaient élu, et pour s'éviter des explications trop longues au gouverneur militaire de la province, avait spécifié qu'il s'agissait d'un agitateur rouge des plus dangereux.[121]

After Atilano's execution, «le calme régnait au village» and the routine of rural life continues to focus on the arrival of «l'express»: «D'ailleurs

[117] Ibid., p. 755.
[118] Ibid., p. 758.
[119] Ibid., p. 758.
[120] Ibid., p. 759.
[121] Ibid., p. 759.

maintenant on aurait la paix pour quelques mois. Les mauvaises influences de lunes étaient écartées ...» [122]

The only trace left of Atilano is the body of a dead eel found by one of the women that he violated. The eel «avait sur la tête une petite excroissance semblable à un arbre miniscule ... Et comme il s'agissait du double d'Atilano, il [the sorcerer] en fabriqua une potion qui devait guérir la stérilité, les rhumatismes, et les enflures des jambes, mieux que la semence même du glissant ...» [123].

The proportion in the figure of Atilano between folk myth and the author's own imagination is difficult to know. However, it is clear that, just as the setting itself and some of the central characters of the story bear the stamp of the authenticity of a familiar reality, the myth of Atilano has some basis in Cuban folklore. Lydia Cabrera, in her compilation of Cuban mythologies, speaks extensively of the great variety of tree myths on the island, and in particular of «este misticismo que despierta la ceiba en todo el país». Atavistic and animistic beliefs about the sacred «ceiba» are widespread:

> Se sabe que de noche las ceibas conversan, andan y se trasladan de un lugar a otro. «Caminan por la sabana»... Su espíritu es tan potente que muchos que van a rogarle, sin llegar a perder conocimiento y sienten su peso en la nuca y les faltan fuerzas para resistirlo... La ceiba... también se encarga de causar la desgracia o la muerte de una persona. Ella hace toda la obra. [124]

Although Carpentier's myth is in a sense the reverse of this popular tendency towards anthropomorphic animism, relating as it does, the transformation from man to tree, the possibility that he was directly inspired by the recollection of legends absorbed in his youth seems likely. We should recall that Carpentier's «first and most important world was not La Habana, but rural Cuba. His father did not only practice the profession of architecture, but also owned two country estates, so that the author spent his entire childhood and a part of his youth in direct contact with the Cuban countryside». [125]

Carpentier's own animistic description of the «ceiba» in *Tientos y diferencias* although long after the short story, reveals his knowledge of the popular myth of the tree: «La ceiba ... sagrada por linaje. Allí está, en lo alto de una ladera, solo, silencioso ... *rompiendo el suelo con sus enormes raíces escamosas.*» [126]

---

[122] Ibid., p. 759.
[123] Ibid., p. 759.
[124] Lydia Cabrera, *El monte* (Miami: Rema Press, 1968), p. 154.
[125] Eduard Houdesek, «Einige Bemerkunger zur Persönlichkeit und zum literischen Schaffen von Alejo Carpentier,» *Wissenschaftliche Zeitschrift der Universität Rostock* WZUR, XIV, 1965, p. 41. Translated by private arrangement by Ulrich Schneider, Harvard University.
[126] *Tientos y diferencias, op. cit.,* p. 40.

Yet if Carpentier derived the suggestion of his story from folk tradition, it is nonetheless a highly personalized example of fantastic expressionism which has been given the form of a myth. Atilano is Carpentier's own monster, individuated by sensuous detail and literary device is also the embodiment of central themes already expressed in *Écue,* particularly that of regression, which recur in subsequent stories.

Louis Vax comments on the proximity to our own psyches of the fantastic monster in fiction:

> Le monstre incarne nos tendances perverses et homicides, aspirant à vivre, libérées, d'une vie propre. Dans les récits fantastiques, monstre et victime incarnent ces deux parts de nous-même: nos désirs inavouables et l'horreur qu'ils nous inspirent. L'au-delà du fantastique est un au-delà tout proche... Le monstre traverse les murs et nous atteint où que nous soyons. Rien de plus naturel, puisque le monstre, c'est nous. Il s'était déjà glissé dans notre coeur...[127]

While the fantastic can respond to an inner reality, it can also be a statement of the absurd contradiction of the human condition:

> Le fantastique ne veut pas seulement l'impossible parce qu'il est effrayant, il le veut parce qu'il est impossible. Vouloir le fantastique c'est vouloir l'absurde et le contradictoire.[128]

Atilano is the expressionistic exaggeration of qualities pointed out in the protagonist of *Écue.* The progression from the dehumanized, magnified eroticism and oneness with nature of Menegildo, to the «Glissant», is almost foreseeable.

Yet in the attempt to discern, in «Histoire de lunes», the balance between the creativity of the author and folk myth, between expressionism and the popular tale, it is essential to see the story within the framework of primitivism. Atilano as the «Glissant» is a conjured reality which Carpentier painstakingly seeks to portray as a germination of a popular imagination, as a collectively imagined phenomenon. The carefully limned ambiguities surrounding the myth are elaborately designed to create in the reader the delicate perception of the story as myth as a creation of the people. The reader is invited to participate in it as if reality: «L'arbre commençait à pousser. Du moins, ce que l'envoûtement faisait pousser comme un arbre... Les gens pouvaient ne pas le voir mais Atilano sentait qu'il remplissait tout le village.»

Therefore we can see in the creation of the «Glissant» a carefully controlled Expressionism, as both the product of the self-conscious myth-making nourished by roots in the Black subculture of Cuba, and of the unfettered imagination nourished in the atmosphere of experimentation of Carpentier's Parisian milieu.

In «Histoire de lunes» the theme of regression and metamorphosis

---

[127] Louis Vax, *L'Art et la littérature fantastiques* (Paris: Presses Universitaires de France, 1960), p. 10.
[128] Ibid., p. 30.

foreshadowed in *Écue* is the focus, and is played out and actually realized. Atilano has a triple identity as man, tree, and, eel. His metamorphosis first into tree, and then upon his death, into eel, seems inspired by the duality of «nos désirs inavouables et l'horreur qu'ils nous inspirent», the horror and forbidden pleasure of «le viol». As the «Glissant» he becomes a force of the pre-conscious, the anti-social, the totally sensual and instinctive existence which fascinates Carpentier in one form or other in all his later work.

Theme

The theme of the subtle battle between religions and customs—between atavism and catholicism, black and white, belief and belief, is in the foreground of «Histoire». As opposed to the monolithic *Écue*, Carpentier uses the counterpoints by a syncretic society to advantage, bringing out ironic contrasts.

For the drama of the violantions and manhunt takes place in a society within a society—the rural «Ñáñigo» world of beliefs and customs within the Hispanic world of bureaucracies and institutions (in *Écue* the white world exists in shadow and institutional effigy). Those bureaucracies and institutions are represented in flesh and blood by «le curé» (the church) and «le maire» (the government). Both figures are forced to react to the strange occurrences of the village, and are forced to project solutions.

The white priest delivers a sermon censoring «les fidèles»:

> Mes frères, commença le curé... Dieu nous a fait différents des animaux... l'homme, dont le front s'élève vers le ciel, peut comprendre et mesurer la grandeur de Dieu. Si tant d'entre vous ne se laissaient aveugler par les ténèbres honteuses de la sorcellerie, des évènements comme ceux qui viennet de se produire ici seraient impossibles...[129] (This passage will be quoted in its entirety on page 82).

The gulf existing in the story between the faiths, which makes the reiteration of «mes frères» ring with irony, and the priest's ineffectual attempt to eradicate atavism are portrayed with mastery here. As will be shown the counterpoint is woven stylistically as well.

In like fashion the mayor must confront the problem of the village. But there is no administrative code for dealing with monsters and metamorphosis. The Black world view, which welds the supernatural and the everyday in its interpretation of reality, is far more complex and rich. Therefore when the mayor must reduce the extravagant events to fit within the framework of judicial procedure, the result is incongruous and absurd: Atilano is labeled a Communist, «pour s'éviter des explications trop longues».

At the execution, Atilano, speaking within his own framework as a

---

[129] «Histoire de lunes,» *op. cit.*, p. 752.

«Ñáñigo» whose actions, far from being criminal, are the result of an «envoûtement», cries out in his perception of the absurdity, his incomprehension of the applied justice: «Vous allez tuer un arbre!» Carpentier, seizing upon the irony, and the anachronism, of the situation, inserts laconically, «un arbre communiste, car le maire... avait spécifié qu'il s'agissait d'un agitateur rouge...». The black humor of the situation suggests a new detachment in Carpentier, and his ability to see both cultures in perspective, weaving counterpoints and observing incongruities with irony.

However at the same time, «Histoire de lunes» signifies primitivistically the triumph of atavism in a manner which foreshadows Carpentier's two great novels, *El reino de este mundo* and *El siglo de las luces*. There the priest and the mayor and were unsuccessful in eradicating atavistic belief, guilty of gross underestimation of its power which led to the downfall of both. The body of beliefs and customs of the «Ñáñigo» «fidèles» in «Histoire de lunes» remains intact. It is a triumph of atavism in that the folkloric imagination manages to preserve its own interpretation of events, in spite of the superior and diametrically contradictory forces surrounding it: administration, clergy, and the passengers from Habana on the daily express.

Carpentier's widening focus in «Histoire» to encompass the syncretic reality of Cuba is a significant step in his evolution as an American writer, and reflects the recognition of a complexity and cultural impurity that by and large he sought to ignore or avoid in *El milagro de Anaquillé* and *Écue-yamba*. As time went on it became precisely this aspect of the Latin American existence that he celebrated above all else. The «ángeles tocando maracas» carved on an abandoned jungle church in *Los pasos perdidos* provoke an extensive eulogy in the narrator. Syncretism became the key to his belief that the Latin American is the truly universal man by virtue of his multiplicity of cultures and the will to assimilate and incorporate diverse elements.

Essential to the understanding of Carpentier's portrayal of syncretic society is the fact that he uses its manifestations for relief and contrast. In the episode of the church, the contrast between the priest's code and that of the «Ñáñigo», makes each stand out in greater relief, particularly with the use of effective imagery. If the story of Atilano were set in a totally Black social context, with no references to the white culture, it would fail to have the impact that it has. Background, contrast, and irony are all gained by the introduction of these disparate elements.

Form

The basic form of the story is a crescendo of violence, beginning with Atilano's violations, which gradually disrupt the social fabric of the town, developing into gang warfare and finally the dual denouement of the solution by the mayor and the townspeople.

On the mayor's side the affair is neatly ended with Atilano's death, but in the richer version of the townspeople, Atilano's death is merely the temporary end of a dangerous lunar cycle:

> D'ailleurs maintenant on aurait la paix pour quelques mois. Les mauvaises influences de la lune étaient écartées, car l'astre en entrait dans un des triangles du ciel qui neutralisent son action néfaste sur le crâne des hommes.[130]

Thus Carpentier suggests the repetitiveness of the primitive world, in which every event reflects an archetypal event which comes to pass again and again. Atilano does not actually die (as Makandal does not in *El reino de este mundo*); he is simply reincorporated into the regressive form of an eel, and ultimately into the fecundating potion made of his body: «il en fabriqua une potion qui devait guérir la stérilité, les rhumatismes et les enflures des jambes mieux que la semence même du glissant». The lunar cycle begins once more in peace.

Thus the execution and the finding of the eel by the townspeople are alternate endings, or frameworks for the story. In the one case, the drama is closed, in the other, it is left open. The value is in the contrast, and in that Carpentier can suggest both without precluding either.

In the disposition of episodes of the story, the arrival of the train is interpolated regularly, as a ritual signifying a state of normality:

> C'était à 12 h. 28, assez exactement, que le train commençait alors à claxonner aigrement. On faisait démarrer le ventilateur au Café des Trois Mages. Et les mendiants, les marchands de fritures ou de prières envahissaient le quai...[131]

It is always the same, this ritual, and it occurs four times in the story. In one sense, the train represents the view to the outer world, it is a window opening from and to the hermetic world of the rural folk. In another way the train establishes the rhythm and a pattern in the story, which the violence surrounding the «Glissant» breaks. At the first serious outbreak of violence,

> ... seuls les enfants allaient à la gare... le ventilateur des Trois Mages [another constant element of the ritual train arrival] tournait d'autant mieux que les réunions s'y succédaient, sans attendre l'heure du train... Sans les cris de Paulita l'idiote qui se mit à hurler au beau milieu de la route parce que le glissant lui avait arraché les vieux croûtons de pain qu'elle portait dans son corsage, on serait aussi insouciant que d'habitude; on irait baver devant les bras nus, les gramophones et les omelettes du pullman.[132]

But then at the height of the gang warfare,

> Ce jour-là, pendant les cinq minutes d'arrêt, les voyageurs de l'express abandonnent leurs wagons et sortirent sur le perron de la gare, cherchant à comprendre ce qui se passait au village. Le ventilateur des Trois Mages *ne tournait*

---

[130] Ibid., p. 759.
[131] Ibid., p. 747.
[132] Ibid., p. 749.

plus, même les deux vieilles Ford restaient cachées dans leur case... Le train repartit plein d'hypothèses et de questions sans réponse.[133]

In this example, then, we can see how Carpentier uses the train as both window and pattern.

Style

When, as in «Histoire de lunes», the entire vision is channeled through a single narrator, the complex question of point-of-view in the Jamesian sense of the novel is usually reduced to the relatively more simple question of author-narrator perspective and distance. In «Histoire de lunes» Carpentier has chosen the indefinite third person—the «on» in French. Carpentier's use of «on» often circumscribes the narrator and the small limited world of the village, suggesting the homogeneity of a collective psyche in a manner befitting a folk tale.

Yet, due to its indefiniteness, the «on» as Carpentier uses it here, gives the narrator a kind of floating identity; he can leave its confines unnoticeably, or return to it, insinuating himself into the collective psyche. Thus the author is, or seems, at various points, witness, participant, reporter, *griot.*

Carpentier's use of the indefinite third person gives the tale an air of familiar authenticity, yet paradoxically, there is a kind of detachment resulting fom the familiarity which permits the narrator a kind of distance from his material. He takes a certain reality for granted, thus precluding excessive description or exclamatory prose. It is a kind of short-cut to the heart of his material. This balanced perspective of familiarity and distance and the attendant economy of means is precisely what is lacking from *¡Écue-yamba-Ó!* The effective use of this kind of double omniscience reappears noticeably in his most perfect tale «Camino a Santiago».

Thus, at the opening of the story, Carpentier establishes the margin between the collective world of the townspeople and the outside world of the train passengers, by placing the narrator within the trivial pattern of the villagers' daily response to the arrival of the express: «On faisait démarrer le ventilateur au Café des Trois Mages... Visages des femmes différents de ceux que l'on connaissait trop.»[134]

The «on» as Carpentier uses it locates and circumscribes, emphasizing the within-without relationship of the town and the train:

> On irait baver devant les bras nus, les gramophones, et les omelettes du pullman. Maintenant c'était les gosses que l'on envoyait mendier à la gare et porter la salade à la tortue du fourgon tandis qu'aux Trois Mages, on astiquait fusils et revolvers, assis en rond autour du ventilateur...[135]

[133] Ibid., p. 755.
[134] Ibid., p. 747.
[135] Ibid., p. 749.

Or it is used for immediacy and drama: «Quand on entendit la voix du quatrième tambour, l'église était déjà vide. Les fidèles marchaient vers la montagne.»[136]

More often, and most significantly, Carpentier uses the «on» as a disguise with which to penetrate the collective psyche, the interior world, of primitive beliefs. From within the «on» perspective Carpentier as a seeming folk raconteur gives an air of confirmed veracity to the fork tradition:

> Quand Jesús le coiffeur devint Saint-Barbe pour quelques jours, on ne l'a pas troublé par des questions inutiles. On leur a mis de la nourriture au pied d'un arbre, et c'est tout. Tandis que les hommes-chevaux, les hommes-boucs, les arbres qui marchent, ceux-là on les crêve, et surtout s'ils violent des femmes et que les femmes y prennent plaisir. Les glissants sont comme les serpents: si on les rencontre sur son chemin et qu'on ne les tue pas, ils deviennent très vieux, et alors ils rentrent dans la mer, tout ridés, tout couverts de bosses et de poils blancs, et comme ils ont horreur du sel, ils maudissent l'homme qui leur a laissé cette chienne de vie... D'ailleurs tout ce qui touche aux influences de lunes ne peut finir que très mal.[137]

This passage has a tone of intimacy with local reality totally missing from *Écue-yamba-Ó*. The device of the indefinite third person was a fortunate solution at this point to the great problems of perspective and tone, a rectification of the previous fumbling attempts to bridge the huge gap between Carpentier's European cultural perspective and the regional scene. This is what the author, true to Breton's observation on modern primitivists, «aun a costa de un milagro» wished to possess in fiction. As in the metamorphosis of Makandal in *El reino de este mundo,* Carpentier seeks to weld his «I»—his lyrical sense of the «merveilleux—to the magical beliefs of a people. The result is the collective epiphany of miracle, metamorphosis, and other transcendent events.

Carpentier's is a sensitivity which must work within the contexts of history or myth. His keen sense of fantasy only thrives where there are time honored fabrications of popular tradition. Yet as in Expressionistic works, the facts or events of «Histoire de lunes» stand alone. The story creates its own aesthetic and meaning without reference outside it, as opposed to allegory or symbolic forms. Thus Atilano's change into tree is not a symbolic event; it does not demonstrate a universal truth, but rather creates its own aesthetic and laws. It is the aesthetic partially molded by the grotesque, a term integral to Expressionism and Surrealism.

One of the most universal components of the grotesque according to Kayser, is the fusion of distinct realms of perception and reality. This is observable from Bosch's canvases, through the tales of Poe and Kafka, and Chirico's abstractions.

---

[136] Ibid., p. 752.
[137] Ibid., p. 757.

6

The grotesque, as as aesthetic and moral category found in Expressionist works, is also a hermetic and non-transcending mode distinct from tragedy, pathos, or comedy:

> As an artistic genre, tragedy opens precisely within the sphere of the meaningless and the absurd the possibility of a deeper meaning —in Fate, which is ordained by the gods... The creator of grotesques, however, must not and cannot suggest a meaning.[138]

This self-sufficient, almost purely aesthetic nature of the story can be illuminated by examining its center—the metamorphosis.

In «Histoire de lunes» the metamorphosis, and thus the tale itself, is but an extended metaphor comparing the uncontrolled growth of a tree, the inexorable and purely biological forces of fecundation, to latent violence of man's own sexuality normally repressed by society. In the story, as in all literary metamorphoses, the metaphor is realized, and the realms are fused in «Le Glissant», the tree-man. I have found this description by Walter Sokel particularly appropriate.

> The function of the metamorphosis is to express utter ambivalence, an empirically impossible task which only an empirically impossible event can perform. Satisfying each of mutually contradictory impulses, the metamorphosis accomplishes the literally impossible. It integrates disintegration, not by reversing or stopping it, but by embodying it.[139]

Let us look at Atilano's transformation:

> Mais c'était à l'heur exacte où les wagons entraient en gare, que l'arbre commençait à pousser. Du moins ce que l'envoûtement faisait pousser comme un arbre. Le corps d'Atilano était plein de terre. D'une terre grasse, suante et rouge, comme celle des champs de canne a sucre. Tout à coup, il sentait la graine éclater dans son cerveau, et des racines tièdes, se durcissant progressi-vement, venaient se faufiler entre ses côtes. Un serpentin vert se déroulait au long de sa colonne vertébrale, pour claquer sèchement, comme fouet, entre ses cuisses. Et l'arbre poussait, plus lourd que l'homme, entrainat l'homme à sa suite, tirant sur des racines bien accrochées à une terre gluante et chaude. «L'arbre te conduira!» —avait crié le sorcier sur le seuil de sa case. Encore fallait-il attendre la tombée de la nuit pour partir... Depuis que ça l'avait repris, Atilano s'efforcait de cacher ses crises. Jamais il ne s'était donné tant de mal pour faire reluire les bottes de ses clients.[140]

And later, as Atilano lies outside the café, listening to the men preparing their rifles and planning the capture of the «Glissant»,

> Atilano était couché sous la vérandah, à l'ombre grandissante du pilier. Il écoutait les propos des hommes d'une oreille tapissée de velours. Les paroles

[138] Wolfgang Kayser, *The Grotesque in Art and Literature* (Gloucester, Mass.: Peter Smith, 1968), p. 186. Trans. Ulrich Weisstein.
[139] Walter Sokel, *The Writer in Extremis* (Stanford: The Stanford University Press, 1959), p. 48.
[140] «Histoire,» *op. cit.,* p. 748.

arrivaient bien à l'escargot, la harpe et le petit marteau qui résonnent quelque part sous le crâne, mais de là au cerveau, le chemin était long. Les racines de l'arbre commençaient à l'envahir. L'arbre poussait. Les gens pouvaient ne pas le voir mais Atilano sentait qu'il remplissait tout le village, ébranlant les murailles et qu'à son ombre une odeur d'amour montait...[141]

As if sprung from «el lodo de sudor y polvos rojizos» that covers the caneworkers in *Écue-yamba-Ó*, as if drawn «del limo a la savia» as the cane itself is personified, Atilano combines the anthropomorphic and the zoomorphic tendencies of that book. As metaphor, Atilano is the aesthetic embodiment of the theme of regression, the incarnate *force vitale* of «las primeras formas» which overflows the positive borders of conventional primitivism and enters the grotesque.

The metamorphosis is the central manifestation of the crossing of the realms of nature which is realized stylistically on a smaller scale throughout the story like the nascent «realismo mágico» in *Écue*.

First of all, while Atilano is portrayed as a combination of the realms of plant and human life, the rival bands of the town are seen in the light of their totemic affiliations:

> Boucs ceux du côté montagne, crapauds, ceux du côté rivière... Et voici que même glissant, même anguille, arbre ou envoûté, il n'avait violé que des femmes boucs, respectant les femmes crapauds.[142]

The two bands, fighting the primordial struggle of right of possesion of «la hembra», lend an air of expressionistic animality to the story. Their identities and actions have been reduced to the totems of goat and toad.

As in *Écue-yamba-Ó*, an animal context is given to people and event, but unlike that novel, its purely image, or imaginative enhancing.

> ...une odeur d'amour montait, en plein midi, de la robe des négresses. Des hennissements se faisaient entendre. Dans un pré les bêtes se labouraient à leur joie.[143]

During the hunt for the «Glissant»,

> Des coups de feu avaient bien claqué dans les ténèbres mais sans autre résultat que de tuer un cochon noir, appartenant au curé. Partout où l'on croyait apercevoir le glissant, on ne trouvait que crabes de terre fuyant dans les herbes, ou grosses couleuvres réveillant des poules pour les faire tomber d'un arbre.[144]

In the first example the animal imagery is sexual, in the second, it is

---

[141]   Ibid., p. 750.
[142]   Ibid., p. 755.
[143]   Ibid., p. 750.
[144]   Ibid., p. 751.

clearly intended to suggest the grotesque and disagreeable. The image of the snake and the chickens parallels «le viol».

The use of animism and personification continues to play an important part in Carpentier's style. Significantly the animism found in «Histoire de lunes» is, as in *Écue-yamba-Ó,* closely associated with ontology, and clearly used in a conscious attempt to impose the primitive's vision stylistically. The following passage which relates the interruption of the priest's sermon by the cult drums, the invasion of the sanctity of the church by the insinuating force of atavism, demonstrates Carpentier's ability to infuse matter with life and draw significant contrasts and relationships among various elements.

> Mes frères, commença le curé sous la conque baroque de la chaire, tandis que la colombe de porcelaine, représentant le Saint Esprit, se balançait au bout de sa ficelle —mes frères. Dieu nous a fait différents des animaux. Les bêtes ont les museau toujours baissé vers le sol, pour mieux nous montrer que l'homme dont le front s'élève vers le ciel, peut comprendre et mesurer la grandeur de Dieu. Si tant d'entre vous ne se laissaient aveugler par les ténèbres honteuses de la sorcellerie, des évènements comme ceux qui viennent de se produire ici seraient impossibles. Le Seigneur est plein de bonté, mais il sait aussi se montrer terrible dans la colère. Souvenez-vous de Sodome et Gommorrhe; souvenez-vous du dernier cyclone; souvenez-vous...
>
> Le curé se torna brusquement vers l'entrée, en serrant les dents. Un roulement sourd, tonnerre sous la forêt, roucoulement d'un pigeon monstrueux, avait éclaté au loin. Puis, coupant un bref silence, une batterie sèche, impérative, envahit l'église.
>
> Une percussion grave entra dans la ronde, pour mieux faire trembler les statues de cire dans leurs vitrines. Un, deux, trois, quatre. Les quatre tambours rituels, cognés dans l'ordre commencèrent à parler. D'abord le Tambour-d'Appel; ensuite, le Tambour-de-Nation et le Tambour-du-coq; puis enfin le Tambour-de-Deuil, qui sert à invoquer les morts.
>
> Quand on entendit la voix du quatrième tambour, l'église était déjà vide. Les fidèles marchaient vers la montagne.[145]

The drums are personified in metaphor, as «pigeon monstrueux» (a surreal image) that «envahit» the church, and later are named individually. Their «voix» is the force that animates this scene, «pour mieux faire trembler les statues de cire dans leurs vitrines». The white wax figures of the Catholic saints tremble animistically, with the vibrations of the cult drummers, suggesting the defensive, weak position of the church in relation to the living force of atavism. The ruling image of «pigeon monstrueux» contrasts effectively with the «colombe de porcelaine», which, «réprésentant le Saint Esprit, se balançait au bout de sa ficelle». The notion of artificiality and fragility is conveyed by the image of the balancing porcelain figure, as opposed to the «pigeon monstrueux».

Thus the counterpoint of elements of a syncretic society is woven through animism and personification in a manner which vividly suggests a struggle.

[145] Ibid., p. 752.

At this point in the narrative the four drums, personified, «commencèrent à parler», evoking the immediate response of the people who empty the church. As in scenes cited in *Écue-yamba-Ó,* but to a greater degree and with more subtlety, Carpentier here expresses the essence of the conflicting styles of life with the aid of annmated objects alone. He is able to suggest violent action without mention of human agents, through the use of animism. This indirect method of dramatization is highly effective, and suggestive of an atmosphere charged with the *force vitale.* The relationship of the animistic trope to «Ñáñigo» mythology which invests cult drums with individual identities and powers, makes the scene doubly effective.

The following scene, which shows «les fidèles» advancing up the mountain in search of the sorcerer's hut, reveals Carpentier's continuing use of animism in connection with reification. This combination produces the crossing of the realms.

> Faces noires et têtes crépues avançaient en groupes serrés par les sentiers rocailleux. La batterie des tambours tournait sous le soleil comme une tempête d'été. Parfois on avait la sensation de s'éloigner de l'endroit où l'on cognait les peaux de bouc tendues à la flamme. Ça venait du nord, du sud; ça montait de la rivière, ou dévalait du grand pylone en coquillages pétrifiés, habité par les vautours et les daims. Ceux qui ne connaissaient pas l'entrée de la faille où se dissimulait la case du sorcier, avec sa corne en paratonnerre, aurait pu errer jusqu'à la nuit parmi les plantes grasses, au risque de s'arrêter sous un gouao dont l'ombre fait grossir une tête humaine à vue d'oeil. Mais on arrivait déjà au chemin blanc, qui conduisait tout droit à l'enclos du Ta.[146]

The disembodiment of the «fidèles» (a form of reification), their reduction to «faces noires et têtes crépues» in combination with the of the drum—«ça venait du nord, du sud; ça montait de la rivière, ou dévalait du grand pylone en coquillages pétrifiés»—gives the impression of a world where latent forces predominate at the expense of man, where there are «plantes grasses» and the trees, «dont l'ombre fait grossir une tête humaine à vue d'oeil». The three verbs of motion—«venait», «montait», «dévalait»—ascribed to the sound of the drums, convey a sense of multiplicity of personified action akin to an invasion.

This tendency to diminish man in relation to forces and even objects is most apparent in the depiction of the carnival in the story. In the carnival there are two floats; one, born by the «Crapauds», carries the local «Vierge» in effigy, while the other belonging to the rival cult, carries the «Saint-Lazare vivant», a living townsman. Carpentier concentrates upon the effigy.

> Quant à la grande Patronne, couronne d'or, vêtue de neuf, et ornée de toutes les boucles d'oreilles prêtées par les fidèles, elle attendait l'instant d'être hissée

[146] Ibid., p. 752.

sur son tronc en demi-lune soutenu par les trois séraphins roses dont on avait
dépouillé le corbillard des enfants, avec la permission de l'Agence des Pompes
Funèbres... On alluma les roulettes à pétards. Des fusées partirent, tandis que
Notre-Dame-des-petites-oreilles poursuivait son chemin, en fixant la foule de
ses yeux sombres. On l'arrêtait devant les maisons où il y avait un malade,
pour la «faire danser.» Puis la procession repartait, dans un vacarme de
cuivres et de cymbales.

La vierge avait parcouru ainsi les rues principales du quartier crapaud.
On arrivait au quartier bouc... lorsque l'on vit apparaître un cortège inattendu
tout en haut de la rue des Libérateurs. Des tambourinaires, des hommes déguisés en animaux, portant de grosses lanternes sur leur ventre, avançaient en
groupe compact, suivis d'une sorte de plateforme en bois, sur laquelle se
dressait un grand Saint-Lazare noir, entouré d'une meute de chiens en plâtre.
Pavillon à l'air, quelques trompettes chinoises élevaient leurs plaintes lugubres,
en tête d'une colonne de femmes qui hurlaient, en agitant des mouchoirs de
couleurs:

«Saint-Lazare vivant! Saint-Lazare vivant!»[147]

Carpentier captures admirably the syncretic confusion of cultures and
realms in the parade—the men disguised as animals, the complaining
trumpets, howling women, and the presiding effigy, «fixant la foule avec
ses yeux sombres». As often in these descriptions, Carpentier touches on
the grotesque.

Of stylistic interest in the story are two examples of synecdoche, a device that increases in Carpentier's works. As I have pointed out this device
is related in an important way to animism. As animism captures the essence
of action through an illusion of spontaneous generation, synecdoche captures the essence of objects, human or inanimate, by focusing on a single
feature as if it were the whole.[148] Carpentier often uses the device cinemato-
graphically, using his prose in a manner suggestive of the close-up.

At the beginning of the story, Carpentier takes over the mind's eye of
Atilano, and arranges visual reality from the angle of a bootblack:

Seul Atilano maudissait l'express. Le matin ça allait encore. Courbaturé, trop
éreinté même pour avoir peur, bêchant du saindoux chaque fois qu'il se
grattait la poitrine ou le ventre, il cirait les bottes du colon américain et les
brodequins du maire; après les souliers du chef de gare, c'était le tour des
bottines vernies de Monsieur Rhadamès, le maquereau français qui attendait
à l'écart ses papiers de naturalization cubaine pour repartir à la Habane...[149]

This sequence helps define the peripheral location and perspective of
the poor bootblack with relation to men who live in the world of shined
shoes. As to them he is merely a bootblack, unaware as they are of the

---

[147] Ibid., p. 757.
[148] W. M. Frohock, *French Literature: an Approach Through Close Reading*
(Cambridge: Schoenoff's Foreign Books, 1970), p. 164.
[149] «Histoire,» p. 747.

strange metamorphosis going on under their eyes, to him they are merely a succession of «bottes», «brodequins», «souliers», and «bottines vernies». This discrepancy, early established in the story, reinforces the theme of clashing worlds which leads up to the absurd twin denouement. This use of synecdoche —or «le tout au moyen de la partie» in Morier's definition[150]—is also a form of reification. Similarly, after the conflict at the church, when the «Glissant» and Saint-Lazare «se roulaient toujours dans la boue» in grotesque but syncretic disharmony, «les uniformes kakis avançaient, en laissant partir une décharge tous les trois pas».[151]

Officialdom, the other world represented by the advancing police, is reified, disembodied by the synecdoche «les uniformes avancaient». This as the previous example, is intended to convey the perspective of the threatened cult members, who in their fear or contempt, see only «uniformes», not individual men. This case combines some of the properties of animism, since the uniforms are given life with synecdoche.

In summation, «Histoire de lunes» is an important link in the evolution of the author because it exhibits a new mastery over his material. In contrast to Écue-yamba-Ó it is a highly artistic story. The contours are imposed by the mind instead of the from life as in Carpentier's first novel. Awareness of the richly syncretic elements of the Cuban reality lends complexity and irony to his work and the effort to forge a style capable of conveying certain central aspects of the Black welt continues with use of animism, personification, reification, and synedoche in the crossing of realms. The tendency towards the grotesque becomes more pronounced as documentary naturalism gives way to a freed Expressionistic force. Nevertheless Carpentier's effort to stay within the bounds of a collective psyche provides the paradox which is central to his evolving style.

[150] Henri Morier, Dictionnaire de poétique et de rhétorique (Paris: Presses Universitaires de France, 1961), p. 439.
[151] «Histoire,» p. 58.

IV. «VIAJE A LA SEMILLA»

Some eleven years after Carpentier began his literary career with the publication in Madrid of the ambitious and flawed *¡Écue-yamba-Ó!,* he published a short story (thirty pages) in a modest edition of one hundred copies in Havana. «Viaje a la semilla», an experimental story that narrates the life of the Marqués de Capellanías in reverse sequence, seems to represent a radical departure from the author's previous tales of «brujos» and cane-cutters. To most critics, it is the logical point of departure in the effort to comprehend the corpus of his mature works.

«Viaje a la semilla» of 1944 is virtually the only story of the early period known to the public, since it was a part of *Guerra del tiempo,* the collection of tales that appeared in 1958. As the other stories in that volume, «Viaje a la semilla» is a highly sophisticated and well-constructed work that operates by artifice at a distance from the raw stuff of reality. The neo-baroque complexity of detail and elegance of language, its hermetic paragraphs that trap essences and correspondances of sensations, bring to mind pasages of *El siglo de las luces.*

These qualities, in addition to the more obvious ones of total change of ambience (to the aristocratic *milieu* of nineteenth-century Cuba) and character type, lead critics to view the publication of «Viaje a la semilla» as a rupture with the author's past efforts. Neither of the otherwise penetrating theses of Klaus Muller-Bergh and M. R. Assardo establish any major connection between «Viaje a la semilla», and earlier works. For the former, Carpentier's change of perspective is «asombroso». Carpentier himself chooses to begin his accounts of his literary career with the publication of «Viajes a la semilla», calling it in several interviews «mi primer cuento».

Yet for the true nature of the tale and its themes to emerge, one must place it where it belongs—some fourteen years before its appearance in *Guerra del tiempo.* «Viaje a la semilla», of 1944, precedes by months the publication of «Oficio de tinieblas», a tale of black sorcery, by two years the appearance of his prize-winning tale «Los fugitivos» which recounts the escape and trials of a Cuban slave, and by five years the appearance of his second published novel, *El reino de este mundo,* the romance of the rise and fall of the Haitian king Henri Christophe. Every work (with the exception of «L'étudiant» of 1928) of the period 1927-1949 is closely tied to black life of the Caribbean.

The themes and stylistic devices, the central preoccupations of «Viaje a la semilla» are a direct outgrowth of the preceding works—Écue-yamba-Ó and «Histoire de lunes»—and closely linked to those that directly follow it. Only in terms of his preceding works can «Viaje» be put into perspective. Thus my conclusion differs greatly from that of M. R. Assardo, who in response to the question, «¿Por qué escogió Alejo Carpentier este método de narrar?», sums up:

> Para darle más interés al relato y para continuar la «guerra del tiempo.» Este procedimiento es más eficaz e interesante que una narración directa. Se puede considerar más como un experimento estilístico que como una exposición filosófica de sus teorías.[152]

The notion that Carpentier's regression in time is «experimento estilístico» and a mere technical device to make the tale «más interesante», that it is therefore wanting in «philosophical» import, is to miss the thematic nature of the tale, and its continuity with previous works. But before discussing this thematic content and its specific relations to other works we must examine the story itself.

Like Don Juan Manuel's famous tale of the sorcerer and the partridges, «Viaje a la semilla» is a tale within a tale, an act of magic compressed within the normal sequences of a familiar and predictable course of events. The difference in the two tales, of course, is that the sorcerer in the former tale creates future time within the present, and the black sorcerer in the latter recreates the past.

The outer, or real, frame of the story is like a shell containing the nucleus and bulk of the narration which is—the magically produced regression. This outer frame of progressive normal time is very brief, comprising the first chapter (two pages) and the last (one page), and relates, quite simply, the progressive demolition of an old colonial house.

As the demolition of the Capellanías' estate progresses, an old black man appears among the debris. When the workers call down from the roof «¿Qué quieres, viejo?», the old man «no respondía. Andaba de un lugar a otro, fisgoneando, sacándose de la garganta un largo monólogo de frases incomprensibles».[153]

The workers ignore him and the demolition continues until dusk when they depart. «Entonces el negro viejo, que no se había movido, hizo gestos extraños, volteando su cayado sobre un cementerio de baldosas.»[154] The magical gestures of the old negro produce the vertiginous reversal of time, the resuscitation of man and matter which make up the nucleus of the story. «Los cuadrados de mármol, blancos y negros volaron a los pisos, vistiendo

---

[152] M. R. Assardo, *La técnica narrativa en la obra de Alejo Carpentier,* Diss., University of California, 1968, p. 148

[153] Alejo Carpentier, «Viaje a la semilla,» *Guerra del tiempo* (México: Compañía General de Ediciones, 1958), p. 77.

[154] Ibid., p. 80.

la tierra. Las piedras, con saltos certeros, fueron a cerrar los boquetes de las murallas.»[155]

The house flies together, and the old man, like a director of a *mise-en-scène,* prepares it for the forthcoming drama: «El viejo introdujo una llave en la cerradura de la puerta principal, y comenzó a abrir ventanas.»[156] The drama begins with the funeral of the marquis: «Gentes vestidas de negro murmuraron en todas las galerías, al compás de cucharas movidas en jícaras de chocolate.»[157]

Thus the transition is subtly made from reality to fantasy, from progression to regression. The old Negro, although it is not stated, is the Capellanías' «calesero» Melchor, «nieto de príncipes vencidos», without whom «la vida no tenía encanto» for the young marquis, near the end of the story.

Melchor is perhaps a composite figure of a «rey mago» in the nativity myth (this symbolic interpretation bears the most weight due to the obvious relationship between Melchor as the child's fantasy figure of the story and the traditional Melchior, «rey mago»), cult king (*La música en Cuba* names such a figure among the «Ñáñigo» chieftains of Habana) and vividly remembered household servant.

As Ti Noel in *El reino de este mundo,* the servant, the human depository of the most intimate of family memories, returns to the ruins of the shattered mansion as the last living witness, as the bridge between death and life, past and present. The influence of Faulkner is not unlikely in Carpentier's conception of these rôles, the most evident parallel being with Jim Bond in Faulkner's *Light in August.*

Through the simple gesture of turning the key in the resurrected house and performing his routine servant's duties—«comenzó a abrir ventanas»—Melchor inserts himself naturally into the nucleus, thus linking the two time frames. In the dark interior of the house, «Don Marcial [the marqués]... yacía en su lecho de muerte, el pecho acorazado de medallas, escoltado por cuatro cirios con largas barbas de cirio derretido».[158] The candles grow «hacia atrás» attaining their original size, until «los apagó la monja apartando una lumbre». In parallel fashion, the marquis returns to life: «pulsó un teclado invisible y abrió los ojos». Then Carpentier enters the mind of the marqués and delivers the reverse impressions of the dying man:

> Confusa y revuelta, las vigas del techo se iban colocando en su lugar. Los pomos de medicinas, las borlas de damasco, el escapulario de la cabecera, los daguerrotipos, las palmas de la reja, salieron de sus nieblas.[159]

155 Ibid., p. 80.
156 Ibid., p. 80.
157 Ibid., p. 81.
158 Ibid., p. 81.
159 Ibid., p. 82.

As the marquis leaves the shadow of death his attitude becomes lighter, unburdened by the fear of god until finally in confession he asks himself, «¿Y qué derecho tenía, en el fondo, aquel Carmelita, a entrometerse en su vida?».[160] Yet, rescued from death, the marquis must pass back through the combined misery of financial insolvency and poor health:

> Don Marcial no se sentía bien. Al arreglarse la corbata frente a la luna de la consola se vio congestionado. Bajó al despacho, donde lo esperaban hombres de justicia, abogados y escribientes, para disponer la venta pública de la casa.[161]

Then the marquis passes into the period of his marriage. After «meses de luto» the marquise returns to life and both are slowly rejuvenated until: «Más fogoso, Marcial solía pasar tardes enteras abrazando a la marquesa ... borrábanse patas de gallina, ceños y papadas, y las carnes tornaban a su dureza.»[162] The honeymoon is described as the rapid dissolving of a state: «Después de un amanecer alargado por un abrazo deslucido, aliviados de desconciertos y cerrada la herida, ambos regresaron a la ciudad.»[163]

The responsibilities of marriage give way—«los anillos fueron llevados al taller del orfebre para ser desgrabados»—and the marquis, freed of yet another burden, enters the stage of carefree bachelorhood. The passage of time leaves no impression on his spirit; the memory of the future does not exist, and Marcial is like an animal relieved of the knowledge of and the preoccupation with his own mortality:

> Una noche, después de mucho beber y marearse con tufos de tabaco frío, dejados por sus amigos, Marcial tuvo la sensación extraña de que los relojes de la casa daban las cinco, luego las cuatro y media, luego las cuatro, luego las tres y media... Era como la percepción remota de otras posibilidades. Como cuando se piensa, en enervamiento de vigilia, que puede andarse sobre el cielo raso con el piso por cielo raso, entre muebles firmemente asentados entre las vigas del techo. Fue una impresión fugaz, que no dejó la menor huella en su espíritu, poco llevado, ahora, a la meditación.
>
> Y hubo un gran sarao, en el salón de música, el día en que alcanzó la minoría de edad. Estaba alegre, al pensar que su firma había dejado de tener un valor legal, y que los registros y escribanías, con sus polillas, se borraban de su mundo...[164]

After months of debauchery and nightly visits to the «Casa de Baile, donde tan sabrosamente se contoneaban las mulatas de grandes ajorcas», Marcial enters into the Real Seminario de San Carlos. However, he is no longer equipped for the world of abstractions and institutional forms:

[160] Ibid., p. 82.
[161] Ibid., p. 83.
[162] Ibid., p. 86.
[163] Ibid., p. 87.
[164] Ibid., p. 89.

El mundo de las ideas se iba despoblando. Lo que había sido, al principio, una ecuménica asamblea de peplos, jubones, golas y pelucas, controversias y ergotantes, cobraba la inmovilidad de un museo de figuras de cera... su mente se hizo alegre y ligera, admitiendo solo un concepto instintivo de las cosas... El gnomon recobró su categoría de duende; el espectro fue sinónimo de fantasma; el octandro era bicho acorazado, con púas en el lomo.[165]

In this tale imagination increases its capacity as the journey towards youth progresses and rationality decreases. Now Marcial

vivía su crisis mística, poblada de detentes, corderos pascuales, palomas de porcelana. Vírgenes de manto azul celeste, estrellas de papel dorado, Reyes Magos, ángeles con alas de cisne, el Asno, el Buey, y un terrible San Dionisio que se le aparecía en sueños, con un gran vacío entre les hombros, y el andar vacilante de quien busca un objeto perdido. Tropezaba con la cama y Marcial despertaba sobresaltado, echando mano al rosario de cuentas sordas. Las mechas, en sus pocillos de aceite, daban luz triste a imágenes que recobraban su color primero.[166]

Carpentier's prose becomes increasingly lyrical and elevated as the era of early childhood and credility approaches. From the magical perspective of childhood, symbols retain their true meaning and secrets hidden from adults are unlocked:

Sólo desde el suelo pueden abarcarse totalmente los ángulos y perspectivas de una habitación. Hay bellezas en la madera, misteriosos caminos de insectos, rincones de sombra, que se ignoran a altura de hombre. Cuando llovía, Marcial se ocultaba debajo del clavicordio. Cada trueno hacía temblar la caja de resonancia, poniendo todas las notas a cantar. Del cielo caían los rayos para construir aquella bóveda de calderones— órganos, pinar al viento, mandolina de grillos.[167]

One day, Marcial is enclosed in his room. Looking out the window he sees that «llegaban hombres vestidos de negro, portando una caja con agarraderas de bronce». The death of his father evokes the vision of «el pecho rutilante de condecoraciones... el sable y los entorchados de oficial de milicias»; this gives a deliberate cyclical stamp to the story, since Marcial's own body lying in state at the beginning of the «relato» was described as having «el pecho acorazado de medallas».

The entrance of Melchor, «el calesero», sent in to entertain the boy on the death of his father, ushers in the stage of the concentrated «real maravilloso» in the young boy's life:

Cuando los muebles crecieron un poco más y Marcial supo como nadie lo que había debajo de las camas, armarios y vargueños, ocultó a todos un gran secreto: la vida no tenía encanto fuera de la presencia de Melchor. Ni

---

[165] Ibid., p. 93.
[166] Ibid., p. 95.
[167] Ibid., p. 97.

Dios, ni su padre, ni el obispo dorado de las procesiones del Corpus, eran tan importantes como Melchor...

Melchor venía de muy lejos. Era nieto de príncipes vencidos. En su reino había elefantes, hipopótamos, tigres y jirafas. Ahí los hombres no trabajaban, como Don Abundio, en habitaciones obscuras, llenas de legajos. Vivían de ser más astutos que los animales... Aquel hombre que dominaba los caballos cerreros con sólo encajarles dos dedos en los belfos; aquel señor de tercio-pelos y espuelas, que lucía chisteras tan altas, sabían también lo fresco que era un suelo de mármol en verano, y ocultaba debajo de los muebles una fruta o un pastel arrebatados a las bandejas destinadas al Gran Salón...[168]

Thus in «Viaje a la semilla», the one human contact of importance is that with Melchor. Melchor, «rey mago», «nieto de príncipes vencidos», or servant, leads Marcial into the universe of «lo real maravilloso» of the black *welt*. Evoked through the magnifying lens of childhood perceptions, Carpentier, as in portions of *¡Écue-yamba-Ó!*, «El acoso», and *El siglo de las luces,* reaches the level of epiphany in this chapter.

After the stage of comradeship with Melchor, Carpentier speeds up the movement of time, passing through stages rapidly. As Marcial grows smaller, «olvidó a Melchor para acercarse a los perros ... la lagartija que decía 'urí, urá' ... el ratón que tapiaba su agujero con una semilla de carey».[169]

The vertiginous return to the womb begins as Marcial's sensations are reduced to the basic ones of pleasure and displeasure:

Ignoraba su nombre. Retirado del bautismo, con su sal desagradable, no quiso ya el olfato, ni el oído, ni siquiera la vista. Sus manos rozaban formas placenteras. Era un ser totalmente sensible y táctil... Entonces cerró los ojos que sólo divisaban gigantes nebulosos y penetró en un cuerpo caliente, húmedo, lleno de tinieblas, que moría... Pero ahora el tiempo corrió más pronto, adelgazando sus últimas horas. Los minutos sonaban a glissando de naipes bajo el pulgar de un jugador.

Las aves volvieron al huevo en torbellino de plumas... las palmas doblaron las pencas, desapareciendo en la tierra como abanicos cerrados... todo se metamorfoseaba, regresando a su condición primera. El barro volvió al barro, dejando un yermo en lugar de una casa.[170]

Progressive time begins again in the next and last chapter with the arrival of the demolition workers «con el día». They arrive to find «el trabajo acabado», the house having been erased by the time regression. Carpentier adds a humorous touch:

Después de quejarse al sindicato, los hombres fueron a sentarse en los bancos de un parque municipal. Uno recordó entonces la historia, muy difuminada, de una Marquesa de Capellanías, ahogada, en tarde de mayo, entre las malangas del Almendares. Pero nadie prestaba atención al relato, porque el sol viajaba de oriente a occidente, y las horas que crecen a la derecha de los relojes deben

---

[168]   Ibid., p. 100.
[169]   Ibid., p. 101.
[170]   Ibid., p. 105.

alargarse por la pereza, ya que son las que más seguramente llevan a la muerte.[171]

By failing to rerun the film, in other words, to restore the house to the condition in which the workers left it on the preceding night just after the arrival of «el viejo», Carpentier brings the magical regressive nucleus into conflict with the progressive frame, producing the workers' natural reaction to the mysterious usurpation of their right to the job of demolition. While the device of insinuating elements of a fantastic frame of reference into a normal one life—the flower in Alfonso Reyes story, «La Cena,—is a well-known device to add credibility, here Carpentier uses the deliberate overlapping of frames to comment laconically on the two types of time regression, that is memory versus progression. The hours that travel «hacia atrás», are countered by «las que crecen a la derecha de los relojes». The latter are those that «más seguramente llevan a la muerte», and in which the majority of men are condemned to live. The former are for «brujos», writers of fiction, and those who believe in memory. These hours too, «llevan a la muerte», but perhaps with less frightening certainty, due to the illusion of the recapture of youth. The parallel of the act of memory of the writer and the arrival at the archetypal «illo tempore» by the primitive in ritual, is, I believe, intended by Carpentier.

The story «Viaje a la semilla» is a vehicle, or as Carpentier would put it, «instrumento», of realization of a task only possible in ritual and fiction —the return to the womb. In other words, the setting itself of the old colonial house accompanies Marcial's «regreso a las raíces de las cosas». This is a truly original aspect of the work; in other works of this nature— Berkeley Square[172] for example—the protagonist is merely transplanted into an earlier epoch.

As the imaginary author Quain, of Borges' early story «Examen de la obra de Herbert Quain», imagines «aquel inverso mundo de Bradley, en que la muerte precede al nacimiento y la cicatriz a la herida, y la herida al golpe»,[173] Carpentier suppresses the laws of causality and here creates a sensory world in which the crusts of age and knowledge are shed like a snake-skin. Acts have no consequences, leave no memory, and the destiny of life is the sensual ego-world of the child and finally the reincorporation into the mother. In this scheme at times Carpentier playfully suggests a reverse causality to striking effect, in which the deathbed seems to cause the patient to feel better; the body of his dying mother, «al sentirse arrebozado con su propia sustancia, resbaló hacia la vida».[174] This process, so strikingly suggestive of the workings of Fate in the same Aristotelian sense that the potential for fire in the wood precedes the actual fire,

[171] Ibid., p. 107.
[172] John L. Balderston, Berkeley Square (New York: Macmillan, 1929).
[173] Jorge Luis Borges, «Examen de la obra de Herbert Quain,» Ficciones (Buenos Aires: Sur, 1944), p. 96.
[174] «Viaje», p. 105.

probably gave Carpentier depth and stimulation for the *Hoc erat in votis* theme of «El acoso».

Thematic content

As we have indicated, there are important relationships in terms of theme and style between previous works and «Viaje a la semilla», in spite of the changes I have mentioned in ambience and social *milieu*. First of all, the function of «el viejo», who may appear the gratuitous stage director or a kind of *deus-ex-machina* who sets things in motions, is more essential than a first reading might suggest. This comes more to light when we establish the fact that «el viejo» and Melchor «el calesero» who appears towards the end, are the same character. The old servant, who by an act of magic makes the wheels of time roll backwards, boards the vehicle of time, reincorporating himself into the family and appearing as the youthful «calesero» near the end of the tale.

Thus Melchor ordains, generates, and participates in the drama; he contains it, temporally and spiritually, as his life-span contains that of the marquis. He *is the framework*. The «merveilleux» of the tale is all bound up with Melchor; the magical act of resuscitation is an extension of Marcial's childhood vision of the powers of the «calesero» as a figure with whom «ni Dios, ni su padre, ni el obispo dorado» could compare, and who was capable of performing «lo maravilloso».

Melchor is the human channel through which Carpentier can infuse the story with the magical atmosphere of an act of «brujería», for the form and nature of the story is a closed, connected, outgrowth of Carpentier's vision of primitive *welts*. Central to that effort, as we have amply seen in *Écue-yamba-Ó* and «Histoire de lunes», is the author's concentration on the phenomena of time and metamorphosis. These preocupations discussed with admirable clarity by Mircea Eliade are often found in relation to primitive world-views:

> The primitive, by conferring a cyclic direction upon time, annuls its irreversibility. Everything begins over again at its commencement every instant. The past is but a prefiguration of the future. No event is irreversible and no transformation is final.[175]

The *marqués* repeats the archetype of his father. Time, since it is cyclical can be reversed, and the elements of life are duplicated. «Viaje a la semilla» is related to the primitivistic vision in the sense that it is the rigorous regressive search for a state of authentic innocence, as is *Los pasos perdidos*. The essential difference is that *Los pasos perdidos* projects the search through time and culture into an *era* of innocence. «Viaje

---

[175] Mircea Eliade, *The Myth of the Eternal Return* (New York: Bollingen Foundation, 1965), p. 89.

a la semilla» is a more singleminded endeavor, projecting the search through the medium of the individual into youth and childhood, rather than taking the wider focus of the universal myths of genesis.

We have seen, in *Écue*, Carpentier's tendency to lyrically evoke childhood. In that novel, the theme of the return to the womb, elaborated in «Viaje a la semilla», was foreshadowed:

> ¡Cuánto hubieran dado por tener el alto de un erizo y poder penetrar también en esos laberintos de paz!... por el hueco de una tapia penetraba a gatas en un jardín de frutales sin podar y hierbas malas, donde puñados de mariposas blancas se alzaban en vuelo medroso.[176]

Carpentier seems to consider man in a state of unfortunate exile from himself. The painstaking route to rediscovery of the self—in both an anthropological and individual sense—is directed at four parallel goals: early man—youth; nature—cultural identity. While some works are directed at one or the other of these goals, others, for example *Los pasos perdidos*, ingeniously combine them in a multifaceted quest for authentic identity.

«Viaje a la semilla», aimed at the rediscovery of the stages of a life, and ultimately, the perspective of youth, is the product of Carpentier's ideas concerning memory:

> Una preocupación de largo tiempo ha sido la identidad que existe entre la extrema infancia y la extrema vejez —la vida puede ser reversible. La memoir ideal consistiría en recuperar una especie de no-conocimiento por el que uno ha pasado. Es decir, yo no soy el mismo hombre que era a los veinte años. Por lo tanto, si miro mis veinte años desde la edad de sesenta que acabo de cumplir, pues he ido adquiriendo cosas que han modificado mi vida, y lo interesante... es el retroceso, es decir, como era en aquella época, cuando no conocía tal literatura... Por lo tanto me parece que la técnica del hombre que escribe memorias y quiere empezar por el principio y llegar hasta hoy es completamente falsa... el hombre que yo era cuando me iba despojando de conocimientos determinados— es una obsesión que aparece en *Los pasos perdidos* y «Viaje a la semilla.» [177]

This story is in these terms an ideal memoir, since through the reversal of time, in each stage of Marcial's life he enjoys a «no-conocimiento» of the previous stage as the author «peels off» («despojar») the extraneous later experiences.

So pointed and programmatic is the story, that it becomes as instrument for this philosophy, thus illustrating Carpentier's notion of the functional end of fiction:

> La novela empieza para mí donde termina la novela... a medida que la novela va avanzando hacia un terreno diríamos de investigación en cuanto al estilo, en cuanto al entendimiento de ciertos medios, es cuando realmente la novela

---

[176] *¡Écue-yamba-Ó!, op. cit.*, p. 184.
[177] Mario Vargas Llosa, *op. cit.*, p. 32.

está cumpliendo su labor. Siempre he ido más allá de la novela... he tratado de establecer una relación de tiempo sin tiempo entre el pasado, el futuro y el presente.[178]

* * *

«Viaje a la semilla» is related to «Histoire de lunes» through the concept of regressive metamorphosis, central to both stories. The agent of this metamorphosis in «Histoire» is myth and imagination; in «Viaje» these forces are driven by the instrument of time and the rigorous recapturing of the stages of a man's life.

Yet in «Viaje's» world where «todo se metamorfoseaba, regresando a su condición primera», man is in a sense only a part of a wider process induced by the harnessing of time:

> Los tallos sorbían sus hojas y el suelo tiraba de todo lo que le perteneciera... Crecían pelos en la gamuza de los guantes. Las mantas de lana se destejían, redondeando el vellón de carneros distantes. Los armarios, los bargueños, las camas, los crucifijos, las mesas, las persianas salieron volando en la noche, buscando sus antiguas raíces al pie de las selvas...[179]

The magic metamorphosis is expanded in this story to include all of the surrounding reality, and man's return to the womb is but one instance of the generalized reincorporation into nature. Thus, as man is «leveled» by death and decay to humus in the normal series, in Carpentier's tale he is accompanied by the plants, animals and objects around him in the reverse temporality, being finally reduced to «semilla», and presumably nothingness.

Together with this original use of time as instrument of metamorphosis is a distinctly Proustian patience and elegance of craft in the recapture of the sensations of the epochs of a man's life indoors. Carpentier's description of his obsession with time in relation to «Viaje»—his vision of the «retroceso» to the «hombre que yo era *cuando me iba despojando* de conocimientos determinados»—has the flavor of Proust's «vie découverte», the goal of the «recherche»:

> La grandeur de l'art véritable... c'était de retrouver, de ressaisir, de nous faire connaître cette réalité loin de laquelle nous vivons, de laquelle nous nous écartons de plus en plus... La vraie vie, la vie enfin découverte et éclairée ... c'est la littérature...[180]

Then in a passage that reminds one of the ruins of the Capellanías mansion before Melchor's act of magic, that act equivalent to the writer's magical gift of memory, Proust praises the strange power of «l'edifice du souvenir.»

---

[178]   Ibid., p. 31.
[179]   «Viaje,» p. 106.
[180]   Marcel Proust, «L'Art et la vie,» *Le Temps retrouvé* (Paris: Gallimard), quoted in *XXᵉ Siècle*, ed. André Lagarde (Paris: Bordas, 1966), p. 258.

Mais quand d'un passé ancien rien ne subsiste; après la mort des êtres, après la destruction des choses, seules, plus frêles mais plus vivaces, plus imatérielles mais plus persistantes, plus fidèles, l'odeur et la saveur restent encore longtemps, comme des âmes, à se rappeler, à attendre, à espérer, sur la ruine de tout le reste, à porter sans fléchir, sur leur gouttelette presque impalpable, l'edifice immense du souvenir.[181]

The arduous reconstruction of the textures of ambience in «Viaje a la semilla» is an element highly characteristic of late works such as «El acoso» and *El siglo de las luces*.

Yet beyond Proust's muted texture, Carpentier's tale recalls the chaotic inversion of «las cosas» and their appearances in Quevedo's *La hora de todos*. This parallel, suggested to me by Raimundo Lida, opens up the possibility for a richer interpretation not only of the moralistic (the «desengaño» of the author, who sees beyond outer reality), but also of the stylistic dimension of Carpentier's story. The reader will hopefully draw the parallel between Carpentier's opening chapter (cited on page 172) and the following excerpt from the section of *La hora de todos* entitled «La casa del ladrón ministro»:

Cogióle la hora. ¡Oh inmenso Dios quien podrá referir tal portento! Pues piedra por piedra y ladrillo por ladrillo se empezó a deshacer, y las tejas, unas se iban a unos tejados y otras a otros. Víanse vigas, puertas y ventanas entrar por diferentes casas con espanto de los dueños, que la restitución tuvieron a terremoto y a fin de mundo. Iban las rejas y las celosías buscando sus dueños de calle en calle... Quedó desnudo de paredes y encueros de edificio, y sólo en una esquina quedó la cédula de alquilar que tenía puesta, tan mudada por la fuerza de la *hora* que donde decía: «Quien quisiere alquilar esta casa vacía, entre; que dentro vive su dueño», se leía: «Quien quisiere alquilar este ladrón, que está vacío de su casa, entre sin llamar, pues la casa no lo estorba.» [182]

Style in «Viaje a la semilla»

El orden y la seguridad del mundo compuesto de cosas iguales a si misma, distribuidas en familias, especies y géneros, resultó sumamente tranquilizador y ¡lo más importante! adecuado para [que] la acción humana se abriera camino, pero hizo palidecer, como si una sutil capa de ceniza se extendiese, al resplandor de la gloria del mundo, de la vida múltiple, inasible, en perpetua metamorfosis... Pero, algunos hombres no se sometieron a esa determinación en que todo quedaba ordenado; guardaban memoria, azuzada por la nostalgia del tiempo perdido, en que las cosas danzaban en libertad y una piedad sin límites les ganaba a quienes está vedado dejar salir de su interior la voz de la alegría, obligados a mostrar su ser solamente bajo un rostro, el de la servidumbre. Si quedó gente que encontraba insoportable esta servidumbre, que es el original verdadero de la separación de clases, de cosas, de

[181] Marcel Proust, *Du côté de chez Swann*, XXᵉ Siècle, Ibid., p. 226.
[182] Francisco de Quevedo Villegas, *La hora de todos, Obras Completas* (Madrid: Aguilar, 1932), pp. 226-270.

especies... Pues en el principio, todo estaba en todo, todas las cosas eran unas y diferentes, multiplicidad sumergida en la unidad, concordia donde nadie, ni nada, era más ni menos...[183]

These words, aimed towards the description of the central fixation of another well-known Cuban primitivist—Lydia Cabrera—also apply to Carpentier, particularly the Carpentier of «Viaje a la semilla». Both are inheritors of the gifts of the «patria inextinguible de la metamorfosis». The recreation of a cosmos of «vida múltiple, inasible, en perpetua metamorfosis» where «las cosas danzaban en libertad» is the principal function of the highly contrived style of the story. As the poetess Cabrera, Carpentier seeks to free things from their limiting categories, and celebrate a pantheistic symbiosis of liberated forms. In «Viaje a la semilla», the symphony of things predominates over man, who often seems trapped in the detailed arabesques of the author's descriptions of teeming objects.

Carpentier's plan is one of some magnitude: to suppress the man-made classifications of genus, in favor of an aesthetic system, which freed from the compartmentalizing of time, allows a creeper to embrace an Ionian scroll, «atraída *por un aire de familia*». The aim of the author is to create an aesthetic realization of the primitive «illo tempore», where «todo estaba en todo, todas las cosas eran unas y diferentes, multiplicidad sumergida en la unidad».

Although the story is already quite removed in terms of setting from the Black world of earlier (and later) works and quite divorced from the ethnographical orientation of those works, the same techniques used so pointedly there in the effort to capture a world-view, are here used independently, are employed successfully in a radically different milieu.

«Viaje», then, demonstrates the author's growing independence from exclusively black themes, and his need to apply his acquired powers of perception to a wider spectrum of settings and epochs.

Yet the core of his vision remains: animism, personification, and reification—the «crossing of the realms»—are at the concentrated and highly polished essence of the story. Metamorphosis is the key to both theme and the style.

A close examination of the first chapter, which contains a concentrated use of the aesthetic principals of «Viaje», will hopefully demonstrate the author's new control of these forces at this time in his career.

As we have stated, the opening chapter (two-and-a-half pages) is in progressive time, and describes the demolition of the Capellanías' house. Although in this section, which, with the last chapter, comprises the «real» framework for the regressive nucleus, nothing «fantastic» occurs, nevertheless a prelude is voiced therein to the entire story.

In Carpentier's detailed description of the carcass of the mansion and the surrounding debris, he is able to suggest the life in dead forms, their

[183] María Zambrano, «Lydia Cabrera, poeta de la metamorfosis,» *Orígenes*, Año VII, no. 25 (1950), pp. 11-15.

appearance of osmosis into nature. Thus this chapter reveals the potential for metamorphosis of objects, the latent forces of return in the forward cycle. This potential is released in the second chapter, when from the «cementerio de baldosas», the house flies together in the magic act of time reversal.

Because it stays within the confines of the magic «in the real»—and is representative of the working within the limitations imposed by the senses which distinguishes Carpentier's style from fantastic and surreal literature, the first chapter is the most significant single part of the story in terms of the author's style. In this chapter Carpentier wisely establishes the climate and potential for the abnormal before «performing» it, thus closing the gap between fantasy and reality subtly, creating a predisposition in the reader to accept what ensues in the second chapter:

> —¿Qué quieres, viejo?...
>
> Varias veces cayó la pregunta de lo alto de los andamios. Pero el viejo no respondía. Andaba de un lugar a otro, fisgoneando, sacándose de la garganta un largo monólogo de frases incomprensibles. Ya habían descendido las tejas, cubriendo los canteros muertos con su mosaico de barro cocido. Arriba, los picos desprendían piedras de mampostería, haciéndolas rodar por canales de madera, con gran revuelo de cales y de yesos. Y por las almenas sucesivas que iban desdentando las murallas aparecían —despojados de su secreto— cielos rasos ovales o cuadrados, cornisas, guirnaldas, dentículos, astrágalos, y papeles encolados que colgaban de los testeros como viejas pieles de serpiente en muda. Presenciando la demolición, una Ceres con la nariz rota y el peplo desvaído, veteado de negro el tocado de mieses, se erguía en el traspatio, sobre su fuente de mascarones borrosos. Visitados por el sol en horas de sombra, los peces grises del estanque bostezaban en agua musgosa y tibia, mirando con el ojo redondo aquellos obreros, negros sobre claro de cielo, que iban rebajando la altura secular de la casa. El viejo se había sentado, con el cayado apuntalándole la barba, al pie de la estatua. Miraba el subir y bajar de cubos en que viajaban restos apreciables. Oíanse, en sordina, los rumores de la calle mientras, arriba, las poleas concertaban, sobre ritmos de hierro con piedra, sus gorjeos de aves desagradables y pechugonas.
>
> Dieron las cinco. Las cornisas y entablamentos se despoblaron. Sólo quedaron escaleras de mano, preparando el asalto del día siguiente. El aire se hizo más fresco, aligerado de sudores, blasfemias, chirridos, ejes que pedían alcuzas, y palmadas en torsos pringosos. Para la casa mondada el crepúsculo llegaba más pronto. Se vestía de sombras en horas en que su ya caída balaustrada superior solía regalar a las fachadas algún relumbre de sol. La Ceres apretaba los labios. Por primera vez las habitaciones dormirían sin persianas, abiertas sobre un paisaje de escombros.
>
> Contrariando sus apetencias, varios capiteles yacían entre las hierbas. Las hojas de acanto descubrían su condición vegetal. Una enredadera aventuró sus tentáculos hacia la voluta jónica, atraída por un aire de familia. Cuando cayó la noche, la casa estaba más cerca de la tierra. Un marco de puerta se erguía aún en lo alto, con tablas de sombra suspendidas de sus bisagras desorientadas.[184]

[184] «Viaje», p. 77.

The symbiotic concert of man-made and natural forms is powerfully conveyed by Carpentier's densely detailed and organic prose. The abundant architectural detail, combined with the very objective use of personification, gives the passage the air of an imaginative medical description of the death and telescoped decay of some noble beast. The naming of things and their relationships predominate; while highly imaginative, the description does not leave its roots in place and objects and the metaphors are highly organic in that their vehicles are severely sculpted to tenor and to tone.

Carpentier, in his effort to convey an atmosphere of decadence, and the triumph of nature over the forms of man, uses images of primordial forms of animal life—the snake, the fish, the octopus. Thus as Atilano in «Histoire de lunes» regresses «de la savia al limo» in the primordial form of the eel, the Capellanías' house undergoes a similar fate, with its «papeles colados que colgaban de los testeros como viejas pieles de serpiente en muda», its «volutas jónicas» threatened by «tentáculos», and the witnessing «peces grises del estanque» in «agua musgosa y tibia».

The immediate agents of the metamorphosis of the house are the workers. Yet through the subtle use of animism Carpentier disembodies their actions, making them seem to generate spontaneously from the materials themselves. This «creative absence» is the key to the effect of this passage: «¿Qué quieres, viejo? ... Varias veces la pregunta cayó de lo alto de los andamios...»[185]

Carpentier eliminates the agent—the workers—and the question animistically «falls» from the rooftop. Then, in the description of the demolition, «ya habían descendido las tejas, cubriendo los canteros muertos», the impression is one of an autonomous act of the shingles, as if they descended by their own will. «Arriba, los picos desprendían piedras de mampostería, haciéndolas rodar por canales de madera, con gran revuelo de cales y de yesos.»[186]

Again, the removing of agent gives the action itself relief, and creates the impression of the operation of an unnamed force upon the building.

In the following example, the extreme range with which Carpentier employs animism can be observed: «Y por las almenas sucesivas que iban desdentando las murallas aparecían—despojados de su secreto—cielos rasos ovales o cuadrados...»[187]

Here Carpentier converts the jagged appearance itself of a turret into action, without there being such an action in fact. The walls, personified by the attribution of teeth, are «desdentadas» animistically by the turrets. The artist's eye, perceiving the rhythm of the turret's jagged design (note the use of the imperfect—«iban desdentando», suggesting the illusory movement inherent in the regular alternating pattern), sees that design as an aggressive action. Thus Carpentier's tendency towards animism goes beyond divorcing movement from agent, and into the creation of illusory action.

The controlled use of personification becomes evident in the images «desdentando» and «despojados de su secreto», both of which convey the

---

[185] Ibid., p. 77.
[186] Ibid., p. 77.
[187] Ibid., p. 77.

brutal violation of the house, suggesting the «soul» of the family dwelling and depository of memory. Yet the next images of «papeles encolados ... como viejas pieles de serpiente en muda» counteracts the personification, linking the demolition to natural processes of the lower species—the sloughing off of worn skin.

> Presenciando la demolición, una Ceres con la nariz rota... se erguía en el traspatio, sobre su fuente de mascarones borrosos.[188]

This device, which we have found to be consistent in Carpentier's prose, furthers the central aesthetic aim of the chapter. The reversal of rôles of the animate and inanimate is made clear by the carefully crafted absence of the workers versus the importance given the inanimate statue of Ceres, personified as «presenciando la demolición ... sobre su fuente de mascarones borrosos», and animated strangely by Carpentier's favorite verb, often used in the creation of ambiguous states —«erguir». As usual with this verb, Carpentier uses the reflexive, «se erguía», suggesting autonomy, and the imperfect, suggesting continuousness, resulting in the effect of a kind of ceaseless imperiousness appropriate for symbol and effigy. The goddess Ceres of fertility presides over the demolition, waiting to reclaim the materials of the house, once borrowed from nature, and destined to return in the «Viaje a la semilla».

The author continues the effect of the «crossing of the realms» in the next device, which is a curious and effective one:

> Visitados por el sol en horas de sombra, los peces grises del estanque bostezaban en agua musgosa y tibia, mirando con el ojo redondo aquellos obreros, negros sobre claro de cielo, que iban rebajando la altura secular de la casa.[189]

Describing the fish, Carpentier personifies them with the verbs «visitados» and «bostezaban», then actually enters the fish, channeling visual point-of-view through them. It is a brilliant utilization of perspective; through the «ojo redondo» of the fish the image of the workers against the sky is like a low-angle photograph.

Also by channeling visual point-of-view through the fish rather than through «el viejo», or the workers themselves, the author heightens the effect of multiplicity and the «crossing of the realms», and the predominant rôle of natural forces.

Complementary to these visual effects, are the animistically conceived auditory effects: «... las poleas concertaban sobre ritmos de hierro con piedra, sus gorjeos de aves desagradables y pechugonas».[190]

The following paragraph demonstrates perhaps most effectively the

---

[188] Ibid., p. 77.
[189] Ibid., p. 77.
[190] Ibid., p. 78.

successful orchestrating of the artist's preferred instruments of animism, personification, synecdoche and reification:

> Dieron las cinco. Las cornisas y entablamientos se despoblaron. Sólo quedaron escaleras de mano, preparando el asalto del día siguiente. El aire se hizo más fresco, aligerado de sudores, blasfemias, chirridos de cuerdas, ejes que pedían alcuzas y palmadas en torsos pringosos. Para la casa mondada el crepúsculo llegaba más pronto. Se vestía de sombras en horas en que su ya caída balaustrada superior solía regalar a las fachadas algún relumbre de sol. La Ceres apretaba los labios. Por primera vez las habitaciones dormirían sin persianas, abiertas sobre un paisaje de escombros.[191]

The passage describes the arrival of quitting-time for the workers, their departure, and the approach of evening. Yet such a prosaic event is subtly dramatized to seem like an act of magic.

By activating the passage of time—«dieron las cinco»—with the verb «dieron» Carpentier emphasizes its causal function, and the ensuing action seems a direct effect of the five bells. Then instead of attributing the action of vacating the premises to the workers, Carpentier reverses the normal hierarchy, of predicate structure, and the cornices and entablatures «se despoblaron» animistically. Following the pattern of activated matter the ladders are seen as «preparando el asalto del día siguiente».

To create the change in atmosphere resulting from the workers' departure, the author is even more indirect, using synecdoche to capture the essence of the absent workers, while not actually mentioning them integrally: «El aire se hizo más fresco, aligerado de sudores, blasfemias, chirridos de cuerdas, ejes que pedían alcuzas y palmadas en torsos pringosos.» The workers are reified and compressed into «sudores», «blasfemias», «palmadas en torsos pringosos».

The house, personified («se vestía de sombras ... las habitaciones dormirían sin persianas ... contrariando sus apetencias, varios capiteles yacían...») fills the abandoned scene the desolation of which is admirably conveyed in the last image of «tablas de sombra suspendidas de ... bisagras desorientadas».[192]

Although the form of «Viaje a la semilla» is outwardly experimental and unique in Carpentier's works, in as much as it reverses time within a fantastic framework, nonetheless there are elements of the structuring of the story which are strongly characteristic of the author's general conception of the form of fiction.

First, and most apparent, is the virtual absence of a story. «Viaje a la semilla», even if recounted chronologically, is not the «story of a man's life» in any normally accepted sense. Nothing really «happens» to the marqués de Capellanías within the one great event of regression to the origins, nor does he «do» anything outside of the rituals inherent in a man's existence—birth, marriage, funeral. There are no anecdotes, no deeds, no

---

[191] Ibid., p. 78.
[192] Ibid., p. 78.

instances of heroism or cowardice, which might break out of the hermetic atmosphere created by Carpentier's sensory impressionism.

The marqués, like a Proustian figure, grows organically from his surroundings, is inseparable from them. Never once during the course of the story does he leave the confines of his house.

The form of the tale, then, despite the linear direction of the reverse chronology, is not the momentum-giving pattern of linked events, or cause and effect; rather it is much closer to a static, spatial conception, a baroque filling of empty time (indeed the division between space and time, blurred in this story, disappears in *Los pasos perdidos,* where each station on the Orinoco stands for a temporal reality).

In «Viaje», the stages of a man's life are separated and limned in with detail and the author attempts to seize the essence of each, through the rendering of the corresponding sensory impressions. The tendency towards static sequence, as opposed to plot, already observable in the division of *Écue* into «Infancia» and «Adolescencia», is here given full expression since the cause-effect relationship is totally repressed by the reversal of time.

Then in terms of form, the plotlessness of «Viaje», that characteristic being one of the salient marks of the author's fiction, is not a result of the time reversal, it is merely accentuated by it.

As in *Los pasos perdidos,* the harnessing of time in «Viaje» has a predominantly thematic function, as the vehicle of regression—a function supported and reflected admirably by form. The theme of regression, touched on and explored in various ways in *¡Écue-yamba-Ó!,* and «Histoire de lunes», is successfully embodied and fully exploited in this story.

V. «LOS FUGITIVOS»

A reader more familiar with *El siglo de las luces* than with works of Alejo Carpentier's early period, might have difficulty imagining the Cuban's byzantine scope, his gift for elegant description and chiaroscuro that coax the word «neo-barroco» from critics, confined to the crude setting ot the Cuban «monte» and to the humble dramatis personae of a runaway slave and a dog.

Indeed the stark subject and the sub-theme of the test of survival of «Los fugitivos»[193] seem more related to a traditionally nordic preoccupation, to the questions posed by Conrad, O'Neil, Hamsun, Faulkner, Jack London, about the nature of man stripped of the remnants of society, and pushed to the limits of endurance and the margins of identity, than to the author's ecumenical «enfoque» as it is generally apprehended.

The apparently marginal nature of the story's subject in relation to the author's corpus may explain the lack of critical attention brought to bear on the finely crafted story. Carpentier himself seems to have abandoned, if not disowned it—a fate shared by others, perhaps less worthy, of his early works:[194]

> Ese relato «Los fugitivos», que publican ahora en todas partes, no me gusta tampoco. Responde, en realidad, a un estilo que no es mío, lo mismo que mi novela *¡Écue-yamba-Ó!* No creo que sean malos como literatura.[195]

Contrary to this somewhat negative testimony of the author we find «Los fugitivos» to be «muy Carpentier» and accord it a key position among his works as a turning point from the early period to the more complex creations of *Guerra del tiempo*. «Los fugitivos» in terms of content, is a variation on the dominant theme of his early works—regression—and in terms of form, an anticipation of the structured, musical nature of Carpentier's best short works of the 50's. Character as musical line, cyclic

---

[193] Alejo Carpentier, «Los fugitivos,» *Narrativa cubana de la revolución* (Madrid: Alianza Editorial, 1968), 25-39.

[194] However, Carpentier has included «Los fugitivos» in the latest edition of *Guerra del tiempo* (Barcelona: Barral, 1970).

[195] Joaquín Santaña, «Los pasos encontrados» (interview with Alejo Carpentier) *Cuba* (1970), p. 48.

recapitulation, leitmotif, echoing, and coda, are elements of composition that reappear most noticeably in «El acoso», an outgrowth of «Los fugitivos» by virtue of shape and content.

As often in Carpentier, the action itself is notably uninvolved and can be recounted briefly. The story takes place in 19th-century Cuba, and the setting shifts from the fugitives' (Perro and Cimarrón) camp to the margins of the sugarmill.

Perro, one of the Marqués' dogs especially trained in the tracking of fugitive slaves, has left the pack during a manhunt, diverted by the scent of a bitch in heat. As Perro, after following the new trail for some time, approaches the source of the scent, the feral snarls of a pack of «jíbaros» (wild dogs) from the hills ahead, send him in the opposite direction. While fleeing the wild dogs, he scents the man who had eluded the Marqués' «jauría». Motivated by fear and a need for security, Perro ignores the impulse inculcated by his brutal training, and lies down beside the sleeping slave. «Más valía permanecer, por ahora, al lado del hombre.» The man and the dog live together, cooperating in the perpetual hunt for food.

One day as Perro and Cimarrón are keeping vigil over a road, the passage of a wagon arouses the dog's playful instincts and his antics cause the horses to bolt. The passengers are thrown against a bridge and killed. Cimarrón, perceiving that «no todo era malo en aquel percance», avails himself of clothes and «cinco duros».

The possession of money marks the beginning of Cimarrón's descent into temptation and ill-fated return to the fringes of the world of man. His frequent forays—«desafiando la misma tralla y las mismas cadenas»—back to the ingenio in search of women and liquor expose the pair to the danger of discovery. Perro becomes alienated from the strange ways of his companion, and when the latter is apprehended after spending «demasiado tiempo en el cuarto de una mondonguera», returns alone to the safety of «el monte», thus ending the partnership. Increasingly Perro regresses to a wild state, until finally the scent of the wild bitch (as at the beginning of the story) leads him in pursuit. This time, however, Perro accepts the challenge, defeating the pack of «jíbaros» in battle and claiming the «hembra» in an act symbolic of the animal's successful regression to a primitive «state of grace» and earning of identity.

Perro is now a «jíbaro» and joins the wild dogs in the hunt. One day «agarraron un rastro habitual ... olía a negro». The pack converges on the man—it is Cimarrón, who has escaped again. Perro circles his old master, torn between three instinctual impulses—the primeval bond between man and dog, the brutal training of the «ingenio», and the natural instinct of the hunt. In spite of the friendly advances of Cimarrón, it is the second impulse that conquers Perro:

> Y cuando era llamado, huía. Y cuando no era llamado, parecía buscar aquel sonido de voz humana que había entendido un poco, en otros tiempos, pero que ahora le sonaba tan raro, tan peligrosamente evocador de obediencias. Al fin Cimarrón dio un paso, adelantando una mano blanda hacia su cabeza.

Perro lanzó un extraño grito, mezcla de ladrido sordo y de aullido, y salto al cuello del negro.

Había recordado, de súbito, una vieja consigna dada por el mayoral del ingenio, el día que un esclavo huía al monte.[196]

The last brief section of the book describes the dogs playfully tugging at the remaining tatters of Cimarrón's clothing. «Durante muchos años, los monteros evitaron, de noche, aquel atajo dañado por huesos y cadenas.»[197]

In order to best grasp the meaning of «Los fugitivos» it is necessary to see this miniature from the broader perspective of other of the author's works. This albeit peripheral approach enables us to see Perro and Cimarrón as microcosmic figures within the world of the author's fiction, transcending the narrow perimeters of the story.

In terms of setting and characters «Los fugitivos» is a direct outgrowth of «Viaje a la semilla», published in Havana in 1944, two years prior to the appearance of the former. Don Marcial, the Marqués de Capellanías, and protagonist of the earlier story, is the peripheral figure of the slaver in «Los fugitivos» and the action stems from events in the family mill. The black «calesero», Melchor, and the dog Canelo, who figure so importantly in «Viaje a la semilla», have their counterparts in Cimarrón and Perro in the later story.

In the regressive *recherche* through time in «Viaje a la semilla», Melchor appears in the evocation of Marcial's (the Marqués) infancy as a figure invested with the rich hues of a child's fantasy: «Ni Dios, ni su padre, ni el obispo dorado de las procesiones del Corpus eran tan importantes como Melchor.» The portrait is enhanced by the primitivistic vision of the author: «Era nieto de príncipes vencidos. En su reino había elefantes, hipopótamos, tigres y jirafas.»[198]

Then, as Carpentier continues the reverse order in that story, «Cuando Marcial adquirió el hábito de romper cosas, olvidó a Melchor para acercarse a los perros».[199] Marcial forgets the world of humans and identifies totally with Canelo: «ambos comían tierra ... se revolcaban al sol ... buscaban sombra y perfume al pie de las alabahacas».[200]

In «Viaje a la semilla», Melchor and Canelo play the key rôles in the evocation—filtered through the limited but enhancing vision of the child—of the rich faith of early childhood, and are representative of meaningful stages in the reversed chronology of an individual life.

In «Los fugitivos» the same basic rôles—the slaver, the slave, and the dog—are cast from a totally different perspective. In the later story, while Don Marcial is a peripheral figure, the slave and the dog are the protagonists, and are independent agents.

However, in spite of the difference in perspective, the symbolic nature of the two characters in both stories is closely related; just as Melchor and

196 «Los fugitivos,» *op. cit.,* p. 36.
197 Ibid., p. 37.
198 «Viaje a la semilla,» *op. cit.,* p. 100.
199 Ibid., p. 102.
200 Ibid., p. 103.

Canelo are Marcial's bridge back to innocence in the evoked time of «Viaje a la semilla», in the later story, Perro and Cimarrón are the narrator's instruments in a search for a related world of purity.

For «Los fugitivos», with its drama of man's cooperation with and dependence on the canine species, the free nomadic existence of the hunter, the taking refuge in prehistoric caves, is all an evocation of an earlier age, of «el hombre que fuimos hace millares de años».[201]

However, Carpentier's ironic sense of fate intervenes and turns from the almost idyllic middle section towards the brutal and pathetic resolution. The parallelism of man and animal turns to contrast—man's attempted evasion is doomed to failure due to his inability to rid himself of the corrupting ties with society. The dog succeeds because of his indifference to such ties, and devours the loser.[202] Although the dog is the agent (which provides the cruel «twist» to the story), the destruction of Cimarrón is man's —society's—work, since «la consigna» of the slaver trips the murderous reaction in Perro's brain.

There are fruitful parallels here with *Los pasos perdidos,* a more complete unfolding of the same drama of failed evasion. In both works, the «trail»—the symbolic route to authenticity—ends with possession of the «hembra» and incorporation into a primitive life. The narrator of *Los pasos perdidos* in a sense integrates the counterpoised destinies of the two protagonists of the short story, since on one hand he possesses the «hembra» Rosario, achieving a «state of grace» yet on the other ultimately fails in his attempted evasion.

When seen through the broader perspective of *Los pasos perdidos* the identity of Cimarrón transcends its immediate context, and the stigmatic condition of slavery becomes symbolic, a cypher for the human condition. The rôle of slave is the most concrete enactment of, the most graphic representation of, the lot of modern man in the context of Carpentier's fiction. The narrator-as-Sisyphus in *Los pasos perdidos,* condemned to the cyclic torture of meaningless work in the metropolis, and the slave of «Los fugitivos», condemned to the beck and call of «la apremiante espadaña» of the «ingenio», are as one in their response to their only alternative —escape. They fall easy prey to «el avión», «la consigna»—the instruments of the society which inevitably reclaims them.

As we have stated, «Los fugitivos» is a variant on the dominant theme of his early works—regression. While in «Histoire de lunes», the protagonist Atilano actually regresses to «las primeras formas» in the fantastically conceived metamorphosis into «Les Glissant»—half-man and half-tree who violates the village women by night—and in «Viaje a la semilla» the laws of time are reversed in the regression of Marcial to the womb, Carpentier's fictional means in «Los fugitivos» are more modest and within limits of realism. An elaborate parallelism is the principal means the author uses to suggest regression. Man and dog are tied together by fate, in action and

---

[201] Vargas Llosa, *op. cit.,* p. 31.
[202] The animal, however, «loses» also because he succcumbs to the «consigna.»

image and are leveled by the test of survival. As described discursively in *Los pasos perdidos,* through the dog, man arrives at a oneness with nature, and extends his power and perceptions:

> El Perro, en cambio, cuyos ojos estaban a la altura de las rodillas del hombre, veía cuanto se ocultaba al pie de las malangas engañosas... era ya un pacto el que ligaba aquí al Perro con el Hombre: en mútuo complemento de poderes, que les hacía trabajar en hermandad. El perro aportaba los sentidos que su compañero de caza tenía atrofiados, los ojos de su nariz, su andar en cuatro patas...[203]

In «Los fugitivos» this phenomenon, in addition to having thematic import, is realized on the aesthetic level as the dog becomes a means of extension of the sensory powers of the artist. During the story Carpentier often locates his perceptions of reality in the superior organs of the animal, penetrating realms of the basic senses actually «atrofiados» in man and suggesting a dehumanized yet richly synesthetic universe of plastic impressions.

The use of generic, unindividuated names for the characters is a manifestation of Carpentier's expressionistic tendency to reduce, to abstract identity, of his desire to mold fable in the vacuum of «un tiempo sin tiempo», without defined contours. This reduction of character, carried to its extreme in «Los fugitivos» serves the theme of regression, because Cimarrón, shorn of individual attributes, is able to effectively incorporate into the primeval scenario created by the author. With the exception of the affection felt by Cimarrón for the dog in the last episode, the sole motivating forces of character and action are the senses—the search for food and sex.

Form of «Los fugitivos»

In a manner strongly related to *¡Écue-yamba-Ó!* and «Histoire de lunes», the form of «Los fugitivos» is wedded to the seasonal cycles of nature. Specifically, the story covers a period of two years, in which the three comings of spring mark decisive moments. In each coming of spring, the freshly awakened senses and drives of the man and the dog—reflected in the transformation of nature—determine the course of each. Man and animal (recall the «Glissant», of «Histoire de lunes», the personified force of cyclical fecundation) are as subject to the seasonal metamorphosis as are the lower realms of nature.

It is the hypersensitive sexual instinct of Perro—awakened in the atmosphere of spring—that triggers his break with the «jauría» in the first page of the story. Then, the following year—«la primavera los agarró a los dos»—Perro and Cimarrón are driven back to the «ingenio» by the insufferable sexual awakening, «la crisis de primavera». This is the turning point

---

[203] Alejo Carpentier, *Los pasos perdidos* (México: Compañía General de Ediciones, 1959), p. 126.

of the story as Perro deserts his corrupted master, who is trapped by his own imprudence.

The arrival of the last spring marks the beginning of the denouement, as the reawakened «celo» of Perro leads to his venture into the wild pack, and to the pathetic ending:

> Con los aguinaldos volvió la primavera. Una tarde en que lo desvelaba un extraño desasosiego, Perro dio *nuevamente* con aquel misterioso olor a hembra, tan fuerte, tan penetrante, que había sido *la causa primera de su fuga* al monte. *También ahora caían ladridos de la montaña.*[204]

Thus the advent of spring is the «eje» of the story, the cyclically returning crisis (note the «también ahora» of the preceding quote, which reflects the author's conscious repetition) which drives the clamoring senses, and sets the gears of action and fate in motion. For not only is the returning spring a cyclical event, but also the actions which it stimulates are cyclical in nature, and finally, so is the large gear of fate which makes one complete revolution in the course of the story, coinciding precisely with the beginning and the end.

Then the mechanism of the story is composed of the «eje» of spring, and in ascending order of magnitude, the meshing gears of action and fate.

The circular Delphic motion of fate—whose plan is inexorably carried out by Perro—is unleashed in the beginning as dog is pitted against man by the «consigna del mayoral». While in their first encounter (and through the idyllic middle section) they temporarily reverse the decree of the «consigna» in friendship, the brutal ending fulfills the original destinies of both, as hunter and the hunted. The original «rastro» has been struck again and the «consigna»—like an unshakeable curse—returns in the dog's mind and achieves its end.

The ending is doubly powerful by virtue of its unexpectedness, yet its formal perfection. The surprise lies in the fact that the reader expects the resumption of friendship of Perro and Cimarrón. The formal perfection of the ending, and thus of the story, lies in the fact that the seeds of Fate—la «consigna», «el rastro», the torn deer—sown carefully throughout, come to their noxious fruition therein, so that the end is all in the beginning and viceversa.[205]

The formal perfection even reaches outside the story; Cimarrón, created out of the «nada» of the blank page, into the «nada» returns, physically erased.

The story is circumscribed, framed by «la nada»—perfect, round, and closed. Undoubtedly it is Carpentier's musical background which influences his predilection for unequivocal resolution (the protagonists of *El siglo de las luces,* and «El acoso» undergo a similar sacrifice).

Within the cyclical structure discussed above, there are other structural elements of great importance. In a manner which clearly anticipates the

---

[204] «Los fugitivos,» p. 35.
[205] The connection with the *hoc erat in votis* theme in «El acoso» is evident here.

organization of *Los pasos perdidos* into palpable stages of regression, Carpentier structures the setting of «Los fugitivos». In this sense, there is a descending linear movement discernible in the creation of setting from the suggestions of opulence and human activity surrounding the «ingenio» in the first part, to the «jungle» of the last section.

In the beginning, Perro and Cimarrón live at the margins of the «ingenio»:

> El valle se desperezaba. A la apremiante espadaña, destinada a los esclavos, respondía ahora, más lento, el bordón, armoriado de la capilla, cuyo verdín se mecía de sombra a sol sobre un fondo de mugidos y relinchos, como indulgente aviso a los que dormían en altos lechos de caoba.[206]

As the duo integrates into the wild nature, their setting seems to travel backwards in time, in consciously wrought stages of regression:

> Vivían en una caverna, bien oculta por una cortina de helechos arborescentes. Las estalactitas lloraban isócronamente, llenando las sombras frías de un ruido de relojes.[207]

In the cave, Perro digs out «un cráneo ... unos restos de alfarería y unos rascadores de piedra que hubieran podido aprovecharse».[208] The finding of these items in the setting of the primitive cave, is not a gratuitous detail in the story.

The descending trajectory becomes more apparent in the description of the next dwelling-place of the pair: «Al amanecer buscaron una cueva de techo más bajo, donde el hombre tuvo que entrar en cuatro patas...»[209]

Projecting even beyond the previous setting, Carpentier suggests here the arrival at a level of animality. Recalling the epiphanic sections of *¡Écue-yamba-Ó!* and «Viaje a la semilla»,[210] where children penetrate a universe of fantastic dimensions also «a gatas», it becomes apparent that the «lowering» of the stature of man signifies in the context of Carpentier's early works the arrival at a state of mystical reincorporation into the universe, perhaps ultimately expressed in Marcial's return into the womb in «Viaje a la semilla».

When Cimarrón is apprehended, Perro's further regression beyond the world of man is suggested by the setting:

> Perro buscaba ahora el amparo de mogotes casi inaccesibles al hombre, viviendo en un mundo de dragos que el viento mecía con ruido de albarda nueva, de orquídeas, de bejucos lombriz, donde se arrastraban lagartos verdes, de orejeras blancas...[211]

---

[206] «Los fugitivos,» p. 28.
[207] Ibid., p. 30.
[208] Ibid., p. 30.
[209] Ibid., p. 30.
[210] The connection between chidhood and primitivism in literature has been discussed with authority by Goldwater. See Robert Goldwater, *Primitivism in Modern Art* (New York: Random House, 1967), pp. 192-216.
[211] «Los fugitivos,» p. 34.

In the final scene, as the wild pack is closing in for the kill, Carpentier transforms the «monte» into a noxious jungle: «... los jíbaros agarraron un rastro habitual en aquellas *selvas de bejucos,* de espinas, de plantas malvadas que envenenaban al herir...».[212]

Thus the regression of Perro and Cimarrón, and then of Perro alone, realized artistically in the structured setting, is a linear, constant element of form offsetting and balancing the cyclical movements of season, and action, and fate.

Style

The key to Carpentier's style in «Los fugitivos» is found in the author's judicious use of point-of-view. In a semi-omniscient relationship to his material, the author shifts smoothly in and out of his characters, giving alternately poetically elaborate direct descriptions, curt linear narrations, and richly impressionistic indirect interior monologue from within the characters. The strikingly equal disposition of these three highly contrasting «voices» of the author gives a balance rather uncharacteristic of the author's style in general, which is usually marked by its unbroken, monolithic quality.

From the vantage point of the dog, Carpentier creates a distorted universe in human terms, which is both deepened sensually and narrowed emotionally; reality is often seen in the story from two feet above the ground and inhaled through the nostrils to the exclusion of other senses. Thus the manhunt (at the beginning) when projected through Perro, is a question of conflicting odors:

> Seguía oliendo a negro... Sin embargo, Perro no pensaba ya en la batida. Había otro olor allí en la tierra vestida de bejuqueras que un próximo roce borraría tal vez para siempre. Olor a hembra.[213]

The world of mankind, through the perspective of Perro, becomes a series of disagreeable olfactory impressions:

> El olor del cura, a pesar del tufo de cera derretida y de incienso, que hacía tan desagradable la sombra, tan fresca, sin embargo, de la capilla. El mismo que llevaba el organista encima, a pesar de que los fuelles del armonio le hubiesen echado encima tantos y tantos soplos de fieltro apolillado. Había que huir ahora del olor a blanco.[214]

These dehumanized, sensory descriptions are merely intensified manifestations of a characteristic trait of the author—reification of the human figure—observable in nearly all his works. Thus the dog's perspective—the «low» perspective—does not differ markedly from that of the omniscient

[212] Ibid., p. 36.
[213] Ibid., p. 26.
[214] Ibid., p. 28.

narrator of «El acoso», since in neither case are people painted from an eye-to-eye level, rather from below, or above.

As we have suggested, these often elaborate descriptive passages of the story, at times filtered through the characters, at times directly from the author, produce a salient contrast and balance with the almost Hemingwayesque narrative line in its concentrated delivery of basic sensations and actions:

> Las sombras se hacían más húmedas. Perro se volteó, cayendo sobre sus patas. Las campanas del ingenio, volando despacio, le enderezaron las orejas. En el valle, la neblina y el humo eran una misma inmovilidad azulosa sobre la que flotaban, cada vez más siluetadas, una chimenea de ladrillos, un techo de grandes aleros, la torre de la iglesia y luces que parecían encenderse en el fondo de un lago. Perro tenía hambre. Pero hacía allá olía a hembra. A veces lo envolvía aún el olor a negro. Pero el olor de su propio celo, llamado por el olor de otro celo, se imponía a todo lo demás...[215]

We may now return to the nucleus of Carpentier's autocritique cited at the beginning of this book: «responde en realidad a un estilo que no es mío». While in the body of this thesis we have seen how the characters and theme of regression relate to other works of the author, Carpentier himself points to the one respect in which «Los fugitivos» does in fact make a significant departure from those.

Radically different stylistic means were chosen by the author here to achieve his «regreso a las raíces».

The pantheistic style of a magical universe, already highly developed by 1946 (as evidenced in «Viaje a la semilla», «Histoire de lunes» and «Oficio de tinieblas») is substituted by an economical and sheer realism, embellished to be sure with spots of luxuriant impressionism.

One does not experience here the disconcerting and subtle deception of the senses and the spirit—created by the persistent use of animism, synecdoche and reification—as in other early works. Often in those years a hair's breadth from the surreal and the openly fantastic, the author here limits himself severely to the reality which one sees, hears, and smells. There are no «engaños al lector», unless one includes the impressionistic use of synesthesia in that category.

The rôle of the dog is the key to the problem. In a sense, that rôle has usurped the rôle of style. By directly attaching man (Cimarrón) to the actions and instincts of the animal through a persistent parallelism, the burden of style—which in the early works, in our opinion, is the phenomenon of the «crossing of the realms» in achieving regression—is lifted as the realms of man and animal are openly mixed at the surface level. As this central function is supplanted, the impetus of style becomes channeled in two separate areas that are counterpoised—the purely narrative and the descriptive.[216]

---

[215] Ibid., p. 26.
[216] Noemí Knapp in an unpublished monograph, «Análisis de 'Los fugitivos' de Alejo Carpentier» (Harvard University, 1970) has pointed out the striking dichotomy of the narrative and descriptive functions in «Los fugitivos.»

8

«Los fugitivos», in spite of the divergence noted, constitutes a microcosm in the corpus of the author, by virtue of the theme, characters, and form. Above all, the brief story exhibits the characteristic that most distinguishes the best stories of the author—that the book ceases being merely literature and becomes «instrumento de investigación» according to the author's own definition of his novels. Instrument of war also, because the author, enlisting the primordial powers—the rivers, plants and animals—tries to defeat his adversary Time, to free man from his incarceration in the Present.

CONCLUSION

This book is the result of an effort to shed light on the little-known early period of Alejo Carpentier's fiction, specifically, from 1927 («El milagro de Anaquillé») to 1946 («Los fugitivos»). We have found, in the five works studied, a significant consistency in terms of style and theme, and in our analysis of the salient features of the young author's work, feel that the never-ending chronicle of the discovery of Alejo Carpentier has been enriched. It is hoped that our observations on the early stories—buried by time and often by the author himself—will stimulate the curiosity of other explorers.

We have tried to participate in the evolution of the author from the contrived and naive social primitivism of «El milagro de Anaquillé», through the naturalistic and primitivistic ¡Écue-yamba-Ó!, the controlled expressionism of «Histoire de lunes», the adventure of time in «Viaje a la semilla», and finally, to the tale of regression and cyclical violence, «Los fugitivos».

We have discovered in all of these tales a fascination with the natural forces of life which finds its thematic expression in the regress, through time or space, to a primary state. In almost all cases, the linear regression terminates in death (or, as in «Viaje», the reverse—birth), yet there is a cyclical direction imposed on the material which suggests the workings of cosmic patterns (the rebirth of Menegildo in Écue, the preserved «semence» of the «Glissant» and the suggested recurrence of the destructive lunar cycle in «Histoire de lunes», the repetition of the fateful «consigna» in «Los fugitivos»). Yet these cycles were limited by the ontological perspective of the stories. In the progression of Carpentier's career, the concentric circles widened, until in El siglo de las luces, the major events of Latin American history—the conquest, the Enlightenment, and seemingly implied, the Cuban revolution of 1959—are envisioned as the ritual regeneration (as opposed to mere regression), the Eternal Return of mankind to a time outside of time. The destructive violence and absurdity in the later Carpentier entails a redemption as it expresses a deep and latent need in society. In the early works, the dark forces unleashed confirm a naturalistic conception of man, embodied with an expressionistic aesthetic.

By pointing up recurring elements of style in these works—devices such as animism, reification, and the broader phenomenon of the «crossing of the realms»—and reinforcing our observations from within the mythical

115

perspective of the stories, we have hopefully developed a fresh awareness of the author's craft at both a functional and a philosophical level. Believing that the most revealing element of an author's work is his use of language, which reflects and illuminates distinct levels of consciousness, we have entertained the hope that our comments on style in the early works of Carpentier might be of use in the broad endeavor of finding clarity of meaning in one of the century's great novelists.

Carpentier, with an unabiding primitivist's enthusiasm, chose his themes and stories from the reality and cultural myths of the traditional segment of Black Cuba. It has been our contention that the truly vital aspect of this early work is the author's attempt to weld the primitive world vision with style, to fuse myth and trope, metamorphosis with metaphor, the belief of animism with linguistic animism, «ñañiguismo» with surrealism. The paradoxical essence of «lo real maravilloso» is precisely this—to reproduce or invent the magic-seeing perspective of the «believers» (for Carpentier, the over-civilized sceptic, these are the true heroes) through the refined use of language.

APPENDIX

«Oficio de tinieblas» is a story which appeared in the December issue of the Cuban review *«Orígenes»* in 1944, and contains interesting elements in common with *«Viaje a la semilla»* of the same year and the earlier *«Histoire de lunes.»*

The story is set in colonial Cuba during the reign of Isabel II, and according to Klaus Müller-Bergh, specifically in Santiago in 1851, *«cuando un terremoto destruyó la ciudad mientras una orquesta tocaba el* Requiem *de Mozart. El título proviene de la liturgia de la iglesia del oficio matinal para el Viernes Santo, que ya señala la preocupación fúnebre del relato.»*

The story begins with a disconcerting report on the state of affairs in Santiago some months before the earthquake. *«El año cobraba un mal aspecto. Muy pocos se daban cuenta de ello, pero la ciudad no era la misma. No estaba demostrado que los objetos pintaran en los pisos un cabal equivalente en sombras. Más aún; las sombras tenían una evidente propensión a quererse desprender de las cosas...».* Shadows begin to abandon their owners. Pigeons cease their cooing, moss quickly overtakes buildings and the tone of the church changes along with the voices of hawkers who give their cries *«con falsete de sochantre en oficio de difuntos... Nada que fuera blanco prosperaba.»* At the end of the first section we are told that *«así andaban las cosas en Santiago cuando se celebraron, con pompa de cruces, pecheras y entorchados, los funerales del General Enna.»* The death of an obscure general, never again mentioned, is placed at the end of the report of these strange happenings, in a seemingly causal relationship to them. As in *«Viaje a la semilla»,* the death of a powerful man is connected to profound changes in the order of things.

In the second section, Panchón, a huge Black whose function is to transport the bass viol to the orchestra in the church, appears carrying the intrument through the streets on his head and playing one lugubrious and monotonous note as he walks. This note leads into the third section, which introduces the musical piece *«La Sombra»* by Aguero, The piece penetrates the whole story. *«En las retretas, en los desfiles, se escuchaba siempre la misma melodía quejosa, girando en redondo como el caballo viejo del tiovivo. Esta repetición transformaba «La Sombra» en su sombra, pues tal era el tedioso hábito de tocarla, que su compás se alargaba, renqueante, acabando por tener un no sé qué de marcha fúnebre.»* Pianos become sick as the piece infiltrates and infects them, and hyperbolically, Carpentier suggests that all objects *«conocieron por simpatía, el contagio de la maldita danza.»*

In the fourth section, *«llegó la época de las máscaras.»* But the carnaval atmosphere was sad and spiritless until *«un tal Burgos»* began to form a chorus of popular singers which became comparsas. The sole function of this assembly of popular types (*«La Isidra Mineto», «La Lechuza», «La Yuquita», «Juana La Ronca»*) seems to have been to sing the following *«copla»:*

> *«Ay, ay, ay, ¿quién me va a llorar?*
> *Ahí va, ahí va, ahí va la Lola, ahí va.»*

The comparsas multiply, and the copla insinuates itself until *«La Sombra»* of Aguero, is apparently drummed out of town.

In the fifth section, preparations begin for a performance of the play, «La entrada en el gran mundo» (the title of which gives a certain Calderonian dimension to the story) but disconcerting signs appear, such as the pendulum-like movement of spiders in their webs.

In the sixth section, the earthquake shatters the city. «Las dos torres de la iglesia se unieron en ángulo recto... Los aleros se embestían... las paredes de las casas dejaban los tejados suspendidos en el aire... los muebles también entraron en la danza.» Reminiscent of the opening scene of «Viaje a la semilla», these passages place us in an atmosphere of baroque instability as in Quevedo's «La hora de todos.»

The shadows, like rats departing from a sinking ship, abandon the city altogether in section seven. Shortly after, «Alguien se desplomaba en una esquina, con el rostro amoratado y la córnea azulosa.» The cholera had struck. Yet a «contradanza» scheduled for that evening was not canceled, and gave rise to a grotesquely conceived death scene in the luxurious surroundings of a palace in carnaval. «La Sombra» had returned.

«Los intérpretes de «La entrada en el gran mundo» entraron, realmente, en el gran mundo», in section eight. Panchón, and the townspeople are occupied in taking the cadavers to the cementery. Yet as the cholera slowly takes its toll, the townspeople sing, «y a mí ¿quién me va a llorar?» in defiance of imminent death.

One morning everything changes, and in section nine, the Spanish ship «La Intrépida» sails into port, a sign of redemption. «De los baules salieron vestimentas blancas y el aire se hizo más ligero.» On the 20 th of December, during a Te Deum in the cathedral, the organist was astonished to hear the copla «La Lola» squeaking and humming from every cart axle on the street. As the now dead Panchón passes by in an ox-cart, «en el juego de pedales se insinuaba «La Lola» ...Pero el oficiante, que era un poco sordo, no reconoció la copla. Creyó que las manos del organista se habían confundido, enunciando los villancicos que ya debían de ensayarse, en vista de la proximidad de las Pascuas.»

What degree of importance can we attribute to the religious trappings and overtones of the story? Is this a tale of divine retribution and forgiveness, related closely, possibly even allegorically, to the Roman Breviary office of Good Friday from which it derives its name?

This writer contends that in spite of the title of the story, and in spite of Carpentier's literary enthusiasm for the Bible, cited in Müller-Bergh's intelligent article as evidence of a strong religious dimension here, we are in a sense «barking up the wrong tree» if we search for a Biblical structure (correlating, for example, the nine sections of the story to the nine sections of the office) or for that matter, any precisely Catholic connotations or allegory in the story. As in «Histoire de lunes» and especially «El acoso» Catholic ceremony and the church itself is used to alternately contrast (often absurdly) or to enhance the artist's own master plan. The only god in evidence in «Oficio de tinieblas» is Carpentier himself, creating disasters and regenerations with a certain «delectación morosa».

On the other hand, Carpentier undoubtedly meant the title of the Office of Tenebrae to set the funereal tone to the work. In fact, the ancient ritual of this office, still performed in traditional cultures, has an interesting choreographic connection to the story. In the original liturgy, after the words were delivered, the priests would close their breviaries abruptly, thereby extinguishing the candles each carried, leaving only one. The ritual was intended probably to evoke the terror of being in the shadow of divine retribution, and the extinguishing of the candles, death itself. In the story, virtually all the lives are snuffed out by the cholera, saving Panchón. Whe he finally dies at the end, the retribution is over and peace returns, much as in «Histoire de lunes.» However, beyond this somewhat narrow application of the possible influence of the office, we have not been able to establish a significant connection. The theme of retribution is, in the last analysis, treated quite lightly here and seems far from confirming the wrathful nature of God. One might point out also, that Carpentier seems to be careful to disassociate the story from the Holy Week ceremony. The death of Christ is not mentioned, whereas it is the death of an obscure general which is accented. The action occurs between August and

December, and the tone of the story is more pagan than Christian with its suggestions of sorcery.

Much stronger here than the desire to follow any transcendent spiritual theme within a tradition, is the artist's age-old infatuation with the drama of the dance of death. As for the anonymous Spanish poet who penned «La danza de la muerte», as for one of the Cuban's favorite writers, Edgar Poe, Carpentier's fascination is with death as it manifests itself on earth. The incongruity of the «desnarigada» making her way through the merry revelers, the costumes and deceits she uses, and the costumes and vain deceits men use to avoid her, are the focus for both Poe and Carpentier (we are thinking of Poe's «The masque of the Red Death»). It is more a mass choreography of death's strangely amusing dance with man, than an inquiry into the meaning of the dance. No individual in the story raises his head to ask why. As in many works by Carpentier, man does not and cannot know the «why» and the artist revels in the mystery and the absurdity, and even supplants death by arranging his own destruction. We have the exquisitely conceived destruction of a town which foreshadows, as if in microcosm, El reino de este mundo in which the entire colonial system of Haiti is wiped out by the obscure forces of sorcery set in motion by Makandal.

More than any other story of Carpentier's, poetic imagery carries the weight of development. The drama of destruction is depicted poetically as the triumph of darkness over white. «Nada que fuera blanco prosperaba.» Clouds depart, and bridal gowns become victims of a rampant fungus. The unspecified force of destruction which later in the story becomes earthquake and cholera, insinuates itself subtly as first a note (here the cuasi-magical role of Panchón is suggested, in a manner parallel to other stories) and then as a piece of music, «La Sombra». Animistically the piece infiltrates, maddens, and sickens the inhabitants, as does the poison in El reino de este mundo. As the composer's name, Aguero, suggests, «la Sombra» is the harbinger of death. Only the vitality of the popular «copla» can defeat the power of the piece. Again, Carpentier sets force against force, and the «choteo Cubano» with its built-in humor and fatalism, triumphs momentarily over death, much as the townspeople in «Histoire de lunes» defeat the noxious «glissant».

Carpentier's first chosen medium was the social ballet. We have found a remarkable consistency in his interest in setting scenes involving masses of people and destructive forces, in which somehow the collective will predominates through its capacity for regeneration. Much as «los Fieles» in «El milagro de Anaguille», «La Lola» conquers the church, insinuating itself in the «juego de pedales» of the organist, perverts the rigidity of the European «contradanza», and even arrests the encroachment of death.

119

OFICIO DE TINIEBLAS

I

El año cobraba un mal aspecto. Muy pocos se daban cuenta de ello, pero la ciudad no era la misma. No estaba demostrado que los objetos pintaran en los pisos un cabal equivalente en sombras. Más aún: las sombras tenían una evidente propensión a quererse desprender de las cosas, como si las cosas tuvieran mala sombra. Una súbita proliferación de musgos ennegrecía los tejados. Apremiadas por una humedad nueva las columnas de los soportales se desconchaban en una noche. Los balaustres de los balcones, en cambio, se llenaban de hendeduras y resquebrajos, al trabajar de rocío a sol, sacando clavos enmohecidos sobre las barandas descascaradas. Algo había cambiado en la atmósfera. Las palomas de los patios se balanceaban sin arrullos sobre sus patitas rosadas, como con ganas de guardarse las alas en los bolsillos. El diapasón de la campana mayor de la catedral había bajado un poco, como si aquellas inesperadas lluvias de enero la hubiesen hinchado, tomando el bronce por madera. Nunca hicieron tan largos viajes la carcoma y el comején. Los pregones se entonaban con falsetes de sochantre en oficio de difuntos. Nadie creía ya en el dulzor de frutos aguados y los aguinaldos dejaron pasar su tiempo sin treparse a los árboles. Nada que fuera blanco prosperaba. Los rasos para vestidos de novia se cubrían de hongos en el fondo de los armarios y las nubes esperaban la noche para irse a la mar, siguiendo las velas de una goleta destinada a morir en una ensenada solitaria. Así andaban las cosas en Santiago, cuando se celebraron, con pompa de cruces, pecheras y entorchados, los funerales del general Enna.

II

Con los barnices encendidos por el sol, el contrabajo iba calle arriba, camino de la catedral, en equilibrio sobre la cabeza del negro. A veces, Panchón alzaba el brazo derecho, alargando el índice hacia una cuerda áspera, que respondía con una nota grave. Hubo un tiempo en que faltaron en Santiago cuerdas de contrabajo. El ritmo del «Trípili» se marcó entonces con tiras de piel de chivo adelgazadas a filo de vidrio. Pero, desde aquellos días, «La Intrépida» había venido a menudo. Y la cuerda aquella, que sonaba en lo alto—pues Panchón era una especie de gigante tonto—era de buena tripa. De excelente tripa, alzada de tono por el calor. Por eso, la nota llenaba toda la calle, sacando rostros a las ventanas y haciendo parar las orejas a las mulas de recuas carboneras.

Panchón llegó a la sacristía. Sesgó el contrabajo para entrarlo por la puerta estrecha. Ya lo esperaba un músico impaciente, dando resina a las crines del arco. Un índice docto interrogó las cuatro cuerdas, con un rechinar de clavijas en lo alto del mástil. Panchón curioso, siguió al contrabajo que se alejaba a saltos sobre su única pata. Olía a incienso. La nave estaba llena de autoridades y abanicos de encaje. En la penumbra creada por las colgaduras de luto, las solapas de seda negra se vestían de reflejos plomizos. Cuando el sacerdote se acercó al catafalco, la orquesta entera comenzó a cantar. Colándose por un ventanal alto, un rayo de sol se detuvo en el cobre de las trompas. Con gestos de bastoneros, los fagotes acercaron las cañas a las bocas. Rodó un largo trémolo en los timbales. Los bajos atacaron, al unísono, una letanía con inflexiones de Dies Irae. De pronto sonaron todos los sables. En un vasto aleteo de rasos, las mantillas cayeron hacia adelante.

Panchón salió de la catedral. Aquellos funerales suntuarios eran cosa distante y ajena. Además, estaba impaciente por beberse los dos reales de vellón que acababa de ganar. Tal vez por ello, no observó que su sombra se había quedado atrás, en la nave, pintada sobre la baldosa en que se leía: Polvo, Cenizas, Nada. Ahí estuvo largo rato, hasta que terminó la ceremonia y la envolvieron las chisteras. Entonces atravesó la plaza y entró en la bodega donde Panchón, ya borracho, la vio aparecer sin sorpresa. Se acostó a sus pies como un podenco. Era sombra de negro. La sumisión le era habitual.

III

A nadie agradaba «La Sombra» de Aguero. A nadie, porque era una danza triste, mala de bailar, que ponía notas de melancolía en los mejores saraos.

Pero, hete ahí que todos la cogen, de pronto, con «La Sombra». Tal parecía que la banda de los charoles no supiera tocar otra cosa. Lo mismo ocurría con la banda de la milicia de pardos. En las retretas, en los desfiles, se escuchaba siempre la misma melodía quejosa, girando en redondo como el caballo viejo del tíovivo. Esta repetición transformaba «La Sombra» en su sombra, pues tal era el tedioso hábito de tocarla, que su compás se alargaba, renqueante, acabando por tener un no sé qué de marcha fúnebre. Pero ahora, la enfermedad alcanzaba los pianos. Bajo los dedos de las señoritas, las teclas amarillas llenaban de sombras las cajas de resonancia. Hubo quien se matriculó en una academia de música, sin más propósito que el de llegar a tocar «La Sombra». Viejas espinetas olvidadas en los desvanes, claves de pluma y fortepianos baldados por el comején, conocieron también, por simpatía, el contagio de la maldita danza. Aun cuando nadie se acercara a ellos, los instrumentos rezagados cantaban con voces minúsculamente metálicas, uniendo las vibraciones de sus cuerdas a las de cuerdas afines. También los vasos, en los armarios, cantaron «La Sombra»; también los peines de los relojes de música; también los tremulantes y salicionales de los órganos.

El parque se había llenado de una gran tristeza. Los currutacos y las doncellas paseaban, cada vez más despacio, sin tener ganas de hablarse. Los oficleides y bombardinos escandían, con voces de profundis, aquella sombra que coreaban doscientos pianos de caja negra, en todos los barrios de la ciudad. Hubo un sinsonte que se aprendió «La Sombra» de cabo a rabo. Pero lo hallaron muerto, de un atorón de cundiamores, cuando su amo—el peluquero Higinio—se disponía a enviarlo a Doña Isabel II, como muestra de las maravillas que aún se daban en esta tierra.

IV

Llegó la época de las máscaras. Fueron aquellos unos carnavales tristes, de niños disfrazados solos, calles desiertas; de comparsas dispersas por un aguacero; de antifaces que ocultaban caras largas; de dominós del Santo Oficio. Las doncellas que fueron a los bailes no hallaron novios. Las orquestas tocaban con desgano. Los músicos de la banda tenían gestos de figuras de teatro mecánico. Los matasuegras eran de mal papel y las cornetas de cartón arrojaban voces de pavo real. Ablandadas por un sudor malo, las caretas dejaban en los labios un sudor a cola de pescado. Los confettis no habían llegado a tiempo y, en las tiendas, las narices postizas se cansaban de esperar. Un niño, disfrazado de ángel, se halló tan feo al verse en un espejo que se echó a llorar.

Así andaban las cosas cuando un tal Burgos, que tocaba el redoblante en las orquestas, recorrió las calles del barrio de La Chácara, dando grandes voces para pedir a los vecinos que formaran un escuadón. En la esquina de la Cruz se reunieron los voluntarios. Panchón fue el primero en llegar, trayendo su sombra. Luego aparecieron la Isidra Mineto, La Lechuza, La Yuquita y Juana la Ronca. Tres botijas abrieron la marcha. Había que cantar algo que no fuera «La Sombra». Súbitamente, una copla voló por sobre los tejados:

> *Ay, ay, ay, quién me va a llorar?*
> *Ahí va, ahí va, ahí va la Lola, ahí va!*

El escuadrón de Burgos fue subiendo hacia el centro de la ciudad. Nuevos cantadores lo engrosaban en cada bocacalle. El Regidor del Consejo, el Síndico de Cofradías, los oficiales de milicias, el celador, varios miembros de la Sociedad Económica de Amigos del País, y hasta el obispo de Santiago, salieron a los balcones para ver pasar el cortejo. Sin poderlo remediar, el maestro de música de la catedral marcó el compás con el pie derecho. Al caer la noche se encendió una enorme farola, que podía divisarse desde los altos de Puerto Boniato. La farola se bamboleaba a la orilla de los tejados, haciendo alto en las tabernas. Luego partía, otra vez, girando sobre sí misma, como el sol matemático de la Máquina Périca, que tanto se usara, cuarenta años antes, en funciones de ópera de gran espectáculo.

En pocos días los escuadrones proliferaron, multiplicándose de modo inexplicable. Cuando llegó el Santiago, más de diez comparsas recorrían la ciudad, al ritmo de la canción que había matado a «La Sombra»:

> *Ay, ay, ay, quién me va a llorar?*
> *Ahí va, ahí va, ahí va la Lola, ahí va!*

V

El 19 de agosto, después del rosario y de una colación de fiambres, hubo gran animación en los soportales del teatro. El poeta y el músico, de corbatas listadas, bien cerradas las levitas al remate de las solapas, recibían en terreno propio. Llegaban doncellas vestidas de encajes y olores, acompañadas de madres que, al quitar el pie del estribo, lanzaban el coche sobre los muelles de la otra banda. Con gran aparato de látigos, de troncos impacientes, de herraduras azuladas por chispas de chinas pelonas, la sociedad de Santiago concurría al ensayo. En cuadernos de colegialas traían sus réplicas las actrices de un día, copiadas con la letra característica de las alumnas de monjas. La joven que habría de interpretar el papel principal de «La entrada en el gran mundo» se adueñó del camerín en que se habían desnudado tantas tonadilleras famosas, émulas de Isabel Gamborino, amantes de hacendados y esposas de actores. Aún quedaban arreboles de color subido en un plato de porcelana blanca y una colada de mastic en el fondo de un pocillo. En una pared se ostentaba una rotunda interjección de arrieros, trazada con carmín de labios. El canapé de seda canario tenía honduras de las que no se cavan con el peso de un solo cuerpo.

El apuntador se deslizó en la concha. Se dio comienzo al ensayo de «La entrada en el gran mundo», que habría de representarse, al día siguiente, a beneficio de los Hospitales. Se estaba en agosto, y sin embargo hacía frío. Nadie pudo observar, por la oscuridad en que estaba sumida la platea, que las arañas se mecían de modo extraño, con vaivén de péndulos desacompasados.

VI

El 20 de agosto, cuando apenas se entonaba el Agnus Dei de la misa de diez, las dos torres de la catedral se unieron en ángulo recto, arrojando las campanas sobre la cruz del ábside. En un segundo se contrariaron todas las perspectivas de la ciudad. Los aleros se embestían en medio de las calles. Tomando rumbos diversos, las paredes de las casas dejaban los tejados suspendidos en el aire, antes de estrellarlos con un tremendo molinete de vigas rotas. Las mulas rodaban por las calles empinadas, envueltas en nubes de carbón, con un casco cogido debajo de la cincha y la grupela azotándoles la crin. Las rosas del parque alzaron el vuelo, cayendo en zanjas y arroyos que habían extraviado el cauce. Y luego, aquella inestabilidad de la tierra, aquel temblor de anca exasperada por una avispa, aquel desajuste de las aceras, aquel cerrarse de lo abierto y abrirse de lo cerrado. Aun corriendo, dando gritos, llamando a la Virgen del Cobre, se advertía que una calle no tenía ya más salida que una alcoba de doncella o un archivo de notaría. A la tercera sacudida, los muebles también entraron en la danza. Pasando por encima de los barandales, los armarios se dieron a la fuga, largando por los vientres abiertos sus entrañas de sábana y mantel. Todas las vajillas explotaron a un tiempo. Los cristales se encajaron en las persianas. Anchas grietas, llenas de peines, camafeos, almanaques y daguerrotipos, dividían la ciudad en islas, ya que el agua de los aljibes, rotos los brocales, corría hacia el puerto.

Cuando la sangre comenzó a ensancharse en las telas, rasos y fieltros, Todo había terminado. Un reloj de bolsillo, colgado aún de su leontina, marcó un adelanto de un minuto corto sobre los relojes muertos. Fue entonces cuando los hombres, al verse todavía en pie, comprendieron que habían conocido un terremoto. Las moscas, salidas de no se sabía dónde, volaron a ras del suelo, más numerosas.

VII

Las sombras se habían cansado de multiplicar las advertencias. Muchas se disponían ahora, a abandonar la ciudad. Al mes de pasado el terremoto, varios transeúntes corrieron hacia la fuente destruida. Una mujer, perfectamente desconocida —probablemente una forastera—, había caído al pie de la estatua de Neptuno, con los brazos y las piernas en aspa. El delfín seguía vomitando un agua turbia, que regaba plantas indeseables, nacidas al amparo de los lutos. El caso se repitió varias veces durante el día, en distintos barrios de la ciudad. De pronto, alguien se desplomaba en una esquina, con el rostro amoratado y la córnea azulosa. Faltaron panaderos a la hora de hornear y muchos caballos volvieron solos a las casas, trayendo un siniestro compás en las herraduras.

El baile anunciado se dio a pesar de todo. El Regidor estimaba que no era oportuno añadir nuevas inquietudes a las muchas que ya habían ensombrecido el día. Tratábase, además, de reunir nuevamente a los intérpretes de «La entrada en el gran mundo», para reorganizar la suspendida función a beneficio de los Hospitales. Todo había comenzado muy bien. Pero, al bailarse la segunda contradanza, una pareja rodó sobre los mármoles del piso. El contrabajista cayó fuera del estrado, con el arco cubierto de espuma, llevándose las cuerdas atadas a un pie. Una mano insegura, al agarrarse de una borla, promovió un derrumbe de terciopelos sobre los jarrones chinos que adornaban la consola del gran salón.

A pesar de que el director siguiera marcando el compás de «La Sombra», los músicos enfundaron sus instrumentos, y, apagando las velas colocadas en el borde de los atriles, se escurrieron hacia las puertas de servicio. Mientras los pomos de sales iban y venían por las escaleras de anchos barandales ,los invitados llamaban a sus cocheros con voces alteradas. Aquella noche fueron muchos los que abandonaron la ciudad para refugiarse en los cafetales más cercanos. Pero el terciopelo de los asientos estaba lleno de un calor malo. En el cielo viajaba una luna verdosa, imprecisa, como desdibujada por un traje de yedra.

VIII

Pronto los intérpretes de «La entrada en el gran mundo» entraron, realmente, en el Gran Mundo. Los hospitales se instalaban en medio de los parques, y era frecuente que un agonizante se quejara de haber sido incomodado, durante la noche, por el rápido crecimiento de un rosal. Tan numerosos eran los cadáveres que para llevarlos al cementerio de Santa Ana se utilizó el carro de un baratillero canario. A su paso se hizo un hábito decir, en son de desafío:

Ahí va, ahí va, ahí va la Lola, ahí va!

El cólera no había disminuido la sed de Panchón. Y hete ahí que en vez de contrabajos, comienza a llevar cadáveres en equilibrio sobre su cabeza. Por hábito buscaba la cuerda, sin hallar más que un borborigmo. Pero las sombras de otros, atravesadas en lo alto, le preocupaban poco. Iban por el aire, dibujando escorzos nuevos al doblar de cada esquina. Sus pocos estudios le habían dotado del poder de descifrar ciertos letreros. Los identificaba por el color de la tinta de imprenta o la disposición de los caracteres. Cuando se tropezaba con un cartel de «La entrada en el gran mundo» saludaba con el cadáver. Había, sin duda, una misteriosa pero segura relación entre esto y aquello.

Panchón comenzó a sentirse menos tranquilo cuando «La Lechuza» y Juana la Ronca cayeron a su vez. Ese día cargó con los cuerpos, tratando de hacer más corto el camino. Pero los girasoles que ahora levantaban las cabezas sobre las tapias del cementerio acabaron por hacerle pensar que su vida era hermosa. Poco a poco, una canción se fue ajustando a su paso:

Y a mí quien me va a llorar?
Ahí va, ahí va, ahí va la Lola, ahí va!

A mediados de octubre, la Isidra Mineto, la Yuquita, Burgos y todos los del Escuadrón yacían, revueltos, en la fosa común. Eran menos sombras en las calles de Santiago.

IX

Una mañana todo cambión en la ciudad. Hubo juegos de niños en los patios. «La Intrépida» entró en el puerto con las velas abiertas. De los baúles salieron vestimentas blancas y el aire se hizo más ligero. Las campanas espantaron las últimas auras que aguardaban en las esquinas y los caracoles tornaron a cantar.

El 20 de diciembre fue el Te Deum en la catedral. El organista estaba entregado a la improvisación cuando, de pronto, se volvió sobresaltado hacia la plaza. Ahí estaba «La Lola» chirriando por todos los ejes. Panchón yacía detrás del cochero, con los pies hinchados, de bruces sobre un haz de espartillo. Poco a poco, el gradual cambió de figura. Algunos advirtieron que los bajos no acompañaban cabalmente la frase litúrgica. En el juego de pedales se insinuaba, aunque en tiempo lento, el tema de: «Ahí va, ahí va, ahí va la Lola, ahí va». Pero el oficiante que era un poco sordo, no reconoció la copla. Creyó que las manos del organillero se habían confundido, enunciando los villancicos que ya debían de ensayarse, en vista de la proximidad de las Pascuas.

ALEJO CARPENTIER

124

HISTOIRE DE LUNES

I

C'était à 12 h. 28, assez exactement, que le train aux longs wagons jaunes s'arrêtait à la gare du village. Les deux vieilles Ford commençaient alors à claxonner aigrement. On faisait démarrer le ventilateur au Café des Trois Mages. Et les mendiants, les marchands de fritures ou de prières envahissaient le quai... Souvent l'express apportait des hôtes de passage. Un politicien vêtu de dril blanc, un capitaine de la garde rurale, un montreur d'animaux savants, ou quelques élèves d'un conservatoire de la ville voisine, en excursion, portant sur la poitrine un ruban de velours rouge avec les mots: *Vive la musique!* inscrits en italiques dorées... Ces cinq minutes d'arrêt étaient l'aliment d'un bavardage sans fin, reprenant chaque jour au début d'un lourd après-midi hanté par l'ombre des charognards, le vol des mites, des taons, des mouches bleues, et l'odeur d'une pluie tiède qui devait tomber quelque part, derrière les rochers qui attirent la foudre. Visages de femmes, différents de ceux que l'on connaissait trop; cravates, gramophones, bras nus, pièces de monnaie. Le nègre du pullman, déposant des omelettes sur les tables. Et, tous les mardis, le bossu du fourgon des postes, qui achetait une salade pour sa tortue. Les blancs du village se faisaient pères de famille sans travail, aveugles ou vendeurs ambulants, à l'arrivée du train. Les noirs venaient simplement pour regarder. Mais dès que la locomotive s'était engouffrée dans le tunnel, on arrêtait le ventilateur, les Ford revenaient à leur garage de chaume, et les hommes allaient s'étendre à l'ombre des cases, en attendant le retour des femmes qui lavaient leur linge à la rivière.

Seul Atilano maudissait l'express. Le matin ça allait encore. Courbaturé, trop éreinté même pour avoir peur, bêchant du saindoux chaque fois qu'il se grattait la poitrine ou le ventre, il cirait les bottes du colon américain et les brodequins du maire; après les souliers du chez de gare, c'était le tour des bottines vernies de Monsieur Rhadamès, le maquereau français qui attendait à l'écart ses papiers de naturalisation cubaine, pour repartir à la Havane. Avec les chinois et les espagnols il n'y avait rien à faire. Les uns se promènent en pantoufles, les autres en espadrilles... Le train amenait souvent des clients. Mais c'était à l'heure exacte où les wagons entraient en gare, que l'arbre commençait à pousser. Du moins ce que l'envoûtement faisait pousser comme un arbre. Le corps d'Atilano était plein de terre. D'une terre grasse, suante et rouge, comme celle des champs de canne à sucre. Tout à coup, il sentait la graine éclater dans son cerveau, et des racines tièdes, se durcissant progressivement, venaient se faufiler entre ses côtes. Un serpentin vert se déroulait au long de sa colonne vertébrale, pour claquer sèchement, comme en fouet, entre ses cuisses. Et l'arbre poussait, plus lourd que l'homme, entraînant l'homme à sa suite, tirant sur des racines bien accrochées à une terre gluante et chaude. «L'arbre te conduira!»—avait crié le sorcier, sur le seuil de sa case. Encore fallait-il attendre la tombée de la nuit pour partir... Depuis que ça l'avait repris, Atilano s'efforçait de cacher ses crises. Jamais il ne s'était donné tant de mal pour faire reluire les bottes de ses clients. Il était le seul cireur du village; il devait défendre ce privilège qui le gratifiait d'un article au singulier. Car on disait: *le*

125

cireur, comme on disait *le* maire, *le* curé, ou *le* Monsieur Rhadamès. Mais, après le passage du train, la volonté d'Atilano se brisait soudain, comme une glace. Il se couchait sur le dos, à l'ombre d'un pilier de la vérandah des Trois Mages, pour laisser croître l'arbre jusqu'à ce que l'ombre, plus longue que le pilier, allât se réfugier dans la maison. Alors Atilano se levait péniblement. D'un pas d'abord traînant, mais qui devenait de plus en plus léger, il traversait la rue aux portes clouées, la rue de l'église, la rue des chinois, la rue de l'épicerie verte, et la rue qui se terminait au bord de l'eau. Il se glissait sous les arbustes épineux, et cherchait la jarre. Il enlevait sa chemise, son pantalon, ses espadrilles. Il s'enduisait le corp de graisse. Puis il attendait, haletant, se frottant les cuisses, que le chant des lavandières cédât le silence aux grillons. Les premières chauves-souris passaient sur les plantations comme une volée de cailloux. Alors il bondissait hors de sa cachette, nu, reluisant, et prenait sa course dans les herbes à pintades, en tenant son sexe à deux mains.

II

Maintenant, à 12 h. 28, seuls les enfants allaient à la gare. Le méchant petit borgne, dont l'œil avait été crevé par un coq de combat, alors qu'il lui rasait le ventre; Barbarita, celle qui sentait si fort; le gros Titi, et Guarina-la-crâne-pelé, qui relevait ses jupes pour montrer aux voyageurs qu'elle n'était pas un garçon. Mais le ventilateur des Trois Mages tournait d'autant mieux que les réunions s'y succédaient, sans attendre l'heure du train. On discutait ferme sur l'extraordinaire événement. Le *glissant* avait fait une nouvelle apparition au village. On ne l'avait su que le septième jour à cause de ces putains de femmes, qui s'étaient chuchoté la nouvelle en se gardant bien de tirer le verrou de leur fenêtre, la nuit. Ah! ça porte chance d'être violée par un glissant, une bête de l'ombre, âme solitaire d'Elegba, bouc à face humaine, quicroit violer, alors que l'on jappe de plaisir, en faisait patiner les phalanges sur son dos graisseux! Prétendre que sa semence de malheur guérit la stérilité, les enflures aux jambes et les rhumatismes, mieux que les emplâtres au sang de poule noire. Saloperies! Sans les cris de Paulita l'idiote, qui se mit à hurler au beau milieu de la route parce que le *glissant* lui avait arraché les vieux croûtons de pain qu'elle portait dans son corsage, on serait aussi insouciant que d'abitude; on irait baver devant les bras nus, les gramophones et les omelettes du pullman. Maintenant c'était les gosses que l'on envoyait mendier à la gare et porter la salade à la tortue du fourgon, tandis qu'aux Trois Mages, on astiquait fusils et révolvers, assis en rond autour du ventilateur. Il y en avait de toutes sortes: à deux canons, à répétition, à balle ou à grenaille. Des Colt 45, et même un mousqueton à tige, de ceux qui vous envoient une ruade à l'épaule lorsqu'on presse la gâchette. La nuit tombée, il n'y aurait plus qu'à grimper aux arbres, s'accroupir derrière la margelle des puits, ou se cacher dans le dépôt des cuivres de la fanfare municipale, dont le chef avait une fille plus chinoise que mulâtresse— ce qui ne pouvait manquer d'attirer le *glissant,* car les noires qui ont du chinois dans le sang sont chaudes comme personne. Et s'il se présentait... «Moi, à quarante mètres je troue une carte à jouer, placée entre les oreilles de mon cheval»... «Moi je vous fais disparaître un oiseau-mouche avec une balle de petit calibre»... «Moi, je vous tranche si proprement le cou d'un vautour, qu'il continue à planer alors que les termites emportent déjà la tête chez elles»...

Atilano était couché sous la vérandah, à l'ombre grandissante du pilier. Il écoutait les propos des hommes d'une oreille tapissée de velours. Les paroles arrivaient bien à l'escargot, la harpe et le petit marteau qui résonnent quelque part sous le crâne, mais de là au cerveau, le chemin était long. Les racines de l'"arbre commençaient à l'envahir. L'arbre poussait. Les gens pouvaient ne pas le voir, mais Atilano sentait quil remplissait tout le village. ébran lant les murailles, et qu'à son ombre une odeur d'amour montait, en plein midi, de la robe des négresses. Des hennissements se faisaient entendre. Dans un pré les bêtes se labouraient à cœur joie. Mais ici l'arbre montait par saccades douloureuses, et comme ses racines serraient chaque fois plus fort, Atilano ne vivait que dans l'attente de la nuit. Et si les fusils visaient juste? Tant pis! Quand le sorcier envoûte pour son compte, la victime ne peut songer au contre-envoûtement. Le glissant reste glissant jusqu'à sa fin. Quand un saint vivant traverse le village, on se garde bien d'aller le réveiller. Quand Jésus le coiffeur devint Sainte-Barbe pour quelques jours, on ne l'a pas troublé par des questions inutiles. On leur a mis de la nourriture au pied d'un arbre, et c'est tout. Tandis que les hommes-chevaux, les hommes-boucs, les arbres qui marchent, ceux-là on les crève, et surtout s'ils violent les femmes et que les femmes y prennent plaisir. Les glissants sont comme les serpent: si on les rencontre sur son chemin et qu'on ne les tue pas, ils deviennent très vieux, et alors ils rentrent dans la mer, tout ridés, tout couverts de bosses et de poils blancs, et comme ils ont horreur du sel, ils maudissent l'homme qui leur a laissé cette chienne de vie... D'ailleurs tout ce qui touche aux influences de lunes, ne peut finir que très mal.

III

Cette nuit-là, en dépit de toute surveillance, le glissant revint au village. A 11 heures, il viola la mulâtresse chinoise, marraine de la fanfare; à 2 heures, la maîtresse du coiffeur Jésus; à 5 heures, alors que les coqs chantaient déjà, il bondit sur le lit de Paulita qui, cette fois, se laissa arracher les croûtons de pain sans donner l'alarme. Les trois femmes le racontèrent car l'envoûté s'était enduit le corps au cambouis, et les taches noires étaient difficiles à laver. Et puis maintenant que tous les hommes savaient, il ne fallait pas encourir le risque de se voir traitées de putains, comme celles qui, jusqu'à présent, n'avaient rien dit. Des coups de feu avaient bien claqué dans les ténèbres, mais sans autre résultat que de tuer un cochon noir, appartenant au curé. Partout où l'on croyait apercevoir le glissant, on ne trouvait que crabes de terre fuyant dans les herbes, ou grosses couleuvres réveillant des poules pour les faire tomber d'un arbre.

A 8 heures, le café des Trois Mages était plein de monde. On ne fit pas tourner le ventilateur, car il faisait encore frais. Atilano déjà installé devant son fauteuil de cireur, regardait la place d'un air absent. Déposant leurs armes sur le bar, les hommes se mirent d'accord sur la seule mesure raisonnable à adopter. Il y avait une façon de connaître l'identité du glissant. On prêta un cheval au petit borgne. Hissé sur une large selle aux étriers trop longs, il partit au galop vers le sentier de la montagne. Puis, comme c'était dimanche et que les cloches se mirent à carillonner, on alla à l'église ou les femmes priaient déjà. L'harmonium attaqua l'hymne national, et le curé fit son entrée, suivi d'un sacristain noir. Monsieur Rhadamès etait assis au premier rang, entre le maire et le chef de gare... Dans des sortes d'armoires vitrées, des Saint-Christophe, des Vierges et des enfants Jésus, souriaient sous leurs perruques de cheveux véritables, tandis que sur l'autel, un Christ terreux, couvert de sang, entr'ouvrait de ses doigts crispés une blessure laissant apercevoir un cœur rouge vif. L'heure du sermon arriva:

— Mes frères, commença le curé, sous la conque baroque de la chair, tandis que la colombe de porcelaine, représentant le Saint Esprit, se balançait au bout de sa ficelle—mes frères. Dieu nous a fait différents des animaux. Les bêtes ont le museau toujours baissé vers le sol, pour mieux nous montrer que l'homme, dont le front s'élève vers le ciel, peut comprendre et mesurer la grandeur de Dieu. Si tant d'entre vous ne se laissaient aveugler par les ténèbres honteuses de la sorcellerie, des évènements comme ceux qui viennent de se produire ici seraient impossibles... Le Seigneur est plein de bonté, mais il sait aussi se montrer terrible dans la colère. Souvenez-vous de Sodome et Gomorrhe; souvenez-vous du dernier cyclone; souvenez-vous...

Le curé se tourna brusquement vers l'entrée, en serrant les dents. Un roulement sourd, tonnerre sous forêt, roucoulement d'un pigeon monstrueux, evait éclaté au loin. Puis, coupant un bref silence, une batterie sèche, impérative, envahit l'église. Une percussion grave entra dans la ronde, pour mieux faire trembler les statues de cire dans leurs vitrines. Un, deux, trois, quatre. Les quatre tambours rituels, cognés dans l'ordre, commencèrent à parler. D'abord le Tambour-d'Appel; ensuite, le Tambour-de-Nation et le Tambour-du-Coq; puis enfin le Tambour-de-Deuil, qui sert à invoquer les mortes.

Quand on entendit la voix du quatrième tambour, l'église était déjà vide. Les fidèles marchaient vers la montagne.

IV

Faces noires et têtes crépues avançaient en groupes serrés par les sentiers rocailleux. La batterie des tambours tournait sous le soleil comme une tempête d'été. Parfois on avait la sensation de s'eloigner de l'endroit où l'on cognait les peaux de bouc tendues à la flamme. Ça venait du nord, du sud; ça montait de la rivière, ou dévalait du grand pylone en coquillages pétrifiés, habité par les vautours et les daims. Ceux qui ne connaissaient par l'entrée de la faille où se dissimulait la case du sorcier, avec sa corne en paratonnerre, auraient pu errer jusqu'à la nuit parmi les plantes grasses, au risque de s'arrêter sous un *gouao* dont l'ombre fait grossir une tête humaine à vue d'œil. Mais on arrivait déjà au chemin blanc, qui conduisait tout droit à l'enclos du Ta.

Trépignant, ricanant, grimaçant, le sorcier tendait son tablier aux fidèles, à mesure qu'ils arrivaient, pour recevoir leurs offrandes. Chair de porc, gâteaux, monnaies, ex-votos catholiques. Il leur crachait sur le crâne une gorgée d'un mélange de rhum, de sang de coq et d'huile, qui remplissait une bouteille suspendue à son cou. Puis tous allèrent s'accroupir sous le grand arbre, au pied duquel Ma Indalesia, la femme du savant, avait déjà disposé des Saints, des Vierges, des poupées ornées de rubans et de plumes, sur une table basse. Les tambours grondaient toujours sous les poings de quatre initiés... Quand tout le monde fut en place, Tata Cunengue s'approcha de sa femme, dont le corps de géante se terminait par une tête minuscule, semblable à un gros raisin sec. Il la coiffa d'un casque de cuir auquel deux longues tresses de cheveux blonds étaient fixées. Empoignant un sabre, il fit une incision horizontale dans le tronc de l'arbre, pour en faire couler une épaisse sève blanche. Il nettoya l'incision avec le bout des tresses et les colla aux paumes de ses mains. Alors, le tambour à la voix aigue énonça la «batterie de ronde». Le sorcier fixait le visage de Ma Indalesia, tandis que le tremblement de ses mains montait le long des tresses vers le casque de cuir. Les femmes commencèrent à torner autour d'eux en se tenant par la taille. Les hommes, levant les bras, formèrent un cercle qui tourna en sens contraire. Puis un chant grave et monotone s'éleva sur les deux rondes:

> *Olelí, Olelá,*
> *Olelí, Olelá,*
> *Jésus-Christ transmetteur,*
> *Olelí,*
> *Obatalá transmetteur,*
> *Olelí,*
> *Allan Kardek transmetteur,*
> *Olelí,*

Sainte-Barbe transmetteur,
Olelí, Olelá...
Olelí, Olelá...

On tournait, on tournait, haletants, hurlants, sans pouvoir s'arrêter. Olelí, Olelá. Olelí, Olelá. Les femmes frôlant les hommes de leurs hanches, de leurs seins. Une odeur de sueur, de sexes, de rhum, tournait avec les cercles magiques. Et on tournait encore, encore plus vite, poussant en avant, traînant les jambes...
— *Oya! Oya! Oya!*
Les fidèles se laissèrent tomber à terre. Ma Indalesia avait roulé aux pieds du sorcier, déshorbitée, l'écume à la bouche, battant l'air de ses jambes osseuses. Alors Tata Cunengue questionna le Saint qui était descendu dans son corps, selon les formules qui servent aux sorciers pour s'entendre avec les Saints.

V

Maintenant on savait. Laissant les femmes autour de Ma Indalesia, qui revenait lentement aux paroles intelligibles, les hommes descendaient vers le village au pas de charge. Un groupe entrerait par le côté rivière, l'autre par le côté montagne, tandis que Jésus le coiffeur et «Main-au-sol» se posteraient à l'entrée de la gare, pour empêcher Atilano de s'enfuir par la voie. On le coucherait devant son fauteuil de cireur, bien proprement, avec une large blessure derrière l'oreille. Puisque en fin de compte le glissant était un arbre, un arbre qu'un mauvais sort avait fait germer d'"une graine placée dans la tête du double d'Atilano; puisque ce double d'Atilano était une grosse anguille de la rivière, et que vouloir trouver cette anguille parmi les milliers d'anguilles qui descendaient le courant était une tâche que le sorcier se croyait incapable d'accomplir, il n'y avait qu'à couper les racines de l'arbre, à la vérandah des Trois Mages. Du même coup on en finirait avec le glissant, l'anguille, la graine et l'"arbre. Et on aurait enfin la paix.
On apercevait déjà les maisons du village, quand le petit borgne s'exclama:
— Au fait... Le glissant n'a violé jusqu'à présent que des femmes-boucs...
Les hommes s'arrêtèrent:
— Tu dis?
— Mais oui! Paulita, bouc. La chinoise à Don Cosmito, bouc. La maîtresse de Jésus, bouc. Et boucs toutes les autres...
Brusquement les hommes se divisèrent en deux camps. La vieille querelle qui subsistait depuis l'époque des indiens parmi les habitants du village, remonta soudain à la surface des réalités. Boucs ceux du côté montagne; crapauds, ceux du côté rivière. Les boucs possédaient leur confrérie *ñañiga* de protection mutuelle: l'*Ensenillen*. Les crapauds lui avaient opposé l'association secrète de l'*Efo-Abacara*. Atilano était crapaud. Il dansait la danse du *diablito* aux cérémonies et jeux de son quartier. Et voici que même glissant, même anguille, arbre ou envoûte, il n'avait violé que des femmes boucs, respectant les femmes crapauds.
— Crapauds puants!
— Boucs, fils de la très grande putain!
Les boucs foncèrent sur les crapauds. Les crapauds lancèrent leur cri. Des têtes se couchèrent sur l'épaule, la jugulaire tranchée d'un coup de machete. Des intestins bouillonnèrent dans les chemises. On entendit des injures et des cassures de lames, tandis qu'au loin les tambours du sorcier roulaient toujours.

VI

Ce jour-là, pendant les cinq minutes d'arrêt, les voyageurs de l'express abandonnèrent leurs wagons et sortirent sur le perron de la gare, cherchant à comprendre ce qui se passait au village. Les rues étaient désertes. Le ventilateur des Trois Mages ne tournait plus. Même les deux vieilles Ford restaient cachées dans leur case. Mais une musique d'émeute incendiait l'atmosphère. Du côté de la montagne, les trompettes chinoises de l'*Ensenillen* projetaient dans le calme ensoleillé leurs vocalises stridentes. A cet appel, répondaient les grelots et les tambours de l'*Efo-Abacara*, du fond des rues qui se terminent au bord de l'eau. Le train repartit, plein d'hypothèses et de questions sans réponses.

C'était simple pourtant. La guerre était déclarée. Les crapauds avaient pris Atilano sous leur protection. A la tombée de la nuit, ils se faufilaient au long des murailles ct des haies du quartier des boucs, couteau en main, pour défendre le glissant de toute agression. Maintenant il pouvait violer les femelles ennemies, avec l'approbation de tous les membres de sa confrérie. On l'aidait même à s'enduire le corps de saindoux, de cambouis ou de graisse d'essieux. Pendant qu'il empoignait quelque femme nue, dont le nourrison prenait la fuite entre les barreaux du lit, d'âpres combats se livraient dans l'ombre; le sang giclait, et souvent les crapauds accourus au bruit de la bagarre, ne trouvaient plus qu'un agonisant, que l'on entraînait par le cou. Des batailles en règle s'étaient déroulées au parc central. On avait dû supprimer les concerts de la fanfare, car, un soir, l'idée malencontreuse de jouer la vieille rumba des «Alliés et les Allemands», avait provoqué une nouvelle échaffourée entre les boucs et les crapauds. Depuis lors on ramassait souvent des cadavres dans les rues. Le capitaine de la garde rurale s'était fait envoyer des patrouilles de renfort par le gouverneur militaire de la province.

Mais le carnaval arriva, et avec lui, la fête de la patronne du village, Notre-Dame-des-petites-oreilles. Le maire attendait impatiemment cette date, dans l'espoir que la procession traditionnelle calmerait les esprits. Et, en effet, le calme sembla revenir au village, quand il fut question de préparer la sortie du char de la Vierge. Les menuisiers, les peintres, les maçons, le fabricant de cercueils, s'offrirent volontiers, crapauds ou boucs, pour travailler à l'ornement des rues. Ils clouèrent des feuilles de palmier sur les façades et tendirent des guirlandes de rafia, couvertes de drapeaux, au bord des toitures. Dans sa case, le pyrotechnicien attitré montait, en grand secret, les pièces destinées au feu d'artifice. Partout on coloriait des gâteaux, on préparait les étalages de saucisses, de beignets, tandis que les banquiers de charade chinoise, de «massue et d'épée», de bonneteau, s'exerçaient la main en criant aux joueurs: «Plus tu la regarderas, moins tu la verras». Quant à la Grande Patronne, couronnée d'or, vêtue de neuf, et ornée de toutes les boucles d'oreilles prêtées par les fidèles, elle attendait l'instant d'être hissée sur son trône en demi-lune soutenu par les trois séraphins roses dont on avait dépouillé le corbillard des enfants, avec la permission de l'Agence des Pompes Funèbres.

A la fin de l'après-midi, quand tout le monde eut bien hurlé aux combats de coqs; après la course aux sacs, l'escalade du mât de cocagne, et la visite aux deux polonaises qui avaient monté un bordel volant, à la sortie du village, il y eut grande cohue au parc central. Les portes de l'église s'ouvrirent, et le char, escorté par la fanfare municipale et les pompiers du commerce, fut traîné dans la rue. Le cortège se mit en marche. La lueur des feux de Bengale monta dans la nuit. On alluma les roulettes à pétards. Des fusées partirent, tandis que Notre-Dame-des-petites-oreilles poursuivait son chemin, en fixant la foule de ses yeux sombres. On l'arrêtait devant les maisons où il y avait un malade, pour la «faire danser». Puis la procession repartait, dans un vacarme de cuivres et de cymbales.

La Vierge avait déjà parcouru ainsi les rues principales du quartier crapaud. On arrivait au quartier bouc, à gauche de l'étalage des «Chemises de Paris», lorsque l'on vit apparaître un cortège inattendu tout en haut de la rue des Liberateurs. Des tambourinaires, des hommes déguisés en animaux, portant de grosses lanternes sur leur ventre, avançaient en groupe compact, suivis d'une sorte de plateforme en bois, sur laquelle se dressait un grand Saint-Lazare noir, entouré d'une meute de chiens en plâtre. Pavillon à l'air, quelques trompettes chinoises élevaient leurs plaintes lugubres, en tête d'une colonne de femmes qui hurlaient, en agitant des mouchoirs de couleurs:

— Saint Lazare vivant! Saint Lazare vivant!...

Il était bien vivant, Saint Lazare. Appuyé sur des béquilles, il faisait tourner une grosse crécelle de sa main gauche. Ses jambes étaient ornées de plaies fraîchement peintes à l'encre rouge. Ah, ce coiffeur Jésus! L'année passée, Sainte-Barbe était descendue dans son corps pour faire entendre sa voix divine aux fidèles. Cette fois, il s'était réveillé en sentant que le souffle de Saint-Lazare parcourait ses membres. Une voix lui chuchotait à l'oreille: «Lazare, lève-toi, et marche». Il était tombé en transe au beau milieu de sa boutique renversant une table couverte de rasoirs et de tondeuses. Alors les compagnons de sa confrérie avaient organisé la procession en toute hâte. De cette façon on aurait quelque chose à opposer à la parade religieuse des crapauds, dont la Vierge, bien que patronne du village entier, n'avait par réussi à préserver les femmes boucs des viols du glissant, malgré les boucles d'oreilles qu'on lui avait prêtées... D'ailleurs cette concurrence dans l'exhibition des Puissances ne comportait aucune hostilité. Les boucs amenaient leur Saint-Lazare vivant, afin qu'il prit sa place dans la grande procession, avec tous les honneurs qui lui étaient dus.

Le curé, voyant arriver l'inspiré sur son tréteau, se mordit les lèvres, car la moindre protestation de sa part pouvait avoir de telles conséquences qu'il valait mieux se tenir coi. Les porteurs du Saint-Lazare se placèrent derrière la Vierge, et le cortège continua son parcours. On fit ainsi le tour du quartier des boucs; puis l'on revint vers le parc central. Mais au moment oú l'on tournait le coin de la rue des chinois, les gros nuages sombres qui se gonflaient derrière les montagnes, depuis midi, crevèrent brusquement. Une véritable muraille d'eau s'abattit sur le village. Les fidèles prirent leur course vers l'église, dont les portes étaient toujours ouvertes en attendant le retour de la Vierge. Cahotant, roulant avec un fracas de tonnerre sur le sol de terre battue, le char s'engouffra dans le temple, sous une averse serrée. Le curé s'empressa de fermer les battants pour pouvoir dévêtir l'image, dont le manteau trempé commençait à déteindre. Le sacristain noir s'approcha de lui:

— Et vous allez laisser dehors le Saint-Lazare vivant?

Il put esquiver un pied que la soutane ne laissait pas monter assez haut. Mais Saint-Lazare cognait déjà à la porte avec ses deux béquilles. Les boucs réclamaient le droit de l'héberger dans l'église. Les chiens de plâtre fondaient sous la pluie comme des morceaux de sucre. Des centaines de mains percutaient sur les larges planches de cèdre. Une clameur d'indignation s'élevait autour de la vieille bâtisse espagnole... C'est alors que l'on vit Atilano sauter sur la plate-forme et renverser le Saint-Lazare vivant d'un grand coup d'épaule. L'inspiré tomba sur les porteurs en faisant tournoyer ses béquilles dans le vide. La place entière s'emplit d'un fracas de bataille. Des hommes, des femmes, roulaient sur les cendres du feu de bengale, blessés, mordus, piétinés. Les deux clans étaient mêlés, on tapait à droite, à gauche, sur la première tête que l'on trouvait à portée de la main... Une fusillade se fit entendre. Deux patrouilles de la garde rurale étaient apparues sur un des côtés de la place. Les uniformes kakis avançaient lentement, en laissant partir une décharge tous les trois pas. A la cinquième décharge le parc central était désert. Boucs ou crapauds, les combattants s'enfuyaient par les rues les plus proches... A la porte de l'église, seuls, le glissant et Saint-Lazare se roulaient toujours dans la boue, en brandissant des tronçons de béquilles.

VII

Saint-Lazare fut mis en liberté quelques heures plus tard, car il ne fallait pas prendre de mesures trop sévères envers un inspiré. Quant à Atilano, on le tira de sa cellule à l'aube pour le fusiller dans la cour de la caserne. Lorsque les Mauser se dressèrent vers lui, il cria:

— Vous allez tuer un arbre!

Un arbre communiste, car le maire, par délicatesse envers les membres des confréries qui l'avaient élu, et pour s'éviter des explications trop longues au gouverneur militaire de la province, avait spécifié qu'il s'agissait «d'un agitateur rouge des plus dangereux, qui aspirait à renverser le gouvernement républicain, en le voulant supplanter par une dictature bolchevique».

VIII

Le lendemain, le calme régnait au village. Les hommes allèrent a la gare pour vendre aux voyageurs les gâteaux qui étaient restés aux étalages après la fête. Les deux Ford sortirent de leur case. Le ventilateur tourna. Et les femmes lavèrent leur linge à la rivière.

La mulâtresse chinoise découvrit parmi les joncs la peau d'une grosse anguille. Elle avait sur la tête une petite excroissance semblable à un arbre minuscule. Les femmes l'apportèrent au sorcier. Il la fit bouillir dans une jarre d'argile. Et comme il s'agissait du double d'Atilano, il en fabriqua une potion qui devait guérir la stérilité, les rhumatismes et les enflures des jambes, mieux que la semence même du glissant. D'ailleurs, maintenant on aurait la paix pour quelques mois. Les mauvaises influences de lune étaient écartées, car l'astre entrait dans un des triangles du ciel qui neutralisent son action néfaste sur le crâne des hommes.

ALEJO CARPENTIER

BIBLIOGRAPHY

I. *WORKS OF ALEJO CARPENTIER*

a) *Poetry, fiction, and theatrical works.*[1]

Yamba-O (Afro-Cuban burlesque). Music by M. F. Gaillard; performed in Théâtre Beriza, Paris, 1928. MS.

La Rebambaramba (Afro-Cuban ballet). Music by Amadeo Roldán. MS. Havana, 1928.

«Mata-Cangrejo» and «Azúcar» (choreographic poems with music by Amadeo Roldán). MS. n.d.

«L'Etudiant» (short story). *Révolution Surréaliste.* Paris, 1928.

Dos poemas afrocubanos, 'Mari-Sabel' y 'Juego Santo' (set to music by A. Garcia Caturla). Paris: Editions Maurice Senart, 1929.

Poèmes des Antilles: neuf chants sur des texte d'Alejo Carpentier (music by M. F. Gaillard). Paris: Editions Martine, 1929.

«Blue» (a poem set to music by M. F. Gaillard). Paris: Editions Martine, n.d.

«Liturgia» (poema afrocubano). *Revista de Avance,* Año IV, Vol. V, No. 50, 15 September, 1930, n.pag.

«Liturgia.» *Antología de poesía negra hispanoamericana,* ed. Emilio Ballagas. Madrid: M. Aguilar, 1935, pp. 65-67.

«Liturgia.» *Orbita de la poesía afrocubana 1928-37,* ed. Ramón Guirao. La Habana: Ucar, García y Cía., 1938, p. 77.

«Liturgia.» *Lira Negra,* ed. José Sanz y Díaz. Madrid: Eugenio Sánchez Leal Impresor, 1945.

«Liturgia.» *Cincuenta años de poesía cubana 1902-1952,* ed. Cintio Vitier. La Habana: Dirección de Cultura del Ministerio de Educación, 1952, pp. 226-228.

Manita en el suelo (Ópera bufa). MS. Paris, 1930.

«Canción» (Afro-Cuban poem). *Revista de Oriente.* Habana, 1931, n.d., n.pag.

«Canción.» *Órbita de la poesía afrocubana 1928-37,* ed. Ramón Guirao. La Habana: Ucar, García y Cía., 1938.

«Canción.» *Lira Negra,* ed. José Sanz y Díaz. Madrid: Eugenio Sánchez Leal Impresor, 1945.

La Passion noire (Cantata, music by M. F. Gaillard, performed in Paris, 1932). MS.

El castillo de campana salomón («Mitología de La Habana», documentary novel probably written in the period 1928-1933). MS.

---

[1] Although some of the entries in this section are incomplete, they represent an effort to present the totality of Carpentier's unpublished and published fictional work. This contribution was considered to have outweighed the drawbacks of presenting incomplete data in some cases.

Semblante de cuatro moradas (novel probably written in the period 1928-1933). MS
¡Écue-yamba-Ó! Madrid: Editorial España, 1933.
¡Écue-yamba-Ó! Buenos Aires: Editorial Xanadú, 1968.
«Histoire de lunes» (short story). *Cahiers du Sud,* no. 157, December 1933, 747-759.
«El milagro de Anaquillé» (Afro-Cuban ballet written in 1927, music by Amadeo
 Roldán). *Revista Cubana,* VIII, April-June 1937.
«Viaje a la semilla» (limited edition of 100 copies). La Habana: Ucar, García y Cía.,
 1944.
«Viaje a la semilla.» *Los mejores cuentos cubanos,* ed. Salvador Bueno. Lima: Im-
 prenta Torres Aguirre S.A., 1959.
«Viaje a la semilla.» *Selección de cuentos cubanos.* La Habana: Editorial Nacional
 de Cuba, 1962.
«Oficio de tinieblas» (short story). *Orígenes,* Año 1, no. 4, December 1944, p. 32.
«Los fugitivos» (short story). *El Nacional* (newspaper), Caracas, edición universario,
 3 Aug. 1946.
«Los fugitivos.» *Narrativa cubana de la revolución,* ed. José Manuel Caballero Bonald.
 Madrid: Alianza Editoria, 1968, pp. 25-37.
El reino de este mundo (novel). México: Edición y Distribución Iberoamericana
 de Publicaciones S.A., 1949.
El reino de este mundo. Lima: Editora Latinoamericana, 1958.
El reino de este mundo. Caracas: Primer Festival del Libro Popular Venezolano, 1958.
El reino de este mundo. Lima: Torres Aguirre S.A., 1959.
El reino de este mundo. La Habana: Empresa de Artes Gráficas, Bolsilibros Unión,
 1964.
El reino de este mundo. México: Compañía General de Ediciones S.A., 1967.
«Semejante a la noche.» *Orígenes,* Año IX, no. 31 (1952), pp. 3-11.
Los pasos perdidos. México: Edición y Distribución Iberoamericana de Publica-
 ciones S.A., 1953.
Los pasos perdidos. México: Compañía General de Ediciones S.A., 1959.
Los pasos perdidos. La Habana: Organización de los Festivales del Libro, 1960.
«El acoso» (extract). *Orígenes,* Año XI, no. 36 (1954), pp. 6-16.
«El acoso.» Buenos Aires: Editorial Losada, 1956.
*Guerra del tiempo: tres relatos y una novela: El camino de Santiago, Viaje a la
 semilla, Semejante a la noche y El acoso.* México: Compañía General de Edi-
 ciones S.A., 1958.
Guerra del tiempo. Habana: Ediciones Unión, 1963.
«El siglo de las luces,» «jornadas» III and IV of the first chapter. *Nueva Revista
 Cubana.* La Habana: Dirección General de Cultura Ministerio de Educación, 1, 3,
 October-December 1959.
El siglo de las luces. México: Compañía General de Ediciones S.A., 1962.
«El año '59» (the first instament of a trilogy). *Casa de las Américas.* La Habana,
 Año IV, no. 62, October-November 1964, pp. 45-51.
«Les Elus.» *Guerre du temps.* Paris: Gallimard, 1967. (the story, datelined «La Ha-
 vane, 13 Juin 1965,» was probably written in Spanish and translated, along with
 the stories of the anterior *Guerra del tiempo,* by René Durand. *Guerre du temps*
 differs from *Guerra del tiempo* in that it omits «El acoso» and includes two new
 stories, «Les Elus,» and «Le Droit d'asile.»)
«Le Droit d'asile.» *Guerre du temps.* Paris: Gallimard, 1967. (This short story is
 datelined «La Havane, 6 Mai 1965»).
«Los advertidos» in *Guerra del tiempo.* Barcelona: Barral Editores, 1971 («Les Elus»
 in Spanish).
Concierto barroco. México: Siglo XXI, 1974.
El recurso del método. México: Siglo XXI, 1974

b) *Essays.*

La música en Cuba. México: Fondo de Cultura Económica, 1946.
Tientos y diferencias. México: Universidad Nacional Autónoma, 1964.
Literatura y conciencia política en América Latina. Madrid: S.A.E.G.E. Alberto Corazón, 1969.
La ciudad de las columnas. Madrid: Editorial Lumen, 1970.
Letra y solfa. Buenos Aires: Editores Nemont, 1976. (collection of articles written by Carpentier for *El Nacional* in Caracas during the 40's and 50's).
Crónicas. La Habana: Instituto Cubano del libro, 1976. (collection of articles written for the Cuban magazines *Carteles* and *Social*).

c) *Interviews.*

Queneau, Raymond. *Anthologie de jeunes auteurs.* Paris: J.A.R., 1955 (the prologue quotes Carpentier on the subject of fictional dialogue).
Pfaff, William. «A Novelist Talks Back.» *Américas* (English edition), XVI, no. 2, Feb. 1957, p. 36.
Poniatowska, Elena. «El Hijo pródigo.» *Palabras Cruzadas.* México: Ediciones Era, 1961, pp. 216-230.
García Suárez. Interview with Alejo Carpentier. *Bohemia,* no. 21, 1963.
Suárez, Luis. «Con Alejo Carpentier.» *Siempre,* no. 543, 20 Nov. 1963, pp. 44-45.
Poniatowska, Elena. Interview with Alejo Carpentier. Sunday supplement of *Siempre,* 67, 25, Dec. 1963, pp. 2-5.
Reyes Nevares, Beatriz. Interview with Alejo Carpentier. *Cuadernos de Bellas Artes* (México), June 1964.
Vargas Llosa. «Cuatro preguntas a Alejo Carpentier.» *Marcha* (Montevideo) 1246, 12-III, 1965, p. 31.
Fell, Claude. «Rencontre avec Alejo Carpentier.» *Les Langues Modernes,* 59 année, no. 3, May-June 1965, pp. 14-17.
Peyrera, Gabriel. «Plática en La Habana.» *Punto de Partida,* Año 1, no. 3, March-April 1967, p. 58.
Carballo, Emmanuel. «Diario Público de Alejo Carpentier.» *Exelsior,* México, 2 June 1968, pp. 3 and 6; June 9, p. 5; June 16, p. 5.
Silva Estrada, Alfredo. «Unas preguntas a Alejo Carpentier.» *Imagen,* Caracas, no. 30, 10 Aug. 1968. p. 3.
Muller-Bergh, Klaus. «Entrevista con Alejo Carpentier.» *Cuadernos Americanos,* México, July-August 1969, Año XXVII, Vol. CLXV.
Santana, Joaquín. «Los pasos encontrados.» *Cuba,* Habana, December 1970.
Carpentier, Alejo. «Una conversación con Jean-Paul Sartre.» *Revista de la Universidad de México.* Vol. XV, no. 6, Feb. 1961, pp. 11-12.

2. CRITICAL STUDIES AND REVIEWS OF CARPENTIER'S WORKS

1. *Anthologies*

Flores, Julio, et al. «El realismo mágico de Alejo Carpentier.» Valparaíso: Ediciones Orellana, 1971.
Giacoman, Helmy F., ed. *Homenaje a Alejo Carpentier.* New York: Las Américas, 1970. (This volume will hitherto be referred to in abbreviated form as *Homenaje.*)
Müller-Bergh, Klaus, ed. *Asedios a Carpentier: once ensayos críticos sobre el nove-*

lista cubano. Santiago: Editorial Universitaria, 1972. (hitherto referred to as *Asedios*).

—————. *Historia y mito en la obra de Alejo Carpentier.* Buenos Aires: Fernando García Cambeiro, 1972.

2. *!Écue-yamba-Ó!*

Fernández, Ricardo. An unpublished thesis on Carpentier. Princeton University, 1969 (first chapter is a study of *¡Écue-yamba-Ó!*).

Fernández de Castro, José Antonio. Review of *¡Écue-yamba-Ó! Tema Negro en las Letras de Cuba.* La Habana: Ediciones Mriador, 1943, pp. 91-95.

Marinello, Juan. «Una novela cubana.» *Literatura Hispanoamericana.* México: Ediciones de la Universidad Nacional de México, 1937, pp. 165-179.

Sommers, Joseph. *!Écue-yamba-Ó!*: semillas del arte narrativo de Alejo Carpentier» in Boulter, C. G. et al., eds. *Lectures in Memory of Louise Taft Semple.* Norman: University of Oklahoma, 1973.

Lastra, Pedro. «Aproximaciones a *¡Écue-yamba-Ó!»* *Eco,* Bogota, XXIII, 1-2, May-June 1971, pp. 50-69.

3. «Viaje a la semilla» (short story included in *Guerra del tiempo.* México: 1958).

Assardo, Maurice Roberto. «'Viaje a la semilla'» in *La técnica narrativa en la obra de Alejo Carpentier* (unpublished thesis). University of California, 1968, pp. 121-149.

González, Eduardo. «Viaje a la semilla.» *Revista Iberoamericana,* vol. XLI, no. 92, July-December 1975, pp. 423-445.

Mocegá-González, Esther. «La circularidad temporal en 'Viaje a la semilla.'» *Chasqui* 3, ii, 1974, pp. 5-11.

Renand, Richard. «Réflexions sur le voyage à la semence d'Alejo Carpentier.» Annales de Bretagne 82, pp. 201-212.

4. «Oficio de tinieblas»

Muller-Bergh, Klaus. «'Oficio de tinieblas' de Alejo Carpentier.» *El Ensayo y la crítica literaria en Iberoamérica* (leaflet «Separata» published by the University of Toronto), 1970.

5. «Los fugitivos»

Janney, Frank. «Apuntes sobre un cuento de Alejo Carpentier: 'Los fugitivos'» in *Asedios,* pp. 89-100.

Pérez-González, Lilia. «El relato 'Los fugitivos', de Alejo Carpentier.» *Papeles de Son Armadans,* no. 75, 1974, pp. 41-54.

6. *El reino de este mundo*

Adams, Mildred. «From Magic Powers.» *New York Times Book Review,* 19 may 1957.

Adams, Phoebe. «Revolution in Tropical Climates.» *Atlantic* CC., no. 2, Aug. 1957. (Review).

Arrigostia, Luis. «*El reino de este mundo».* *La torre* (Puerto Rico), XV, no. 58, 1967, pp. 244-250.

Baro, Gene. «Early-day Drama in Haiti.» *New York Herald Tribune Book Review,* XXXIII, no. 43, 2 June 1957, p. 7. (Review).

Bazin, Henri. «Conjurations.» *L'Information* (Paris), 18 Sept. 1954. (Review).

Blanzat, Jean. «Le Royaume de ce monde.» *Le Figaro Littéraire* (Paris), 11 Sept. 1954.

Castroviejo, Concha. Review of *El reino de este mundo*. *Ínsula*, Año 22, no. 248-9, July-Aug. 1967, p. 17.

Cau, Jean. Review of *Le Royaume de ce monde*. *Temps Modernes* (paris), Vol. X, no. 107, November 1954, pp. 755-756.

Dorfman, A. «El reino de este Carpentier.» *Ercilla* (Santiago de Chile), 1676, 19-VII, 1967, p. 28.

Glissant, Edouard. «Alejo Carpentier et l'autre Amérique.» *Critique: Revue Générale des Publications Francaises et Etrangères* (Paris), dixième année, no. 105, February 1956, pp. 113-116.

Hilton, Ronald. Review of *El reino de este mundo*. *Hispanic American Report*, Vol. XI, no. 1, Jan. 1958, p. 119.

Lalou, René. «Le Royaume de ce monde.» *Nouvelles Littéraires* (Paris), 8 Dec. 1954, n.pag.

Maldonado Denis, Manuel. «Alejo Carpentier y *El reino de este mundo*.» *Marcha* (Montevideo), XXVII, 17 Dec. 1965.

Pickrel, Paul. Review of *El reino de este mundo*. *Harper's*, CCXX, no. 1286, July 1957, pp. 87-88.

Picón-Salas, Mario. «El reino de este mundo.» *El Nacional* (Newspaper), Caracas, 27 Nov. 1949, n.pag.

Pontiero, Giovanni. «The Human Comedy in *El reino de este mundo*.» *Journal of Interamerican Studies* (Miami), vol. 12, no. 4, Oct. 1970, pp. 527-538.

Price, Martin. «Some Recent Fiction» (review of *El reino de este mundo*). *Yale Review*, XLVII, no. 1, Autumn 1957, n.pag.

Rodríguez Monegal, Emir. «Lo real y lo maravilloso en la obra de Alejo Carpentier.» *Revista Iberoamericana*, vol. 37, 1971, pp. 619-649.

Volek, Emil. «Análisis e interpretación de *El reino de este mundo* y su lugar en la obra de Alejo Carpentier.» *Unión*, Año 6, March 1969, p. 98.

7. «Semejante a la noche»

Assardo, Roberto. «Semejante a la noche o la contemporaneidad del hombre.» *Cuadernos Americanos*, Vol. 163, no. 2, March-April 1969, pp. 263-271.

Fernández, Sergio. «El rescate de Elena.» *El Día* 21 Feb. 1968, p. 9.

Freustie, Jean. «De Troie a St. Domingue.» *Le Nouvel Observateur*, no. 123, March 1967, pp. 38-39.

Quesada, Luis Manuel. «Semejante a la noche: Análisis evaluativo.» *Homenaje a Alejo Carpentier*. New York: Las Américas, 1970, pp. 227-243.

Volek, Emil. «Dos cuentos de Alejo Carpentier: dos caras del mismo método.» *Nueva Narración hispánica*, Vol. 1, no. 2, 1971, pp. 7-19.

8. *Los pasos perdidos*

Alonso, Juan Manuel. *The Search for Identity in Alejo Carpentier's Contemporary Urban Novels:* An Analysis of *Los pasos perdidos* and «El acoso.» Dissertation, Brown University, 1967.

Ayora, Jorge. «La alienación marxista en *Los pasos perdidos*.» *Hispania*, no. 57, 1974, pp. 886-892.

Blanzat, Jean. «*Le partage des eaux* de Alejo Carpentier.» *Le Figaro Littéraire* (Paris), 7 Jan. 1956, n.pag.

Bosquet, Alain. «Alejo Carpentier.» *Combat* (Paris), 19 Jan. 1956.

Bueno, Salvador. «Alejo Carpentier, novelista antillano y universal.» *La Letra Como Testigo*. Santa Clara, Cuba: Universidad Central de las Villas, 1957, pp. 153-179.

Campos Jorge. «Alejo Carpentier y sus pasos hallados.» *Ínsula* (Madrid), no. 118, 15 Oct. 1955, n.pag.

Dorante, Carlos. «Alejo Carpentier y Herman Hesse: Mejores autores en Francia del mes.» *El Nacional* (Caracas), 1956, n.d., n.pag.

Esquenazi-Mayo, Roberto. «Música y narración en Alejo Carpentier.» *Revista Hispánica Moderna,* XXI, no. 2, April 1955, p. 146.

Esquenazi-Mayo, Roberto. «*Los pasos perdidos.*» *Ensayos y Apuntes.* La Habana: Editorial Selecta, 1956, pp. 117-119.

Fernández, Mauricio. «Los pasos perdidos de la casa verde.» *Zona Franca,* Año 4, no. 54 (1968), p. 51.

Fouchet, Max Paul. «Le Prix du meilleur livre étranger.» *Le Temps* (Paris), première année, no. 51, 16 June 1956.

González, Eduardo. «*Los pasos perdidos,* el azar y la aventura.» *Revista Iberoamericana,* no. 38, 1972, pp. 585-613.

González Echevarría, Roberto. «The Parting of the Waters.» *Diacritics,* 4, IV 1974, pp. 8-17.

Gullón, Germán. «El narrador y la narración en *Los pasos perdidos.*» *Cuadernos hispanoamericanos,* no. 263, pp. 501-509.

King, Lloyd. «A Note on the Rhetorical Structures of *Los pasos perdidos.*» *Reflexión* 2, vol. 1, no. 1, pp. 147-152.

Loveluck, Juan. «*Los pasos perdidos:* Jasón y el nuevo vellocino.» *Atenea* 149, 399 (Jan-Mar. 1993), pp. 120-134.

Müller-Bergh, Klaus. *La prosa narrativa de Alejo Carpentier en Los pasos perdidos.* Dissertation, Yale University, 1966.

——————. «En torno al estilo de Alejo Carpentier en *Los pasos perdidos.*» *Homenaje a Alejo Carpentier,* ed. H. Giacomán. New York: Las Américas, 1970.

Paulding, Gouverneur. «A Novel of City and Jungle.» *The New York Herald Tribune Book Review,* XXXIII, no. 15 (1956).

Peavler, Terry J. «The Source for the Archetype in *Los pasos perdidos.*» *Romance Notes* (University of North Carolina), no. 15, 1974, pp. 588-597.

Quigly, Isabel. «New Novels.» *Spectator,* no. 6699, 16 Nov. 1956, p. 690.

Redman, Ray. «Journey into Time.» *Saturday Review,* XXXIX, no. 42, 20 October 1956. (Review of *Los pasos perdidos*).

Rey del Corral, José. «*Los pasos perdidos* de Alejo Carpentier.» *Boletín Cultural y Bibliográfico* (Bogotá), 10 (4), (1967), pp. 857-863.

Rodríguez Monegal, Emir. «Dos novelas de Alejo Carpentier.» *Narradores de esta América.* Montevideo: Alfa, 1961, pp. 147-153.

Santander, T. «Lo maravilloso en la obra de Alejo Carpentier.» *Atenea* (Chile), XLII, Vol. CLIX, 409, July-September 1965, pp. 99-126.

Silva Cáceres, Raul. «Una novela de Alejo Carpentier.» *Mundo Nuevo,* no. 17, Nov. 1967, p. 33.

Silva Sánchez, María Teresa. «*Los pasos perdidos,* una búsqueda de sí mismo a través del tiempo.» *Boletín Cultural y Bibliográfico* (Bogotá), Vol. IX, 1966, pp. 507-510.

9. «El camino de Santiago»

Foster, W. «The Everyman's Theme in 'El camino de Santiago.'» *Symposium* XVIII (1964), pp. 229-238.

Fry, Gloria. «El problema de la voluntad y el acto en 'El camino de Santiago.'» *Revista de estudios hispánicos* (Alabama), vol. III, no. 1, April 1969.

Magnarelli, Sharon. «El camino de Santiago.» *Revista Iberoamericana,* vol. 40, 1974, pp. 65-86.

Rodríguez-Alcalá, Hugo. «Sentido de 'El camino de Santiago.'» *Humanitas* (Monterrey), (5), (1964), pp. 245-254.

Verasconi, Ray. «Juan y Sisyphus in Alejo Carpentier's 'El camino de Santiago.'» *Hispania* XLVIII, pp. 70-75.

Volek, Emil. «Dos cuentos de Alejo Carpentier: dos caras del mismo método artístico.» *Nueva narrativa hispanoamericana,* vol. 1, no. 2, 1971, pp. 7-19.

10. «El acoso»

Assardo, Roberto. «El efecto de la disgregación temporal en 'El acoso' de Alejo Carpentier.» *Revista de letras,* vol. 6, 1974, pp. 74-86.

Bueno, Salvador. «Reseña de 'El acoso.'» *Universidad de La Habana* XXVII, no. 164, Nov.-Dec. 1963, pp. 188-190.

Carlos, Alberto. «El anti-héroe en 'El acoso'.» *Cuadernos Americanos,* Vol. 29, no. 1, Jan. 1970, pp. 93-204 (also in *Homenaje,* pp. 365-385).

Giacomán, Helmy. «La relación literaria entre 'La Heroica' y 'El acoso.'» *Cuadernos Americanos* Vol. CLVIII, no. 3, México, May-June 1968, pp. 113-132.

González León, Adriano. «El acoso.» *Revista Nacional de Cultura* (Caracas), Vol. XIX, no. 120, Jan.-Feb. 1957, pp. 176-177.

Labrador Ruiz, Enrique. «Reseña de 'El acoso.'» *Revista Cubana* XXXI, no. 3-4, July-December 1957, pp. 159-161.

Marinello, Juan. «A propósito de tres novelas recientes.» *Meditación Americana.* Buenos Aires: Ediciones Procycon, 1957, pp. 57-77.

Márquez Rodríguez, L. «'El acoso' y la renovación de la novela en América.» *El Nacional* (Caracas), 9 May 1957, p. 6.

——————. «Tres vertientes en la crisis de un perseguido en la novela 'El acoso.'» *Actual,* Vol. II, no. 3-4, Sept. 1968, pp. 218-223.

Rodríguez-Monegal, Emir. «Dos novelas de Alejo Carpentier.» *Narradores de esta América.* Montevideo: Alfa, 1961, pp. 147-53.

Sucre, Guillermo. «Alejo Carpentier o el acoso del ser.» *El Nacional* (Caracas), 25 April 1957.

Volek, Emil. «Análisis del sistema de estructuras musicales e interpretación de 'El acoso' de Alejo Carpentier.» *Homenaje a Alejo Carpentier,* ed. Helmy Giacomán. New York: Las Américas, 1970.

Weber, Frances. «'El acoso': Alejo Carpentier's War on Time.» *PMLA* LXXVIII, 4 (September 1963), pp. 440-448.

11. *Guerra del tiempo*

Vidal, Hernani. «Arquetipificación e historicidad en *Guerra del tiempo.*» *Nueva narrativa hispanoamericana,* Vol. 3, no. 2, 1973, pp. 245-256.

12. *El siglo de las luces*

Castellanos, Rosario. «Incursión por *El siglo de las luces.*» *Juicios Sumarios.* Xalapa: *Cuadernos de la Facultad de Filosofía, Letras y Ciencias de la Universidad Veracruzana* (1966), no. 35, pp. 160-164.

Desnoes, Edmundo. «*El siglo de las luces.*» *Casa de las Américas* 4, 26, Oct.-Nov. 1964, pp. 100-109.

Dumas, Claude. «*El siglo de las luces,* novela filosófica.» *Cuadernos Americanos,* Año XXV, CXLVII (1966), pp. 187-210.

Galey, Mathieu. «Un roman comme nous ne savons plus en écrire.» *Arts* (Paris), 27 June 1962.

Kilmer-Tchalekian, Mary. «Synthesis as process and vision in *El siglo de las luces* and *Cien años de soledad.*» DAI 35: 5411 A, 1975.

——————. «Ambiguity in *El siglo de las luces.*» *Latin American Literary Review,* Vol. IV, no. 8, 1976, pp. 47-57.

Lask, Thomas. Review of *El siglo de las luces. Books of the Times (New York Times)*, Vol. 112, no. 38537, July 1963, p. 17.

Leante, César. «Un reto a la nueva novela.» *Revolución* (Habana), Año 9, no. 2848, 8 April 1965, n.pag.

López Nussa, Leonel. «Goya en *El siglo de las luces*.» *La Gaceta de Cuba,* January -1964, n. pag.

Marinello, Juan. «Un homenaje excepcional.» *Bohemia* (Habana), Año 56, no. 32, 7 Aug. 1964, pp. 94-95.

Martoq, Bernard. «Las dimensiones de la historia en *El siglo de las luces*.» Dissertation, Faculté des Lettres d'Aix-en-Provence, 1964.

Nadeau, Maurice. «Antilles fabuleauses: couvrant les clameurs disparates de l'histoire, le chant profond du port.» *L'Expres* (Paris), dixième année, no. 575, 21 June 1962, pp. 34-35.

Oramas, Ada. «Diálogo con Alejo Carpentier.» *Mujeres* (Habana), Año 5, no. 10, October 1965, pp. 14-17.

Ortega, Julio. «Sobre *El siglo de las luces*» in *Asedios.*

Pérez Minik, Domingo. «La guillotina de Alejo Carpentier.» *Insula* XXI, CCXXXIII, p. 3.

Rama, Ángel. «*El siglo de las luces:* coronación de Alejo Carpentier.» *Marcha* (Montevideo), Año 25, no. 1206, 22 May 1964, pp. 1 and 4.

——————. «Una revolución frustrada.» *Marcha,* Año XXV, no. 1207, 29 May 1964, pp. 29-30.

Raphael, Frederick. «Questions of Upbringing.» *Sunday Times* (London), 17 February 1963, n.pag.

Sánchez, Luis Alberto. «*El siglo de las luces*.» *México en la cultura,* no. 906 (supplement of *Novedades*), 31 July 1966, p. 3.

Sommers, Joseph. «Alejo Carpentier's *El siglo de las luces*.» *Books Abroad* XXXVIII, (1964), p. 56.

Sucre, Guillermo. «*El siglo de las luces*.» *Revista Nacional de Cultura* (Caracas), no. 180, April-May 1967, pp. 84-87.

Tijeras, Eduardo. «*El siglo de las luces*.» *Cuadernos Hispanoamericanos,* April 1967, pp. 199-204.

13. *El recurso del método*

Egúsquiza, Juan. *El recurso del método* (review). *Revista de crítica literaria* (Lima), Año 1, no. 2, 1975, pp. 142-144.

Peavler, Terry. «A New Novel by Alejo Carpentier.» *Latin American Literary Review,* Vol. III, no. 6, Spring 1975.

Selva, Mauricio de la. «Con pretexto de El recurso del método.» *Cuadernos americanos,* no. 196, 1974, pp. 266-277.

14. *Concierto barroco*

Mejía Duque, Jaime. «Los 'recursos' de Alejo Carpentier.» *Casa de las Américas,* Vol. 89, pp. 155-157.

Müller-Bergh, Klaus. «Sentido y color de *Concierto barroco*.» *Revista iberoamericana,* Vol. XLI, no. 92, July-December 1975, pp. 445-467.

Oviedo, José Miguel. «Un grabado preciosista de Alejo Carpentier.» (Review). *Revista iberoamericana,* Vol. XLI, no. 92, July-December 1975, pp. 665-667.

15. *General*

Barreda-Tomás, Pedro. «Alejo Carpentier: dos visiones del negro, dos conceptos de la novela.» *Hispania,* no. 1, Nov. 1972, pp. 34-44.

Cheuse, Alan. «Memories of the Future: a Critical Biography of Alejo Carpentier.» DAI 35: 6659A-60A, 1975.

Colavita, Federica. «El sentido de la historia en la obra de Alejo Carpentier.» DAI 35: 6659A-60A, 1975.

Díez, Luis. «Carpentier y Rulfo: dos largas ausencias.» *Cuadernos Hispanoamericanos,* no. 272, pp. 338-49.

Dorfman, Ariel. «El sentido de la historia en la obra de Alejo Carpentier.» *Imaginación y violencia en América.* Santiago: Ediciones Universitarias, 1970, pp. 93-137.

Escrivá de Romaní, Manuel. «Alejo Carpentier recurre a René Descartes.» *Camp de l'Arpa,* Vol. 17-18, pp. 49-51.

—————. «Componiendo barroco sin excusas.» *Camp. de l'Arpa,* Vol. 10 pp. 25-27.

Fuentes, Carlos. *Carpentier o la doble adivinación* in *La nueva novela hispanoamericana.* México: Joaquín Mortiz, 1969, pp. 48-58.

Goirdano, Jaime. «Unidad estructural en Alejo Carpentier.» *Revista Iberoamericana* XXXVII, no. 75, Apr.-June 1971, pp. 391-401.

González, Eduardo Gumersindo. «El tiempo del hombre: huella y labor de origen en nuestras obras de Alejo Carpentier.» DAI 36: 923A-924A, 1975.

González Echevarría, Roberto. «Notas para una cronología de la obra narrativa de Alejo Carpentier 1944-1954», in *Lectures in Memory of Louise Taft Semple.* Norman: Univercity of Oklaoma Press, 1973, pp. 201-214.

—————. «Isla a su vuelo fugitivo: Carpentier y el realismo mágico.» *Revista Iberoamericana,* Vol. 40, 1974, pp. 9-63.

Hidalgo, Jorge. «El tiempo y las formas en tres obras de Alejo Carpentier.» DAI 35: 5406A-5407A, 1975.

Levine, Suzanne. «Lo real maravilloso de Carpentier a García Márquez.» *Eco,* Vol. 20, no. 120, pp. 563-576, April 1970.

Mazzioti, Nora, ed. *Historia y mito de la obra de Alejo Carpentier.* Buenos Aires: Fernaando García Cambeiro, 1972.

Müller-Bergh, Klaus. «Corrientes vanguardistas y surrealismo en la obra de Alejo Carpentier.» *Revista Hispánica Moderna,* Vol. 35, 1969, pp. 323-340.

—————. «Reflexiones sobre los mitos en Alejo Carpentier», in *Homenaje,* pp. 275-293.

Pérez de la Riva, Juan. «70 aniversario de Alejo Carpentier.» *Revista de la Biblioteca José Martí* (La Habana), Jan.-April 1975.

Picado-Gómez, Manuel. «En torno a Carpentier.» *Revista de la Universidad de Costa Rica,* Vol. 41, pp. 213-221.

Rincón, Carlos. «Sobre Alejo Carpentier y la poética de lo real maravilloso.» *Casa de las Américas,* Vol. 89, pp. 40-65.

Rodríguez-Puértolas, Carmen. «Alejo Carpentier: teoría y práctica.» *Eco,* Vol. 17, no. 98, pp. 171-201, June 1968.

Ross, Waldo. «Alejo Carpentier o sobre metamorfosis del tiempo.» *Universidad Antioquía* (Colombia), Vol. 45, no. 171, Oct.-Dec. 1968, pp. 133-146.

Sánchez-Boudy, José. *La temática novelística de Alejo Carpentier.* Miami: Editorial Universitario, 1969.

Santander, Carlos. «El tiempo maravilloso en la obra de Alejo Carpentier.» *Estudios Filosóficos,* Vol. 4, 1968, pp. 107-129.

Uriarte, Fernando. «El criollismo alucinante de Alejo Carpentier.» *Mapocho* (Santiago), Vol. 5, no. 1, 1966, pp. 90-101.

Volek, Emil. «Alejo Carpentier y la narrativa latinoamericana actual: dimensiones de un realismo mágico.» *Cuadernos Hispanoamericanos,* no. 296, pp. 319-342.